Refael (Rafi) Benvenisti

Economic Life at the Dawn of History in Mesopotamia and Ancient Egypt

Refael (Rafi) Benvenisti

Economic Life at the Dawn of History in Mesopotamia and Ancient Egypt

The Birth of Market Economy in the Third and Early Second Millennia BCE

Translated from Hebrew by
Naftali Greenwood

DE GRUYTER MAGNES

Published in Hebrew by Magnes Press, 2014.
Hebrew title:
הכלכלה בשחר ההיסטוריה: מוסדות כלכליים במסופוטמיה באלף השלישי ותחילת האלף השני לפנה"ס

ISBN 978-3-11-106510-6
e-ISBN (PDF) 978-3-11-106553-3
e-ISBN (EPUB) 978-3-11-106585-4

Library of Congress Control Number: 2022952124

Bibliographic information published by the Deutsche Nationalbibliothek
The Deutsche Nationalbibliothek lists this publication in the Deutsche Nationalbibliografie; detailed bibliographic data are available on the internet at http://dnb.dnb.de.

Cover image: Human with a Sila Bowl. The Sila bowl (standard one liter bowl, a unit of Sumerian money) is the symbol of the word “ba” in Sumerian, which means wages, or alternatively rations. Mesopotamia. Clay Tablet. Pictographs drawn. Early writing tablet recording the allocation of beer. Iraq. Late Prehistoric period. 3100 – 3000 BC. British Museum. London. England. United Kingdom. akg-images.
Printing and binding: CPI books GmbH, Leck

www.degruyter.com

Foreword

This book was written by an economist of the classical school who uses the tools of Institutional Economics.[1] He ventured into the world of historians, Assyriologists, archaeologists, and anthropologists. His purpose—to interpret their areas of interest using a model other than the primitive-substantive[2] one they customarily apply. Some of these traditional scholars claim that societies in ancient Mesopotamia were organized by rulers into large, family-based, groups of people, centered around the temple and the palace. They worked together in agriculture, manufacturing, and services for subsistence rations only and lived in primitive conditions. According to these scholars, there were no markets and no exchanges between people based on prices determined by the markets; nor were there universal means of exchange (money). People exchanged goods and services among themselves for social reasons (favors and status building), using equivalencies (prices) of certain chosen goods set by the authorities. Credit was given for administrative reasons to traders and others who were ordinary workers of the organization; thus, credit was an administrative means of social transfer of resources, and interest was a simply a token of gratitude. In the language of one of the proponents of this model, the "key elements in such an ideal type of household economy are the unity of labor, living together within a household, and consumption with no prices, no wages, no rent, no profit or capital."[3]

This writer does not dispute the findings and translations of the documents these esteemed researchers present, but he does allow himself to dispute their interpretation of the findings, applying another model, the formal-modern one. This model maintains that people living in Mesopotamian societies during the third millennia BCE lived in ordinary families, worked in large organizations (the temple and palace) for wages and salaries paid by barley and other goods as a means of exchange (money). They exchanged their surpluses as a means of exchange in numerous markets for other goods and services that they sought, using prices established in the markets. The large organizations (the temple and palace) where

1 There are several study areas that use the term Institutional Economics. In this book, the study area, called sometimes New Institutional Economics, is the framework used to analyze the economic history of Mesopotamia and the Old Assyrian Period. A description of the study area and its tools appears in the subchapter "Institutional Economics Theory," page 165.
2 The society is at a primitive stage of development. Its economic activities are substantive in nature, and its economic structure is embedded with social institutions. The temple and the palace are dominating the society. See later the subchapter "Economic Models that Explain the Era," page 167.
3 Renger 1994, 170.

https://doi.org/10.1515/9783111065533-001

large agriculture products producers and manufacturing units (like textile and leather products) managed their large profits and surpluses and the balance of their means of exchange (barley, copper and silver) by storing them and exchanging them for infrastructure and services including defense. They were engaged in trade with other regions with the help of professional traders. Credit (calculated by the means of exchange of the period—barley, copper, and silver) was an established institution among people and organizations for production, trade, and consumption; interest was the price for using it. Traders were private entities and operated for profits. Property rights to protect people's assets and capital and help them in the use and exchange of these assets, goods and services in the market were certainly present and operative.

The book identifies the presence of important economic institutions, such as property rights, the market, and credit systems in documents from Mesopotamian and ancient Egyptian societies as far back as the third millennium BCE. It also offers a different interpretation of Sumerian documents on the rewards for labor from working in the temple and the palace. Some researchers did not discern that barley was the form of payment in Sumerian society, which was used to pay various workers using a volume unit of barley called the sila (one liter). Barley played a dual role in Sumerian society—as food and as a means of exchange, that is, money in units of volume. Similarly, copper was used for the manufacture of tools and weapons and as an instrument of payment, money in units of weight. These payment instruments were used to set prices in trade, as units of measurements in the accounts of the palace and the temple, and for deferred payments (credit). Acknowledging standard measures of barley as instruments of payment for services rendered (and not only as a way to feed the population) fundamentally transforms the terms of the debate over the structure of the economy and the economic institutions of that era.

In a summary, there is a big difference in interpretation of the economic and social reality of the period between the two sides. When the writer sees people working for wages for the big organizations (the temple and the palace) and paid in the currency of the period—barely, the opponents see free redistribution of food rations (barely) to serfs of the palace and the temple. When he sees market exchanges with prices set by the markets, they see reciprocity (social exchange) done with equivalencies (prices) set by the authorities. When he sees ownership of assets (and capital) identified by clear instruments of means of exchange (money), stamps, cones and kudduru stones, or long-term exclusive renting of assets, they see no money and assets owned (or held) by the societies (or the temple and the palace) but used by primitive serfs. Or alternatively, the opponents acknowledge the existence of some of the market signs and ownership of assets, but say that because of the huge size of the temple and palace economies, the market-based activities are a very small part of the economy of the period and form an insignificant part of it. Both sides can not substantiate their claims because there is no overall economic data for the period and most of the written evidence was discovered in the temples and palaces. The debate looks more like an exchange based on interpretations, beliefs and points of view than a scientific debate. In any way, the book is an attempt to contribute to the debate by presenting a new organized analysis of the economic institutions of the period and compare it to the results emerge from using the other models.

The writer thinks that the book is unique in that it represents the first systematic use of the analytical tools of modern Institutional Economics and Transaction Cost Theory to profile the economic institutions that influenced the economies of Mesopotamia and Egypt in the third millennium BCE. In the course of the research, it became clear that the market economy institutions of the Old Assyrian trade in the early second millennium BCE were the successors of similar institutions in Mesopotamia at the dawn of history.

This book also contributes to the discussion of the Old Assyrian trade. It tries to organize the discussion of the traders' documents by creating a profile of the economic institutions (the "rules of the game") that the traders used. By characterizing these institutions and comparing them with modern ones, this book imparts a better understanding of this commercial phenomenon. Sometimes the writer will argue with scholars of trade about using definitions from the world of modern accounting instead of those established by Assyriologists who investigated the era and translated its documents.

The book owes its origins to a doctoral dissertation entitled "Economic Institutions in Old Assyrian Trade in the Twentieth to the Eighteenth Centuries BCE," approved by the Senate of the Hebrew University of Jerusalem in 2012. In the writer's research, it was his aim to prove that the Assyrian economic institutions in Mesopotamia appeared in periods preceding the Old Assyrian trade. In this book, the writer extends the investigation back to the economy at the dawn of history, the period beginning in the second half of the fourth millennium BCE—that of the great agricultural and urban revolution in Mesopotamia. Also researched ancient Egypt, where an agricultural revolution also took place at that time with the same economic institutions.

As the writer delved into the era, he was increasingly drawn into the great debates over the structure of the Mesopotamian and ancient Egyptian economy and society. His training as an economist simply would not allow him to automatically accept Karl Polanyi's primitive-substantive model (Polanyi 1957, 1977), which so many researchers embrace as conventional wisdom. Polanyi's model, originating in anthropology, is based on studies in the Pacific islands and in Africa, and also draws on the social models of Karl Marx, Max Weber, and Moses Finley (Finley

1973). According to these models, factors of production in Mesopotamia and ancient Egypt belonged to a society comprised of extended families living on a subsistence basis and operating in an economy in which a certain social behavior was embedded. The writer saw the matter differently, viewing the ancient Sumerians and Egyptians as people whose mindsets and motivations resemble our own, and as people who established economic institutions that we can recognize today, with, of course, the inevitable adaptations to changes in technology and culture.

Institutional Economics and Transaction Cost Economies are the tools that helped him profile and scan for the market economy institutions of Mesopotamia and Egypt, analyze them, and explain how they were used. The staggering wealth of Old Assyrian trade documents persuaded him that quoting them, could provide strong support for his views that the institutions of the Assyrian traders, like those of their Mesopotamian and ancient Egyptian precursors, were institutions of a market economy. His assumption was that if institutions such as property rights, markets, instruments of payment, organization, and finance, which appear in documents from the time, functioned then in a manner that is recognizable until today, and were socially enforced, then their economy was indeed a market economy. To substantiate this position, The writer delved deeper into the primitive-substantive model still used by researchers publishing histories of that period.

The book is structured to present in the beginning the historical background of the amazing agriculture and urban revolutions in Mesopotamia in the Fourth Millennium BCE. The later chapters are structured chapters to discuss the different economic institutions. In the end, the writer provides a few sub-chapters on background subjects, such as the description of the theory of Economic Intuitions and the main theories that are used by historians and other researchers of this period. In addition, he gives example of similar economic systems in ancient Egypt, and a trading organization—the Hanseatic League that is quite similar to the Old Assyrian one.

In the beginning of each chapter, the writer presents the definition and structure of the economic institution discussed. The discussion is especially extensive regarding three subjects: property rights, the market, and credit. It is in these subjects that the writer has deep differences with the proponents of the primitive-substantive model. It was important to note how the model the writer uses differs from that of these other thinkers. The detailed discussion was undertaken to help formulate a shared understanding of the economic institutions discussed among scholars from different fields. For this the writer relied on the well-established sources of *The New Palgrave: A Dictionary of Economics* and *The New Palgrave: A Dictionary of Economics and Law.* Afterwards, he explains the appearance and details of the institutions in the Early Mesopotamians periods, and at the end the writer describes the appearance and structure of the Old Assyrian economic institutions and the way they appear in the Old Assyrian documents.

Having completed this study, it is my pleasant task to thank all those who helped me along its journey. First among them are the instructors who accompanied the research: Professors Israel Ephal, Jacob (Kobi) Metzer, and Rehav (Buni) Rubin. Professor Ephal earned my immense gratitude for his continuous help in designing and implementing the research plan. He helped me to navigate the research program to meet its goal, despite the difficulties of planning an interdisciplinary study that straddles three important departments (Geography, History and Economics) at the Hebrew University of Jerusalem, examining a period in history that is not at the center of attention in Israel's universities, and wielding the tools of Institutional Economics, which are still in their early stage of their development. Professor Metzer is thanked for his useful comments and guidance in Institutional Economics, and Professor Rubin for helping to fit my interdisciplinary research into the framework of the Department of Geography. I thank the other members of Research Program Approval Committee, who guided me and approved my program of study: Professors Ephraim Kleiman, Nathan Wasserman, Nathan Sussman, and Nadav Neeman. Their questions and comments were invaluable in helping me design the research.

The translation of the Hebrew book was done professionally and very accurately by Naftali Greenwood and the excellent editing have been done with great care by Susan Doron both of Academic Language Experts.

I want to thank De Gruyter and Magnes Press for the publication of this book, and their senior staff Julia Brauchand of De Gruyter and Johnathan Nadav and Yael Klein of Magnes for their help in this endeavor . Special thanks are due to Alice Meroz for her excellent work on the index of the book and the preparation of the book for publication.

I am grateful for the work done by Joachim Katzmarek and Matthias Wand from Datagroup for their work on the publication of the book.

Last but far from least is my family: my late wife Ruthie; my children, Yaron, Tamar, and Michal; and my grandchildren, Harel, Maya, Niva, Eden, Omer and Shira, who saw their father and grandfather disappear on lengthy visits to such an old period in history and return with his captivating stories that may not have been so fascinating for them.

Contents

Sources

To study the economy of third-millennium BCE Mesopotamia, the writer consulted the works of leading researchers of that era who based their work on primary sources. To select them, he availed himself (among other sources) of a bibliography produced by Professor Norman Yoffee for a seminar on the 'Mesopotamian Economy in Antiquity', given at the University of Michigan in 2006.[1] The writer also predicated his work on studies by Assyriologists who deal with economic phenomena and interpret them on the basis of the primitive-substantive model,[2] an accepted convention in anthropological research. Using formal-modern model[3] and Institutional Economics, the writer interprets the findings quite differently than they do.

The researchers on whom the writer relies most published their works in the second half of the twentieth century—describe the society and the economy of the Uruk era (late fourth millennium BCE) by drawing on findings and tablets unearthed in archaeological excavations.[4] That period was the heyday of two large organizational structures—the palace and the temple—and the evidence from the tablets and inscriptions found describes their activities in production and payments to employees. Englund holds that these organizations were engaged in production and redistributed subsistence rations to their members, in the third millennium BCE. According to Nissen, barley was an instrument of payment at that time, exchanged in the market for other goods by means of the standard measure (one liter) of hand-made beveled-rim bowls.[5]

Other researchers describe the socioeconomic structure of the Sargon and Ur III empires (third millennium BCE) as continuations and refinements of those of earlier periods.[6] These scholars consider this structure the dominant one in all parts of southern Mesopotamia and in the Ur III Empire. That period also witnessed economic activity by individuals outside the palace and temple framework, including private ownership and leasing of means of production, but it was very

---

1 It appeared in the past (2014), at the University of Michigan site: http://sitemaker.umich.edu/nyoffee/files/economics_sem_06_readings.pdf

2 Polanyi 1957. Social institutions are embedded in the economy. The society is primitive and engaged in subsistence activities.

3 Based on classical economics. Modern economic institutions are recognizable.

4 Nissen 1988, 65–127; Englund 1998, 15–236; Van de Mieroop 2004a, 19–38.

5 Nissen 1988, 84–5.

6 For example: Foster 1977, 31–43; Foster 1982; Foster 1983, 147–75; Steinkeller 2004, 91–111 Renger 1984, 31–123; Renger 1994, 157–208; Renger 2003, 15–137; 31–123; Van de Mieroop 1992.

https://doi.org/10.1515/9783111065533-002

limited in scale. This is also the prevailing view among researchers who published in the 1990s and at the beginning of the current century.[7]

However, in more recent studies a consensus has grown among researchers that the model that best describes the Mesopotamian economy in the early second millennium BCE is a formal-modern one that encompasses intensive private sector activity.[8] Property rights during that period were held mainly by the private sector. Although the economic organizations of the palace and temple continued to function, they did so on a relatively smaller scale. In fact, the Mesopotamian economy of the time was marked by markets in which goods, properties, and means of production were exchanged, often by using agreed-upon instruments of payment, foremost silver, copper and barley. Investment capital, loans, and agreed-upon interest rates were recognized and private traders engaged in local and interregional trade.

In the book, the writer draws upon publications about traders' archives discovered in several locations in Asia Minor, Mesopotamia, and Syria. They document in great detail trade relations, means of exchange (use of precious metals such as silver) and credit, the relationships between the production stage and exchange, and relations with the authorities. Other important sources are legal systems discovered in Eshnuna and Babylonia (the Code of Ḫammu-rapi[9]) that include clauses pertaining to private commerce.

The largest trove of tablets relating to private trade was found in Kanesh, Anatolia, in the archives of Assyrian merchants up to the eighteenth-century BCE, all written in cuneiform in an Old Assyrian dialect of Akkadian.[10] Tablets have been appearing in the antiquities market since the nineteenth century. In 1926, Friedrich Hrozný traced their provenance to a site called Kültepe, near the town of Kayseri in central Anatolia. The city, identified as ancient Kanesh, has been intensively excavated since 1948; this work was overseen until 2005 by the late Turkish archaeologist Tahsin Özgüç, and since than by Fikiri Kulakoğlu. The excavations uncovered approximately 18,500 clay tablets, some still awaiting deciphering and research at museums in Turkey. In addition, around 5,000 documents have been found in unauthorized excavations since the late nineteenth century, and they are widely scattered among museums and private collections. Documents produced by traders and persons mentioning trade have also been found elsewhere in Anatolia—in small quantities, in Alişar, Boğazköy, Acemhöyük, Kalehöyük and

---

7 See, for example, Postgate 1995; Kuhrt 1997; Van de Mieroop 2004a.

8 Van de Mieroop 2004, 54–64; Silver 2004, 65–87; Steinkeller 2004, pp. 91–111; Jursa 2010, 13–26.

9 Wasserman And Bloch 2019, 18–19. Discussion on the Name. (Hebrew)

10 The records in the archives can be classified in several broad categories: Letters 30–50 %; legal documents 30–40 %; Lists, memorandums and notes 20–30 %. Veenhof 2013, 37–38.

Kayalipinar. In all, they mention about forty localities that had Assyrian trade colonies.[11]

Several important studies[12] have been published cataloguing what is known about the subject of the Old Assyrian trade: the important recent general studies of Klaas Veenhof (2008); Ian Dercksen's (2004, 2014) work on the Old Assyrian trade and its institutions; Mogens Larsen's (2015) detailed descriptions of the institutions of the city of Assur and of the Assyrian colonies in Anatolia; and Gojko Barjamovic's studies on various aspects of trade and the geography of Anatolia (2011). These works, in addition to Cécile Michel's comprehensive opuses (2003, 2005/6, 2011, 2015), which include an up-to-date bibliography of the ancient documents and studies about them, as well as further research by her, yield research into various aspects of the Old Assyrian trade. Added to these and other recent studies is earlier work of Paul Gareli (1963) and of Louis Orlin (1970), among the first to describe trade as an enterprise of private trading houses and to explain various aspects of how trade was financed. Veenhof's numerous big studies (1972, 2003a, 2008 and more) describe many aspects of Assyrian trade, including what was traded, how caravans were organized, how trade was financed, instruments of finance, communication, and the Assyrian legal system. Works such as Hertel's (2013) concern themselves with law and jurisprudence, and Larsen (1976) gives a detailed account of the institutions of Assur city and the Assyrian colonies in Anatolia. These studies are only a small portion of the vast corpus that deals with the phenomenon of the Old Assyrian trade.

All of these studies were conducted by Assyriologists and have focused mainly on deciphering the old documents on tablets, translating their terminology, and describing and clarifying the business and private processes that took place, using terms from the fields of sociology, economics, law, and finance for the purpose of translating the documents. They described the economic institutions and explained how they operated, but without conducting a systematic economic discussion of them based on economic institutions models. Consequently, their characterizations are incomplete, as they did not use research tools from the field of Institutional Economics either to analyze what institutions in that society enabled the trade phenomenon, or to explain why traders used these institutions and what their contribution was to the success of trade.

Research into these documents has been led in recent years by a group of scholars—Gojko Barjamovic, Jan Gerrit Dercksen, Karl Hecker, Thomas Hertel, Bert Kouwenberg, Guido Kryszat, Mogens Trolle Larsen, Cécile Michel, Ed Stratford

---

11 Dercksen 2008a, 110.
12 See the large bibliography at the end, and Michel 2003, 2005/6, 2011, 2013.

and Klaas Veenhof and others—who have devoted over thirty years to this mission.[13] The first book published under the auspices of their project is an archive of the trader *Aššur-nādā* (Larsen, 2002). Additional such archives of merchants from Kanesh have been published, for example, by Veenhof (the trader *Kuliya*) and Larsen (*Šalim-Aššur*) (Larsen, 2010; Veenhof, 2010) and others. English translations of many other documents from the other merchants' archives appear in the aforementioned works.

In the chapters that follow, the writer defines and characterize the important economic institutions that influenced Old Assyrian trade by presenting traders' documents that have been researched and published. He analyzes why these institutions were used and assess their impact on the transaction costs and profitability of the traders' business activities. Quoting from the traders' writings, he explains the structure and form of the institutions and their operations. These quotations were obtained from two main sources. The first comprises collections of traders' documents that appear in Mogens Larsen (2002) and William Gwaltney (1983), and in the books and studies of Veenhof,[14] Larsen,[15] Dercksen,[16] Michel,[17] and others.

The writer second source of quotations is the Chicago Assyrian Dictionary (CAD).[18] Each word that appears in the dictionary is accompanied by multiple quotations harvested from documents from several periods, including those of traders in the Old Assyrian era that have been translated into English. The quotations in the dictionary that trace to that era were chosen carefully by the editors of CAD. In order to best determine the meaning of a word, all of its occurrences are aggregated along with enough texts to establish its meaning in a specific context.[19] These lexemes, extracted from the traders' vocabulary, describe phenomena from the fields of market activity, instruments of payment, organization, funding, and enforcement, all as identified and translated into English by those who researched the primary documents. Accordingly, the quotations should be treated as accurate representations of the phenomena described. In certain cases, the quo-

---

13 The research efforts were done under the umbrella of the project 'Old Assyrian Text Project' (OATP) at the University of Copenhagen.

14 Veenhof 1972.

15 Larsen 1967.

16 Dercksen 1999, 85–99.

17 Michel 1997, 285–300.

18 The *Chicago Assyrian Dictionary* (CAD), a project on the Akkadian language and its idioms, undertaken by the University of Chicago since 1921. It comprises twenty-two volumes.

19 CAD $A/_1$, xi–xii.

tations are compared with the contents of the original documents as translated in published studies such as those of Gwaltney (1983) and Larsen (2002).

The definition and characterization of economic institutions in the book was done with the aid of *The New Palgrave: A Dictionary of Economics* 1987, 2018 and *The New Palgrave: A Dictionary of Economics and Law,* 1998. The very long and detailed discussion of the economic institution in the beginning of each chapter was meant to make it clear what is the institution that is being discussed in light of different definitions that appear in the other economic and social models used by other researchers.

Last but not least are the sources for the discussions on Institutional Economics[20]. The main source was the works of Douglas North, who was one of the founders of the theory of Economic Institutions and received the Nobel Prize for his contribution to the building of the theory and other fields of economics. The Conclusion of the book is built around his books *Structure and Change in Economic History* (1981) and *Understanding the Process of Economic Change* (2005). The writer also used the works of Avner Grief on Medieval Trade and economic institutions and Oliver E. Williamson works on New Institutional Economics. The chapter in the Conclusion called "The Institutional Economics theory" is included in the book to help the readers with the elements of this rather new theory.

Names of places, proper nouns, and months of the year in the quotations from the Assyrian traders' documents appear with the following abbreviations attached:

MN = name of month
GN = General Name. A general name with a number denotes multiple locations.
PN = Personal Name. A personal name with a number denotes multiple people.

Words in Akkadian and the Assyrian dialect of Akkadian appear in *italics.* Use is made of diacritical marks that denote, per convention, ' – a; (š) – sh, (ṣ) – ts, (ṭ) – t, and the Semitic (ḫ) – het. Diacritics above letters denote the length of a vowel: (ū), (û).

Sumerian words appear in ordinary Latin characters—ba.

Transliterations have been provided to facilitate pronunciation of names, rulers and places.

In the quotations, brackets denote additions to the translation made to create continuity in the text and explanations. Appearing dots means missing text.

20 Sometimes mentioned as the *New Institutional Economics.*

Introduction

Historical background

In the sixth millennium BCE,[1] northern Mesopotamia became populated by members of what later became known as the Halaf and the Hassuna civilizations.[2] Building larger settlements than those erected by the first farmers in the Neolithic era, these new inhabitants also created a material culture characterized by unique buildings and ceramics. Differences in size in the dwellings in these settlements reflected not social stratification, but mainly family size. Already in the Neolithic era, the central role of granaries was evident in these early societies. Some scholars attribute to granaries a central role in creating social organizations responsible for amassing and distributing cereals, as well as defending the granaries themselves from bandits. Two important institutions—temples and palaces—were later established near the granaries.[3]

Some researchers claim that settlement and social development in southern Mesopotamia were profoundly influenced by the great climate changes that the region experienced in 5000–2000 BCE, reflected in monsoon activity, temperature volatility, and levels of precipitation. These changes affected the flow of the major rivers on the Mesopotamian plains—the Tigris and the Euphrates, leading, in turn, to changes in the locations of riverbanks and channels. Sea levels were about three meters higher than they are today; the coastline was approximately 200 kilometers northwest of that of today; the cities of Ur and Eridu were evidently coastal, and Uruk was not far from the shore. All these changes affected social organization in southern Mesopotamia, forcing these societies to adapt their residential forms and agricultural methods to the new environmental conditions. They had to construct irrigation systems to contend with the changes in climate, precipitation, sea level, coastline, and watercourses. Gradually, between 2000 and 1000 BCE, the shore retreated to where it is today and the climate stabilized.[4]

In southeastern Mesopotamia, as in the northern part of the region, organized settlement began in the sixth millennium BCE. These settlers are known as the Ubaid civilization and by their ancient name, Eridu, for the place where they were first identified. This culture was typified by ceramics production, a special way of building, and urban (or large village) settlement across a wide swath of

1 Nissen 1988, 39–127; Oates 1976, 121–126; Van de Mieroop 2004a, 80–118; Kuhrt 1995, 74–117.
2 Nissen 1988, 39–64; Van de Mieroop 2004a, 15–16.
3 Mayshar et al., 2011, 43.
4 Zarins 1992, 56–67.

https://doi.org/10.1515/9783111065533-003

southern Mesopotamia. Traces of agriculture based on barley and wheat, helped along by simple irrigation techniques, have been found in Ubaid villages. The manner of building in the settlements suggests a distinct form of social organization, possibly arrayed around common agricultural activity, digging and maintaining irrigation canals, and sustaining religious institutions. The archaeological remains reveal a social stratification based on hierarchy, a division of roles, and a concentration of power resulting from the growth of social structures. This social stratification finds expression in the emergence of larger residential buildings among a certain part of the population, probably of those of high social status. Also typical of this culture are the large structures, including temples, that were found in the vicinity of Eridu and that date from the middle of the sixth millennium BCE onward. Judging by their shape, they also presumably served as administrative centers and central locations of granaries.

Remains of this culture have been discovered across a broad area in the central Zagros Mountains, in northern Syria, along the Mediterranean coast, and along the shores of the eastern flank of the Arabian Peninsula as far as Bahrain. The wide dispersal of these remains in many settlements along important routes may suggest commercial activity accompanied by merchant colonies on the fringes of the settlements, on the trade routes, and in destinations.[5] Commerce was evidently based on barter in metals (chiefly copper), lumber for construction, stone for monumental-scale construction and sculpture, and gems from peripheral areas, all of which were exchanged for agricultural products, such as dried food, dried fish, dates, wool textile, and hides from southern Mesopotamia. This culture lasted for a long period of about two millennia without experiencing any perceptible change. However, the archeological findings from the time may allude to a process of change in agriculture and urbanization and the initial formation of the large social and economic structures that typify Mesopotamia of the late fourth and the third millennia BCE.

The Urban Revolution in the Fourth Millennium BCE Mesopotamia

Scholars disagree about the reasons for the formation of large urban settlements during this period of the fourth millennium BCE and beyond.[6] The main explana-

5 Remains of documents related to traders in colonies and their relations with rulers of settlements were found in Ebla in later periods (middle of the third millennium BCE onward).
6 Oats 1976, 135–6.

tions they proffer are the aforementioned climate changes and intensive irrigation activity that made it necessary to design, organize, and operate large organizations and systems that facilitated the division of labor and specialization and the generation of large surpluses for use by the inhabitants and their organizations. Some scholars claim that the existence of an agricultural system based on a water delivery system that is centralized and about which information is transparent encourages centralized rule, whereas one in which information about the water supply is vague promotes decentralized rule. A system of the first type existed in Egypt, where the Pharaohs had information about the level and timing of flooding of the Nile. In the system in Mesopotamia, by contrast, information about the irrigation was diffused among different sectors of the population in different places.[7] Another reason for the development of larger urban settlements was burgeoning large-scale trade among regions specializing in agriculture, mining, and processing of the raw materials these activities yielded. Additional contributing factors were the advent of religion as a mainstay of the inhabitants' lives, the creation of a ruling system related to it, and the establishment of large religious and governmental centers. There is a tendency to attribute the urban development to all of these factors and to suggest that in each period, one of them was dominant in its impact on development.

In the early fourth millennium BCE, a new group of people appeared in southern Mesopotamia[8]—the Uruk culture,[9] which is identified with the Sumerian people. Although scholars disagree about their origin, the predominant view is that they were a non-Semitic people that took shape as a group in southern Mesopotamia or reached it from the Persian Gulf region and developed there due to climate changes and the technological and cultural innovations these engendered.[10] The Uruk/Sumerian culture was typified by distinct ceramics—simple, utilitarian, unadorned—that were manufactured in large quantities, and is also known for its hand-made beveled-rim bowls.

The large-scale urban settlement activity that was characteristic of the Sumerians took place in the northern part of southern Mesopotamia, in the vicinity of the ancient cities Kish and Nippur, and in the south, around the cities Uruk and Ur. This activity may have first appeared not in Uruk but in Kish, situated north of Nippur in the northern part of southern Mesopotamia. This conjecture is based on the list of Sumerian kings that begins with the monarchs of Kish.[11]

7 Mayshar et al. 2011, 40–42.
8 Nissen 1988, 65–128; Van de Mieroop 2004a, 19–38.
9 Today: Warka, Iraq.
10 Reade 1997, 221–29.
11 Wilcke 1989, 557*ff*; Michalowski 1983, 237*ff*, Potts 1997 57*ff*.

The Uruk settlements were larger than those found in the previous period. The city of Uruk sprawled over more than 200 hectares and had a population in the tens of thousands. It grew over the course of several periods, most notably during what archaeologists call Uruk VI (3400–3100 BCE). It was then that the complex of the great temple of the goddess Eanna was built and written tablets first appeared.

In the period that followed (3100–2900 BCE), known as the Uruk III or Jamdat Nasr period, writing became more sophisticated and economic organizations may have expanded in size and complexity.[12]Changes in technological and social organization unfolded over a period of some 1,000 years.[13] Technology evolved in the design and construction of large irrigation systems and facilities to run them; the organization of agricultural fields; methods and implements for ploughing and seeding (a combined ploughing and seeding device);[14] the introduction of a seeding cycle and the use of six-row barley (instead of the two-row species);[15] the establishment of large and complex organizations, including far-reaching specialization in individuals' economic activities; the institutionalization of a volume measure of barley (the sila) as a prime universal means of exchange in the local market, along with weight units of copper for large assets and interregional trade;[16] the construction of large central granaries;[17] the advent of writing and the complex cylindrical seal as instruments of control, identification of property rights, and communication in complex organizations;[18] the invention of the wheel and its use in the manufacture of pottery and in carts for freight and passenger transport; and the expansion of domestication and use of donkeys for transportation, especially trade over long distances.

The dramatic changes in productivity in agriculture, crafts, and transportation created an infrastructure for the massive restructuring of employment and society, and Sumerian society underwent rapid specialization. Large organizations with hierarchical administration and thousands of wage laborers took shape, specializing

---

12 The first part of the period is named for a civilization whose remains were found at Tel Jamdat Nasr, south of Baghdad. A large city, temples, and large quantities of clay tables with information about production and redistribution-in the temple have been found there. The dating is 3100–2900 BCE.

13 Liverani 2006, 15–19; Nissen 1988, 60.

14 Potts 1997, 84*ff.*

15 Six-row barley, considered a mutation of the two-row barley that occurs commonly in nature, was used mainly in northern Mesopotamia in dryland agriculture. The Sumerians identified the mutation and introduced it widely in southern Mesopotamian irrigation agriculture. Ibid., 58*ff.*

16 For discussion of volume measures, see the chapter on markets.

17 Some emphasize the social aspect of the granary, which overcame the seasonality of grain farming and the volatility occasioned by changes in nature.

18 Postgate 1995, 51*ff.*

in agriculture, fishing, hunting, and sheep and cattle grazing. This was accompanied by increasing specialization in crafts and services. Metalworkers, woodworkers, potters, weavers, leather workers, jewelry and statue makers, and producers of mats from reeds began serial production in specialized crafts shops. Workers specialized in construction, tarring, brewing, trade, and transportation, and temple and palace staff became specialized in delivering religious, administrative, defense, and personal services. Some skilled workers were self-employed; others worked for organizations. These organizational and social structures would continue for thousands of years.

Researchers of that era explain the advantages of large-scale landholding—as practiced, for example, in rural communities and the palace and temple organizations—for meeting the need to centrally determine what and how to produce. It was also necessary to invest in a central administrative system, researchers claim, in order to maintain the irrigation system, invest in land betterment, tools, and beasts of labor, and to systematically implement the seeding cycle.[19] The organizations that arose needed to make decisions about what to plant and sow, when to sow and reap, and how to organize agricultural labor. The evolving specialization process had to be organized and decisions about storing surplus produce, as well as decisions about investing in shared irrigation and storage facilities, had to be made. Such matters were evidently resolved by assemblies of elders and general assemblies, out of which an assemblies' leadership and a monarchy eventually emerged.[20]

The expansion of agricultural production generated considerable surpluses of barley that were stored in large granaries owned by the economic organizations. With barley being such a common, vital, and easily measurable scarce commodity, it became the means of exchange (money) of the period. Large organizations paid workers (as documented in later periods) in the "coin" of a daily and monthly quantity of barley—measured in volume units and differentiated by sex, age, occupation, and the worker's standing in the hierarchy. The monthly wage was double the physical subsistence rations, high enough for workers to accumulate barley in containers in their homes and to barter the surplus for other goods and services, with the help of standard measurement bowls supplied by the authorities and standard sacks. The organizations, growing more barley than they needed to meet their payrolls, stored the surpluses accumulated in large granaries and storage facilities that they managed. In addition to paying their employees with the surpluses, the organizations exchanged them with producers of goods and services

---

19 43 Ibid., 183–90.

20 Jacobsen 1943, 165–6; North 1981, 93–4.

for the temple and the palace. These organizations also invested their surpluses (by paying wages and acquiring materials) in the temple and the palace, as well as in various infrastructures (irrigation systems, walls, roads, and bridges), and interregional trade. The Uruk/Sumerians' commercial activity, analogous to the process described above regarding the Halaf and Hassuna civilizations that preceded them, led to the establishment of merchant colonies along and at the terminuses of the trade routes.[21] The Sumerians lived in settlements in specific areas, remains of which have been found along trade routes from southern and western Iran to as far as the Mediterranean coastlines and today's eastern Anatolia.

Clay tablets from the Jamdat Nasr era reveal a set of accounts of production and redistribution of barley and other commodities. Barley was measured in units of volume; the basic unit—the sila—is a liter (*qûm*—in Akkadian and kav—in ancient Hebrew)[22] and was measured in standard beveled- rim bowls. The bowls, came in various sizes, were mass-produced with a crude hand design.[23] Found in the relevant archeological strata in very large quantities, they are among the most important indicators of the era.[24] The large number of bowls (some intact) found in the waste sites of the time suggest that they were inexpensive to make and commonly used among the populations at large.[25] It is likely that the bowls were also used for eating by the common people, whose diet seems to have included ground or minced barley porridge with legumes, vegetables, oil, lard, fish, and salt, with spices added.[26] The large organizations used the barley measures to record quantities of production and barley payments in the system. An emblem of the sila is one of the first cuneiform marks that accompanied the quantity measures of production and barley payments on the organizations' tablets from that period. The markings of a human head next to a beveled-rim bowl denote the Sumerian syllable—ba—payment of wage (or, as other researchers call it, "redistribution of ration").[27]

The existence of a standard means of exchange, backed and inspected by the authorities, facilitated the development of exchange in the markets and lowered

---

21 The development of these regions probably resembled that appearing in writings from the Ebla era (2400 BCE) and that of the Old Assyrian trade (1900–1700 BCE).

22 Gelb 1982, 585–590. At certain times, the sila may have been 0.8 liter and the gur may have been 240 liters.

23 Half-sila and two-sila bowls have also been found.

24 Nissen 1988, 83–85.

25 That some were found intact in garbage dumps may also suggest that the large organizations distributed them at no charge as a standard measure.

26 The common diet of the time also included bread, fermented barley beer, sometimes fruit such as dates, and occasionally meat. See Limet 1987, 132–147.

27 Gelb 1965, 230–243 and Englund 1998, 184–8.

transaction costs considerably. At that time (much as in later eras) additional commodities—such as other foodstuffs (like oil), textiles, wool, and copper—probably served as instruments of payment that were measured by standard weights.[28] Metals (largely copper at first) that were also measured by weights were apparently used for barter for large assets, such as houses, plantations, large ceramic implements, and copper implements, or in interregional trade.

Uruk/Sumerian society became a city-state that appears to have self-organized in an oligarchic structure composed of a military and religious leader and two types of civil assemblies,[29] one of "elders" (community notables) and another of "the people" (everyone else). Constant tension prevailed between the assemblies and the military and religious rulers.[30] The priest-king (en in Sumerian) headed the administration and the army.

In the early third millennium BCE (2900 – 2350), Mesopotamia entered an era of city-states[31] known as the Early Dynastic (ED) period. It is customary to divide this epoch into I (2900 – 2750 BCE), II (2750 – 2600), IIIa (2600 – 2450), and IIIb (2450 – 2350). It is also customary, however, to treat this period politically and socially as a single period divided into subperiods corresponding to political units that were prominent at different times.

Various sources shed evidentiary light on this era, including archaeological findings that support attempts to describe the culture, the social structure, and day-to-day life. Archaeological strata from that time have begun to yield discoveries of cuneiform documents on clay tablets or stone in Sumerian (c. 2900 BCE); large numbers of administrative documents in excavations of palaces and temples;[32] political documents of rulers describing their reigns; and literary documents (mainly religious) from later eras, describing the early periods. Documents belonging to private citizens, pertaining to property and other rights, among other artefacts, have been unearthed as well. Documents of later provenance, including lists of Sumerian kings describing the dynasty from the Uruk period to the early second millennium BCE, when the tablets were written, have also been discovered. However, the information they yield is imprecise and, therefore, of little historical

---

28 Silver apparently came into first use as a means of exchange in the middle of the third millennium BCE.

29 The political structure of ancient Sumerian society emerges implicitly from stories about the era in the great eposes discovered in documents from the early second millennium BCE. Interestingly, this structure very closely resembles that of coeval Assyrian society. See the Chapter on Enforcement, page 141.

30 Bailkey 1967, 1213.

31 Nissen 1988, 129 – 64; van de Mieroop 2004a, 39 – 58.

32 Postgate 1995, 51 – 70.

value.[33] In addition, literary recounting of the deeds of kings and gods from the Uruk era (fourth millennium BCE) have been found.

The documents from different periods portray nation-states where gods dwelled and kings served them. The temple and the palace were surrounded by a hierarchical organization similar to that of the Uruk era. This organizations were populated by priests who served the deity, clerks who served the king, and soldiers arrayed in armies. Clerks ran economic systems that included agricultural production, crafts shops, and service organizations, such as trade and transportation. Production was organized on the basis of units subordinate to superintendents. There were also artisans and self-employed persons, such as fishermen, hunters, brewers, tavern keepers, forwarders, and more. Produce was gathered in granaries and storerooms managed by the clerks.

The city-states conducted diplomatic relations in ways including alliance formation, inter-family marriages, exchanges of gifts, and meetings. While the entire population of southern Mesopotamia saw itself as part of the Sumerian nation and culture, not all relations, were friendly. Rulers throughout the region routinely warred with each other, conquering each other's cities and causing great bloodshed.

The climatic features of northwestern Mesopotamia, Syria, and eastern Anatolia differed from those in southeastern Mesopotamia. The more abundant precipitation in the northwest made rain- fed agriculture possible, leading to changes in the development of the region. Settlements were less centralized in the northwestern region, and nation-states evolved later than they did in southern Mesopotamia. The region's large cities, such as Nagar, Mari, Tuttul, Carchemish, Ebla, Ugarit, and Byblos, developed in approximately the mid-third millennium BCE. The population of this region had a different origin, with the most prominent group, the Amorite, evidently originating in Eastern Turkey/northwestern Syria. The Amorites were nomadic tribes that migrated as far as central Mesopotamia. Lacking a written language of their own, they left inscriptions in Akkadian.[34]

In the late third millennium BCE (2334–2004), two large imperial entities arose in Mesopotamia in succession: the dynasty of Sargon, king of Akkadia, and the Third Dynasty of Ur (Ur III).[35] The Sargon dynastic empire (2334–2154 BCE) sprawled from the Lebanon range to southwestern Iran, its rulers building a

33 Van de Mieroop 2004a, 43–50.

34 43 Ibid., 183–90.

35 Nissen 1988, 165–97; van de Mieroop 2004a, 59–79; Kuhrt 1995, 44–73.

new city in central Mesopotamia—Akkad.[36] In the areas they occupied, they set up a new system of governance, retaining conquered rulers as regional governors and burdening the populations with heavy taxes that were sent to the imperial capital. The Akkadian rulers also took over the existing religious system by replacing the temple high priests with their own men and women, and placed the administrative system under organized control by introducing new bookkeeping methods. The official language of the empire was Akkadian;[37] Sumerian became a language of religious ritual and of literature. The Akkadians did, however, preserve the traditional Mesopotamian economic system, apart from attempts, such as that of King Manishtushu of Akkadia (r. 2269–2255 BCE), to create small private farms for supporters of the rulership.[38]

When the Akkadian empire waned, several rulers gained strength, including Gudea of Lagash Around 2100 BCE, the Akkadians succumbed to Ur-Nammu's Third Dynasty of Ur. These new rulers considered themselves gods and the Ur cities had temples to many deities arranged in a hierarchy of sorts. The Ur III dynasty left behind masses of documentation in the form of inscriptions and documents written in Sumerian on clay tablets. More than 40,000 of these tablets have been published; roughly three times as many languish in museum archives and collections awaiting publication. These written materials describe the empire's military campaigns, religious hymns, and paeans to the kings; they also report production and distribution activities undertaken by the large organizations. Clerks' correspondence with rulers on ongoing matters appears as well. The largest number of documents, however, concerns the management of the large temple and palace organizations.

The Ur III rulers controlled much of Mesopotamia—from southern Syria to southern Iran—and reinstated Sumerian as the language of the bureaucracy. The empire was composed of two important regions. One included Sumeria and Akkadia in Mesopotamia, comprising some twenty districts—the core of the empire. These areas were controlled by governors drawn from notable families in these regions and appointed by the kings of Ur. The other area, a military zone controlled by generals from the army of Ur, stretched from the east to the Tigris River.

---

36 This city (Agade—Akkad) remains undiscovered because it was probably razed to the ground immediately after the eponymous kingdom fell. It is hypothesized to have been located near Baghdad and perhaps can be found under that city's suburbs.
37 The Akkadian later became the *lingua franca* in the Middle East and the mother language of many other cultures.
38 See below, Chapter on Property Rights, page 27.

Beyond it were vassals' kingdoms of the Ur Empire.[39] The ruling system was two-tiered, with a civilian bureaucracy headed by governors and a military apparatus presided over by generals, using a highly centralized operating mechanism, with both governors and generals subordinate to the king. An elaborate tax system was run by an army of clerks, and the city of Puzriš Dagan[40] was a hub for taxation and record-keeping of the goods and livestock that reached the city as tax revenue or war booty. The empire also had a system of regional specialization in animal husbandry and manufacture of basic goods.

* * *

Agricultural settlement in villages started in Mesopotamia in the sixth millennium BCE. The agriculture of the early society of southern Mesopotamia, the Ubaid culture, was based on barley, wheat, and simple irrigation methods. Large temples and evidence of administrative and grain storage centers have been uncovered in centers of settlement. The inhabitants engaged in trade and remnants of the culture have been found in many settlements in specific regions—from the Zagros Mountains and the coast of the Persian Gulf in the east to the shores of the Mediterranean in the west. In the fourth millennium BCE, a new civilization appeared, the Uruk. Evidently of Sumerian extraction, it was typified by urban settlement in large cities, spacious temple complexes, and a society undergoing both technological and social change. The Sumerians engaged in far-reaching trade and established merchant colonies in multiple settlements across the Middle East. In the third millennium BCE, the Early Dynastic (ED) period, city-states (such as Kish, Lagaš, Umma, Ur, Nippur, etc.) developed under military and religious rulers. Many documents have been discovered from this era, most in troves in the vicinity of public buildings, that describe the culture, social structure, and daily life, as well as economic institutions, such as property rights, exchange and trade, means of exchange, credit, and more.

The last part of the third millennium BCE was typified by large empires in Mesopotamia—Sargon of Akkadia (24th–22nd century BCE) and the Ur III dynasty (22nd–21st century BCE). These polities, like those preceding them, were typified by large organizations. Governance under the Third Ur Dynasty was highly centralized and much documentation has been left behind. Researchers proffer two main theories to explain the socioeconomic structure of the time. The first is primitive-substantive society was tribal and functioned as an insular economy for suste-

39 The socioeconomic structure of the time is the subject of debate; see chapter on the Economic Models that Explain the Period, page 167 below.
40 Today: Drehem.

nance purposes. The means of production belonged to extended families organized in large units, and social, not economic motives activated individuals. There were no markets, means of exchange, or credit; interregional trade took place as a result of political exigencies. The second theory, the formal-modern, describes a society that maintained economic institutions of property rights, markets, exchange, credit, wage labor by individuals, and interregional trade for profit, using volume units of barley and weight units of copper and silver as instruments of payment (money).

Regardless of which theory is correct, there is no doubt that there were considerable technological innovations during the fourth and third millennium BCE that influenced social, economic and political developments for a long time.

Technological Changes

An agricultural revolution in the second half of the fourth millennium BCE triggered far-reaching technological changes that would continue to have an impact on the Mesopotamian economy and society in eras to come.[41] The changes set off a massive increase in productivity in the economic systems of Mesopotamia, very high natural increase in birth rates, far-reaching changes in social structure and residential patterns, and rural-to-city migration. The changes included major developments in agriculture such as: new irrigation systems; novel planning and division of fields; adoption of the six-row barley mutation and seed rotation; the invention of ploughing and planting devices;

the potter's wheel, and the wheel; construction of carts; and the domestication of the donkey for long-range riding and transportation. The irrigation system included canals of various sizes and devices that controlled the flow of water to the fields. There was a major expansion of cultivated land; fields were planned out in lengthy strips with a specified number of furrows to enhance ploughing and seeding efficiency, and ox-drawn ploughs mounted with seeding devices were invented.

All these innovations enhanced cultivation and improved agricultural productivity many times over.[42]The technological changes and the establishment of large organizations facilitated

specialization and scale economies in agricultural and crafts production. Crafts started becoming more standardized and duplicable. Archaeologists have

41 Potts 1997; Postgate 1995.

42 The Sumerians attained an output thirty times greater than the quantity sown.

also found large craft workshops. As discussed, the introduction of volume units of barley as "money" and the large-scale manufacture of standard volumes (the beveled-rim bowls) simplified exchange and improved its efficiency.

The invention of writing and the cylindrical seal allowed for more efficient management of the large socioeconomic systems that had materialized and of the mechanisms used to enforce economic institutions.[43] The invention of the wheel and its use for producing pottery and building carts revolutionized pottery production and transportation of high-volume, low-value products.[44]

Due to the aforementioned revolution in pottery production, it could be produced more efficiently in workshops, thus making it possible to transport farm produce from fields to granaries and workshop output to and from central storerooms. Growing domestication of the donkey and its use as a beast of transportation tripled long-range transportation efficiency and allowed interregional trade to expand. These developments, as stated, led to immense improvements in productivity and encouraged rapid increases in population, standards of living, and countryside-to-city migration. Indeed, many urban settlements in southern Mesopotamia were established at this time.

The second half of the third millennium BCE saw additional dramatic changes in the technologies used in Mesopotamia and adjacent areas. New metals came into extensive use and major developments in writing and communication occurred. In the middle of that millennium, the supply and use of copper, silver, and gold continued to expand.[45] Another important technological change at this time was the diffusion of the production and use of a tin-based bronze alloy, replacing the natural copper-arsenic alloy and creating a basis for demand for tin throughout the Middle East. The Old Assyrians, for example, maintained contact with areas in today's Iran, where tin for the bronze industry was sourced. Trade between Assur and Kanesh (in Anatolia)—took place in tin and woolen textiles from Assyria, which were bartered for silver and gold from Kanesh. In Anatolia, trade satisfied the demand for tin for the manufacture of bronze, and in Mesopotamia and Assyria, precious metals were needed as means of exchange, ornamentation, and accumulation of assets.

The source of tin in Bronze Age interregional trade has been extensively investigated by scholars,[46] With some tracing tin to the Herat area of southwestern Afghanistan and the Kandahar region in the eastern part of that country, pursuant to discoveries of cassiterite in river sediments and layers of stone. According to the

43 Some 6,000 tablets with primitive writing from the Uruk era have been found.

44 The invention of the wheel traces to the fourth millennium BCE.

45 Moorey 1994, 218–40.

46 Muhly 1973; Potts 1994, 153–9.

findings, sizable quantities of tin appeared in use and in production of bronze in approximately the middle of the third millennium BCE. One scholar notes the connection between the appearance of gold and of tin in large quantities in Mesopotamia in the late third millennium BCE. The two metals appear in river settlement in Afghanistan, thus explaining why they are often mentioned together in trade documents.[47]

Silver first appears in large quantities in archaeological strata from the fourth millennium BCE.[48] The second half of that millennium saw growing demand for silver and gold as a means of exchange and assets. Silver joined barley and copper as a standard "currency." Measured in agreed-upon units, an official exchange rate of the Gur was established—300 sila of barley = 1 silver shekel. Measures of silver were used for recording in the accounts of the temple and palace. The growth of the supply of silver from Anatolia and the East made the precious metal available for expanded use as means of exchange in Mesopotamia.[49]

In the second half of the third millennium BCE, rapid change also occurred in the development of writing,[50] tablets, tablet envelopes, and seals.[51] This precipitated a major change in information technology, as it became simple, safer, and more efficient to share, store, and retrieve information. As a result, transaction costs and trade-related risks fell. At this time, writing, writing tablets, and seals ceased to be used exclusively by the palace and temple scribes and bureaucrats; now other population groups used them as well, chiefly those engaged in trade and credit. Furthermore, these writing instruments became important means of communication and control for those who engaged in long-range trade.[52]

At this time, the use of cuneiform writing changed as a result of developments in writing that caused the number of signs in use to contract to 120, some of which were in only very limited use. According to scholars, the number of signs in use among businesspeople was even more severely restricted (80). Writing instruction appears to have taken place in two ways: in school or with the help of parents and friends. One may hypothesize that writing proficiency was common among the merchant class and that each family had several literate members, some of whom were called scribes.[53]

---

47 Some scholars, such as Yenar, argue for the existence of a source of tin in Anatolia, in addition to imports from Assur. Muhly 1985, 275–91; Yenar 2000, 71–117.
48 Potts 1994, 160–7; Moorey 1994, 235–6.
49 Powell 1996, 224–42.
50 Pursuant to the writing revolution in late fourth-millennium BCE Uruk.
51 Teissier 1984, xxi–xxiv; Postgate 1995, 64–70.
52 Charpin and Dodd 2010, 7–24.
53 Kryszat 2008, 231–3.

A further advance at this time took place in the structure of the clay tablet on which the documents were written. An envelope, on which a summary of the contents of the document was inscribed, was added to the tablet; the envelope was sealed by the authors of the document and by witnesses, using a personal seal.[54] Traders stored their tablets in crates and jars that were sealed and marked according to the subject matter and placed in security rooms in the house; this systematic archiving system enabled them to quickly retrieve any desired document.[55]

In economic terms, the change in writing technology lowered the transaction costs of transferring deeds from hand to hand and region to region and enhanced the safety of the process by documenting it in a written agreement attested to by witnesses. The phenomena of writing and communication media also made it possible for traders to generate 'information asymmetry' and, as a result, to limit the supply of merchandise in the market and keep prices and profits high. A similar phenomenon occurred in the Middle Ages, for example, with the expansion of the use of standard Latin in contracts and credit documentation.[56]

* * *

The rapid technological changes in the fourth and third millennia BCE created an infrastructure for sweeping transformations of Mesopotamian social and economic life. In agriculture, elaborate irrigation systems were introduced, productive fields were organized, and tools for cultivation and seeding were transformed. In the social domain, large organizations with advanced specialization were formed and writing to document their activities was invented. In transport, the wheel was invented and then the cart, followed by the-domestication of the donkey. These changes gave productivity, trade, and urbanization a powerful push forward. Another immensely important change was the use of barley and copper, and subsequently of silver, as means of exchange in the markets, which enhanced exchange and interregional trade. In the second half of the third millennium BCE, rapid change also occurred in the development of writing and writing instruments.

Interregional Trade in the Third and Second Millennia BCE

There is evidence of active interregional trade already in the Neolithic period. In archaeological excavations of the layers of this period in the Land of Israel and

54 Teissier 1984, 66; Larsen 1977, 89–105.
55 Teissier 1984, xxi–xxiv; Postgate 1995, 64–70.
56 Blum and Dudley 2003, 213–38.

elsewhere, tools using volcanic glass of east Anatolia origin from the ninth or eighth millennium BCE have been found, along with precious stones, such as lapis lazuli from Afghanistan. Seashells of Mediterranean origin have been found in the Baltic region and amber from the Baltic zone in southern Europe.[57]

The societies of third millennium BCE Mesopotamia were largely agrarian, based on irrigation and animal husbandry.[58] There were also crafts activities that included the production of woolen textile, leather processing, and wood and metal products manufactures. Given the natural conditions in Mesopotamia, building materials (wood and stone), metals (copper, silver, gold, and tin) and precious stones had to be imported from other regions. They were obtained in exchange for local food products, agricultural raw materials like wool and leather, and crafts products, such as woolen textiles and garments.[59] (See map page 183)

Testimonies about this trade appear in documents from the temples, palaces, and houses of leading traders. The hymns and eposes of the Sumerian gods include descriptions of trade with remote regions such as Meluha (*meluḫḫa*), identified with the Indus River valley, Magan (*Magan*), identified with Oman, and Dilmun (*Dilmun*),[60] identified with Bahrain Island. The middle of the third millennium BCE saw the emergence of large trade centers in southwestern Syria and northwestern Mesopotamia, such as Gebal (Byblos), Ebla, and Mari. Documents from this period have been found in excavations of their sites, foremost in a large library in Ebla. They include accounts of traders, letters, and trade agreements with town rulers along the trade routes. Trade took place with Sumer, western Syria, Anatolia, and Egypt. Mainly land-based, this trade included food products, agricultural raw materials, tin, woolen textiles, copper, and silver. Ebla, in the 24th century BCE, had colonies of traders in main market towns and agreements with local rulers that covered their civil and trade rights and protection.[61] Trade documents from the period of the Akkadian kingdom provide similar information about trade at that time,[62] while trade documents from the Ur III period yield comparable data about the trade regions, products, prices, and credit documents.[63]

The volume of regional trade was affected by the level of economic activity and the demand for the products. The appearance of new technologies, such as the alloying of copper with tin to bronze, created demand for new commodities

57 Wright 1969, 75. It is possible that both served as means of exchange.
58 Ashtour 1995, 1401–20; Larsen 1987, 47–56; von Soden 1994, 123–30; Barjamovic 2018, 133–67.
59 Leemans 1977, 1–10.
60 Kramer 1977, 59–66.
61 Pettinato 1986, 86–97, 113–119, 149–153, 167–170, 229–237.
62 Foster 1977, 31–43.
63 Oppenheim 1954, 6–17.

such as tin. There is a theory that trade influenced the culture in places where it developed, as languages, modes of behavior, and institutions were disseminated by interaction among the participants in trade. Indeed, the spread of cuneiform writing and the Akkadian language cannot be understood without acknowledging the activities and interactions of the traders.[64]

Overland transport in the ancient world was based on three modes: humans, animals, and carts.[65] To facilitate this transport, the donkey was tamed in the late fourth millennium BCE. The donkey's ninety-kilogram carrying capacity and its loading by means of sacks mounted on the animal's back tripled an individual trader's transport capacity. For riding, men used donkeys, horses, and mules.[66] The latter two were more expensive and therefore were used for riding by the rich and the notables. Traders preferred to move goods of high value and low volume using donkey convoys as haulers.[67]Transport of high-volume and low-value products, such as wool, cereals, and copper was done with the aid of carts and oxen. Oxcarts were developed after the invention of the wheel in the fourth millennium BCE. To overcome limitations in the overland transport of high-volume and low-value products such as wood, stone and cereals, vessels were developed in the river valley and the coastal settlements. Overland transportation was costlier than marine transport due to lower speed, lower volume per unit of transportation, higher passage costs, such as taxes and road services, and greater security risks.[68] The advantage of water transport explains the prosperity of Persian Gulf and Mediterranean port towns such as Ur,[69] Dilmun, and Gebal (Byblos).[70] Each population center was connected to a port for the purpose of long-distance trade. Among the population centers in Iran, Anatolia, and Mesopotamia, for example, overland trade was conducted with the aid of donkeys and by riverboats as much as possible. Overland transport was common in high-value, low-volume goods such as tin, silver, gold, precious stones, and textiles.

Researchers of third millennium BCE Mesopotamia are in disagreement over the question of trade organization. Some subscribe to social explanations of exchange and the organization of society around the temple and palace organizations; they see long-distance trade as mainly conducted by public officials and a

64 Leemans 1977, 2.
65 Astour 1995, 1402–1403; Littauer and Crouwel 1979.
66 Michel 2004, 192.
67 Michel 2004, 193.
68 Casson 1974, 176.
69 In the third millennium BCE, Ur was situated near the Persian Gulf.
70 Gebal (Byblos), on the shore of the Mediterannian, was the main hub of Egyptian and Lebanese sea trade in wood and gold in the third millennium BCE.

political exchange between rulers conducted in special places—"trade ports" where prices were managed and official traders operated.[71]

Others describe this trade as an act of exchange for profit based on market-set prices. Traders used silver and gold as means of exchange and went about their business in accordance with agreed-upon institutions that facilitated investment, credit, and agreements to establish trade organizations and partnerships. The authorities intervened in trade in order to enforce property rights, control traders' behavior in the markets in regard to weights and measures, the quality of precious metals (means of exchange), and agreements on the establishment of judicial and enforcement institutions.

* * *

From this description, one can see that the Old Assyrian trade marked the continuation of the flourishing interregional trade movement during the third millennium BCE, if not earlier, during the late Uruk period of the second half of the fourth millennium BCE. The trade movement was in hands of traders who practiced this profession with goods provided to them on credit by the rulers or from their own sources. Trade was conducted with the help of copper and silver as a means of exchange and verbal and written agreements between the trade parties. Traders were aided by local authorities in and en route to market towns, enjoying protection and the right to settle, go about their lives, and trade under secure conditions.

The Background of the Old Assyrian Trade

The Old Assyrian Kingdom evidently came into being in the third millennium BCE. Very little is known about its initial period; most historical data about it dates to the beginning of the second millennium BCE. However, a recent account of the situation in the third millennium BCE reveals the presence of nonmedian people in the country between the two rivers in Mesopotamia. The people were called *Ammurum* in Akkadian or the Amorites. They did not leave any written inscriptions or tablets in their language but their presence is manifested in the thousands of Amorite names mentioned in numerous documents and inscriptions. A list of the Assyrian kings found on five tablets from the 8th-to the 10th century BCE, mention seventeen kings as tent dwellers i. e., nomads. This together with their names denote their inclusion in the Amorites people.[72]

71 Meijer 2001, 325–340; Yoffee 1981, 1–9.
72 Wasserman and Bloch 2019.

The city of Assur was situated at the intersection of southern Mesopotamia, northwestern Iran, and Syria. Old Assyrian trade in the early second millennium BCE spanned vast distances (see map page 184). Tin, in which the Assyrians traded, appears to have reached Assyria from today's northern Iran (or possibly Afghanistan), textiles came from southeastern Iraq (Babylonia), and silver originated in eastern and Western Turkey (Anatolia). In Assur, Assyrian merchants exchanged silver for tin and textiles and hauled them some 1000 kilometers by donkey convoy in order to exchange them back for silver and gold in Anatolia. Inside Anatolia, the merchants engaged in local trade in copper and wool, which subsequently were exchanged for silver and gold. Copper came mainly from mines in northeastern Anatolia and silver largely from the southwestern parts of the region. The Assyrian trade proceeded on the basis of agreed-upon "rules of the game" (institutions) that helped to lower traders' costs and boost their profits.

The Old Assyrian trade, documented in 23,500 tablets, found mostly in the city of Kanesh, Anatolia,[73] took place between the second half of the twentieth century BCE and the late eighteenth-century BCE—240 years or so,[74] corresponding to the first half of what the literature calls the "Old Babylonian" era (2000–1600 BCE). During that time, the city-states of Mesopotamia, Syria, and Anatolia enjoyed an efflorescence that began with the crumbling of the empire of the Third Dynasty of Ur, which engulfed all of Mesopotamia, at the end of the thirtieth century BCE.

When the Third Dynasty disintegrated, Assur city developed self-rule. King Puzur-Assur I was apparently the first monarch of the dynasty inaugurating the "Old Assyria" era. Old Assyrian trade between Assur and Anatolia evidently began under King Erišum I of Assyria (r. 1972–1933 BCE) or, perhaps, at the time of his father, Ilušma.[75] At first, itinerant merchants from Assur apparently conducted this trade; only afterwards, during the reign of Erišum, was the colony in Kanesh established.[76]

The main institutions in Assur (*ālum*)—the general assembly (*puḫrum*), the town house (*bēt ālim*), and the eponyms (*limmum*)—were established at this

73 Additional coeval documents have been found in small quantities in Alişar, Boğazköy, Acemhöyük, Kalehöyük and kayalipinar. A few royal inscriptions and documents from that time have turned up in Assur. Dercksen 2008a, 110.

74 Next to Kültepe, near the city of Kayseri, on the Anatolian high lands in Eastern Turkey; see map below, page 183.

75 Dercksen 2008a, 110 ff and Larsen 2015, 92*ff.*

76 The chronological framework of the period is based on archaeological and philological data. Archeaological evidence shows five occupational levels, only two (II and Ib) rich in textual data. A refinement of the chronology was possible with the list of Assyrian kings, the lists of names of year-eponyms and the traders' documents. (Veenhof 2003b and Barjamovic et al., 2012)

time.[77] Notables (*rabiūtum*—or the elders) played a central role in the town assembly and they convened as a council. Governance was administered by an oligarchy composed of the notables and the king, who was the first among equals and was the secretary of the assembly and also responsible for matters of religion and war. The eponym (*limmum*), an elected clerk, managed the town house (*bēt ālim*) organization where economic and legal matters were conducted and deliberated upon. The legislative and judicial system was run by the assembly, the council, and special committees formed from their number. Society in Assur developed special cultural and linguistic (an Old Assyrian-Akkadian dialect) indicators that lent it the name "Old Assyria."[78]

The Assyrian colony in Kanesh was active in two periods. The first, known in archaeology as Level II of Kanesh, began around 1945 BCE and lasted about 110 years, until 1835 BCE.[79] According to documents that have been found, the period when trade was most active-began in 1890 BCE and lasted twenty-eight to thirty-two years, until approximately 1860 BCE.[80]

Researchers trace the three-decade spurt in activity to a small number of families whose heads died at the end of that period, and to the lack of a supporting environment for the continuity of commercial activity. The proposed explanation for the waning in activity includes, among other things, the lack of systematic bookkeeping, the absence of rules or a tradition of intergenerational transfer of business, the lack of shared resources that would help families move when imperiled, the absence of rules of succession that would abet intergenerational transfer of property in a way that would allow commercial activity to continue uninterruptedly, and total reliance on a well-developed credit system that based itself on the special status of the trader who headed it.[81] During level II period it has been estimated that about five to eight hundred Assyrians lived in Kanesh.[82]

The first period of activity ended with the destruction and torching of the colony and the palace in the wake of a violent occupation in the year 1825/4 BCE. After a few years, the second period of the trader's activity, known as Level Ib, began in 1832 CE and lasted about 130 years, through the reign of King Šamšī-Adad I (1808–

77 See below, chapter on Enforcement, page 141. The Assyrians tended to count years in accordance with each year's eponym. In Kaneš, there was also a weekly eponym. Archaeology turned up lists of eponyms, the first of whom was elected in the first year of the reign of Erišum I—1972 BCE.

78 Veenhof 2008, 20–2.

79 Michel 2020.

80 Barjamovic et al., 2012; Larsen 2015, 6*ff.*

81 Brajamovic et al., 2012.

82 Michel 2015a, 72.

1776 BCE), until around 1700 BCE, when the colony was abandoned.[83] Only several hundred documents from that period have been preserved; they do not explain why the inhabitants of the colony left.

It is evident from the documents left that there was a change in the procedures of the trade. The most Important one is the disappearance of the investment "sack" the *naruqqum.* It can be speculated that the conquest of Assur by *Šamšī-Adad* I brought major political changes in Assur. The oligarchy of the traders was replaced by the king and the gold resources in the temple were used for different uses like financing the palace and the security activities of the small empire of the king. These changes led to limited resources available to the trading activities, smaller volume trade and reduced size of the traders' houses.

* * *

The Old Assyrian trade was geographically vast, including the area from today's northern Iran and southern Afghanistan to central Turkey. The traders transacted their business across distances of more than 1000 kilometers and swapped textiles and tin for silver and gold. The trade began at the end of the Third Ur Dynasty in the end of the third millennium BCE and ended toward the end of the eighteenth-century BCE. In their activities, the Assyrian traders used economic institutions that had come into being in the third millennium BCE and advanced them with the help of political institutions of the merchant oligarchy that had formed in Assur.

83 Veenhof 2008, 31–34; Michel 2020, 80.

Chapter 1
Property Rights

Property rights are rights that can be applied by those holding them to commonly accepted uses of scarce resources.[1] They are defined as institutions that regulate the relationships within society about the use and possession of property and other rights.[2] That is, property rights are socially defined and enforced and they confer permission to use some or all of a right to a property and to use property in a certain way.[3] Property rights help people determine their expectations about their conduct with others with respect to rights to property. Namely, may third parties infringe owners' right to use their property by theft, confiscation, or unauthorized use? Can one preclude others from harming or using one's property? Individuals' expectations find expression in social covenants, statutes, procedures, and customs.

In the modern era, there are two central philosophical approaches to property rights.[4] One, propounded by Locke, Hume, Kant, Hegel, and others, sees property rights as natural rights that belong to individuals, prevailing over rights determined by the state and by statute, and reflecting individuals' freedom and supremacy over nature. According to this approach, the individual should be free to establish ownership of property by means of his or her labor.

The second approach, espoused by Hobbes, Rousseau, Marx, Weber, and others, supports the concept of social ownership established by society, the state, and the law to ensure the attainment of other goals. In Marxian theory, recognition of property rights allows the material world to take control of the individual, causing inequality, suffering, and estrangement. For these reasons, Marxists hold that property rights over the means of production should be done away with. Researchers of antiquity fall into both schools.

There are those who stress the social aspect that refers to a society in which ownership of the means of production (particularly land) belongs to society. The constituents of such a society are actors in a primitive-substantive social organiza-

---

1 Although the approach to and discussion of this topic belong to the discipline of economics, it is conventional to treat them within a legal context as well. The principles are similar in both fields. "The underlying phenomenon in any economic consideration, any attribution of economic value, is that of scarcity. (Gross 1994, 2) This concept relates to the continual gap between people's needs and available sources with which to satisfy them. Demsetz 1998, 144–55.

2 Namely, "rules of the game."

3 Alchian 1987, 1029–31.

4 Getzler 1996, 639–69.

https://doi.org/10.1515/9783111065533-004

tion operating in an economic framework reflecting entrenched social motives and without a market economy. Other antiquity scholars describe a society that allows individuals to acquire proprietary rights for the use of the means of production (foremost land) and that has market economy institutions. Today, in the Western world, researchers invoke both approaches—defending private ownership while dealing with questions of social justice, equality, and general efficiency.

Property rights theory is one of the foundations of Institutional Economics. It describes the incentives of both the individual and society in Institutional Economics and the market economy. The existence of well-defined property rights and a system that enforces them is a *sine qua non* for the existence of markets in means of production, assets, goods, and services. In these markets, property rights are exchanged and their prices are set. When a property is sold in the market, two sets of rights are exchanged; it is the value of these rights that determines the value of the asset exchanged.[5]

Long-term property rights ("ownership" or "use") encourage holders of property to invest in improving its condition, as in, for example, building on it, planting fruit trees on it, or increasing its production capacity as agricultural land. These rights ensure that the owner of the property will retain it long enough to recoup the investment along with an appropriate return.

Holders of property can also use it to obtain loans for personal use or investment, for example, by mortgaging it in return for a loan. Property rights are protected and acknowledged as vital in facilitating access to the capital market and securing credit when such is given; they are especially important when individuals from different cultures engage in long-term trade. To conduct trade and mitigate its innate risks, property rights must be defined and assured by means of customs, laws, and agreements.[6]

It is the role of economic institutions such as property rights to lower the costs of exchange transactions and enhance the security of the holders of rights. Defining property and clarifying it to parties interested in carrying out an exchange reduces the parties' transaction costs by obviating some of the need to spend money to obtain information on the partner to the exchange, as well as by lowering the risk associated with consummating the transaction.[7] An enforcement system also reduces expenses and the risks of not realizing the transaction. The costs of defining and enforcing property rights must be lower than the utility gained by the existence and activation of the rights.

5 Demsetz 1967, 347–59.
6 Demsetz 1966, 62; Demsetz 2002, S653–72.
7 Niehans 1987, 676–79.

Transaction costs are contingent on the type of asset being exchanged and on the social framework (customs, etc.) within which the exchange takes place. A distinction is made between ex-ante expenditure, that preceding the transaction, and ex-post. Ex-ante costs include those related to drawing up, negotiating, and securing a contract that addresses hypothetical situations that may arise. Collateral against breach of the contract may find expression in various forms—for example, encumbering other properties, third-party guarantees, or even an offer of joint ownership. Ex-post expenses, those incurred after the contract is signed, may pertain to adjusting the contract in the event of a deviation from it, negotiating an amendment to the contract, managing the contract, and exercising collateral.[8]

Property rights also lower the transaction cost of investing in properties. Pledging properties, for example, makes it possible to mitigate risks to lenders and lowers the price of the capital obtained. Recognizing and honoring property rights not only reduces the risk of investing in properties, but also increases the return on investment.

Holding property rights confers the right to use the bundle of rights associated with properties, in full or in part. There are three main rights: to use the property and enjoy its fruits (profit, income, benefits);[9] to deny others access to or unauthorized use of the property and the ability to influence the exercise of the rights; and to transfer, without interference, control of the set of rights to others—by bequeathing, selling, gifting, lending, or investing. These elements of the package of rights in a property may be held separately by different parties. Thus, the right to use a property may be held by one person for a short time (rental) or a long period (leasing); the property may be owned by another actor (the society, an institution, or an individual); and the right to transfer the property may be limited by some other actor.[10]

A distinction is made among different kinds of ownership and of property—land and other fixed property (e.g., houses, fixtures, mines, etc., otherwise known as "real estate"); chattels such as furniture, implements, and jewelry; and intellectual property: copyrights, patents, and so on. There are also vested rights, given by authorities for the performance of a specific economic activity, such as fishing, felling timber, sailing, and so on.

In antiquity, people also had ownership rights to human beings, and slavery was recognized. Slaves were defined as property of two kinds. The first type of slaves amounted to full-fledged property in which the prerogatives over them in-

8 North 1997, 127–60.

9 Including the right to make new and as yet undefined uses of the property.

10 In Israel, leasing is long-term rental (more than five years).

cluded the right to sell, encumber, and bequest; they were mainly prisoners of war. The other group comprised slaves who had been summoned due to the exercise of collateral for loans or who had been given over by their families; they were used to generate income and their owners were limited in what they could do with them. Certain slaves could be redeemed.

Property rights may be held by society, organizations, or individuals. Hence, ownership may be public (society, extended family, village, the state), private (a person, a partnership, a ruler), or an organization. As noted above, private property right is one awarded to a person who controls the use of scarce resources.[11] To own a property, one must own a considerable portion of the bundle of rights in the property.[12] Some distinguish between personal property and private property. Personal property serves the individual and his/her household. Private property is generating a gain for its owner when used (as a means of production). Certain social scientists who do not recognize private property refer to this distinction, claiming that there were times in history when the private right to own a means of production, such as land, did not exist, and insisting that such property was held by society.

Property rights are created and change, are used and exchanged. New rights arise as the result of new land use, ideas, inventions, agreements among public entities, and new uses. Property rights acquire meaning in a lengthy process of definition that entails investment in expression, documentation, and creation of enforcement mechanisms.[13] There are cases in which the rights are exclusive but limited in their transfer use. In other cases, the right to transfer property is unrestricted but the price is limited—for example, if maximum and minimum prices are fixed. Rights may be limited in time if, for instance, they are susceptible to threat of confiscation or revocation by edict. Limits may also be placed on certain kinds of competition among sellers of rights or on transference of rights to certain population groups.

The system of creating and enforcing property rights can be analyzed through two prisms: one, the "private order," which governs individuals' behavior where no rules of the game are dictated; and, two, individuals' behavior in a situation where authorities dictate the rules.[14] The rules of the "private order" are created by groups of individuals sharing a common background, who coordinate expected be-

---

11 The change in ownership of property flows from the need to internalize the costs associated with the use of the property and from the creation of a shortage.

12 Demsetz 1998, 145–6.

13 Ibid., 151–2.

14 See below, discussion in the chapter on Enforcement, page 141.

havior among themselves, and create a social system for disseminating information.[15]

Rules of the game (institutions), in contrast, are handed down "from above" in a political process, imposing control over economic life because they are defined and enforced by governing authorities. This happens, for example, when property rights are allocated, amended, and enforced with official assistance. According to the 'state' theory, the state maximizes society's wealth by means of a contract that limits certain individuals' activity relative to others in order to increase economic growth. This theory posits that property rights are developed in order to limit individuals' actions with property for the sake of greater economic efficiency. "Top-down" institutions recognize agreements between individuals and activate a system of enforcement, such as courts of law and bureaucracies. Political systems, however, are not always equal to the challenge of safeguarding property rights; sometimes they spawn other institutions that neither acknowledge nor support these rights.[16]

Property rights are anchored in agreements between people.[17] A land sale contract, for example, creates property rights to the land and deposits them with the buyer; a will establishes rights to a deceased person's assets that an heir may invoke. Assets may also be created as the result of written and oral agreements for the transfer of property to others in the form of loans, deposits, or collateral. In such agreements, an asset, such as money, is handed from one person to another and an obligation to repay it on a certain date is created. This undertaking *per se* is an asset that comes with defined and protected property rights.[18]

Property rights, as stated, are recognized and enforced by official authorities. They may also be created by court rulings that recognize holders of rights to a given asset. In most studies about property rights and exchange, it is assumed that rules governing contractual disputes exist. The courts, aware of these rules, put them to deliberate and sophisticated use. This makes litigation more predictable and thus less costly.[19]

* * *

In summary, property rights regulate relations within a society with respect to the use and ownership of assets. There are two approaches to this issue of property rights. One views them as natural rights that reflect individuals' freedom to create

---

15 Grief 2005, 428–52.

16 North 1981, 7–8.

17 See discussion in the chapter on Enforcement, page 141.

18 See discussion in the chapter on Credit and Finanace, page 104.

19 See discussion in the chapter on Enforcement, page 141.

and use rights. The second holds that private property rights cause inequality and social injustice, claiming that such rights actually belong to society and, therefore, private property rights in the means of production should be rejected. Ownership of rights to property confers the right to use these rights. The principal rights are use, exclusion of others, and transfer of the property to others. The rights can be held by society, organizations, or individuals. Having property rights and a system to enforce them is a *sine qua non* for the existence of markets. In markets, property rights are exchanged and their prices are set. Rights are established and enforced as the outcome of systems of social, private, and public arrangements. Agreements between people create the possession of rights; disputes concerning them are litigable in courts of law and enforceable by governing authorities.

Property Rights in Mesopotamia

Documents and archaeological findings attest to the existence of property rights as an economic institution in third- and early-second-millennium BCE Mesopotamia. In fact, their existence was crucial for exchange, credit, and investment in assets and means of production in that part of the world. Property rights belonged to the "private order" and "rules" that political institutions dictated. They were recognized and identified, *inter alia*, by stamps, seals, stakes, sale documents and border stones, and enforced with respect to goods, services, assets, and means of production.

The existence of property rights in assets such as houses, slaves, and other personal property is undisputed among researchers.[20] Archaeological excavations have uncovered documents pertaining to the sale of assets, inheritance, and marriage that attest to the existence of property rights in ancient Mesopotamia. Researchers do, however, disagree about property rights in land as a means of production. Those advocating a social approach contend that land (the means of production) was owned by large organizations (extended families) that worked it jointly for subsistence, and that some of the organizations' land was handed over for cultivation for subsistence farming to tenants who held positions in the organizations. Other scholars argue that there is evidence of the existence of extensive rights to the use of private land as a means of production. Much of the land, they claim, was held in long-term leases by palace and temple office-holders, and land rights were bequeathed and sold under certain conditions.

20 Scholars who follow the social approach call these assets "personal."

The structure of property rights in Mesopotamia appears to be an ancient one, dating from the fourth millennium BCE, if not even earlier, and evidently originated in the great urbanization—the transition to permanent settlements, allocation of fields for cultivation, and accumulation of property. Land use rights were presumably established then, too. Indeed, rights of exclusive use were set forth within the confines of settlements, created and managed by leaders— "elders"—on the basis of oral agreements.[21] In the new settled framework, the main vocation was agriculture; people formed social organizations in order to take advantage of the river water to irrigate crops using sophisticated irrigation systems. Scholars of the social approach contend that this self-organization took place in large family units called *bītum* (households) that held and cultivated the land jointly. Tribal or village heads of the extended family allocated the land. Inheritance customs were such that rights to fields were co-owned by a large number of family members. Cultivation, however, was the labor of the few; the rest of the family engaged in other occupations.[22]

The earliest written testimony of property rights is evidently the Stele of Ušumgal, which documents the sale or granting of three fields, three houses, and some livestock in the presence of the witnesses in the Early Dynastic period (2900–2700 BCE). The archaic script, however, is such that the substance of the transaction cannot be determined.[23]

During most of that era, only a small portion of land was privately owned.[24] Although written material about private ownership of farmland exists, scholars note the paucity of documents and struggle to reconstruct the structure of land ownership. The documents originate in institutional, not personal, archives. Several artifacts attest to family and community ownership of land; they indicate that transferring title to land between families and communities is presumed to have been complex and rare. Large-scale changes of land ownership in the urban era involving large palace and temple organizations were conducted by kings.[25]

According to documents from the Bau temple in Girsu from the Early Dynastic period (mid-third millennium BCE),[26] the organizations' lands—those of the temple and the palace—were divided into three portions.[27] One part, "god's land" (67 per-

21 This structure is still accepted in some less-developed societies.
22 Gelb 1979, 3–4.
23 See in Metropolitan Museum, https://www.metmuseum.org/art/collection/search/329079
24 Renger 1995, 269–19; Wilcke 2003, 163–72.
25 Gelb et al., 1991.
26 Postgate 1995, 183–90.
27 Deimel 1931.

cent of total cultivated land of the temple), was worked by laborers, who received a wage (or a ration)[28] in the means of exchange of the period—barley, dates, oil, wool, and textile. Another part (25 percent of the land) – "wage or ration land" was held by officeholders, priests, or members of the military. They cultivated the fields for their own use in return for services that they gave the organization—the king. Land held by officeholders was allotted by the king, was forbidden for sale, and was inheritable only if the sons remained in the same function or service as the original officeholder. The holders of use rights to the land could transfer them to others by leasing. The third portion of the organization's land, 8 percent of the cultivated land of the temple ("Tenant land"), was leased under an arrangement in which the farmer shared the harvest with the organization or paid a regular annual leasing fee.[29]

An important study on property rights in the third millennium BCE (Early Dynastic Period I up to Ur III), presents documentation of sales relating to quite a large number of properties,[30] including documentation concerning rights of ownership in real estate that were found among the economic documents at Tel Fara, otherwise known as ancient Šuruppak. These documents (kudurru stones), on which are recorded the sale process, its terms, and the boundaries of the parcel, all inscribed in ancient Sumerian. They deal with transferring use rights in property, such as fields or other land from the ruler's palace or the temple, to individuals or between individuals. These documents must be interpreted with caution due to their abridged writing style, the absence of words that are crucial for understanding the text, and the ancient Sumerian language employed. In most cases, the documents were discovered in palace or temple archives.[31]

Foster describes the situation in the Akkadian period (the reign of Sargon).[32] At that time, as in the previous era, the palace and temple lands belonged to three parties: the palace and the temple (controlled by the king), cultivated by farm workers; the organization's workers, who received land for their own cultivation; and peasants, who received it under tenancy. Additional land was owned by private families. Land possessed by workers of the organization who held rights could be leased but not sold. It was inheritable provided the heir continued to hold his father's position in the organization.

28 According to the social approach the allocation of the products (rations) to the workers was part of a redistribution process.
29 Postgate 1995, 186.
30 Gelb et al., 1991.
31 Ibid., 1–13, 19; Martin, 1988, 85–103; Wilcke, 2003, 143–4, 163–8.
32 Foster 1982; Foster 1983, 147–75.

On the obelisk of Man-ištūšu, we find the description of a purchase of land by Man-ištūšu, king of Akkad, in 2270 BCE. The sellers were an extended family (a household); their exact identity is difficult to determine due to the profusion of sellers' names on the obelisk. It is hypothesized that Man-ištūšu wanted to acquire the land in order to apportion it among his people or restructure its ownership—from households to individuals—thereby facilitating the handling of encumbrances.[33]

Steinkeller, van Mieroop, and others describe the state of property rights under Ur III (late third millennium BCE).[34] According to their descriptions, royal lands were owned by the palace and the temple and were managed by the king. The structure of palace and temple ownership of cultivated land had not changed since the period preceding the Akkadian kingdom. The land (at the temple of Namḫani, for example) was divided three ways: two-thirds cultivated directly by the temple, one-fourth as "sage fields," and 8 percent as "Tenant fields."[35] No written documentation of land sale transactions has been found. The absence of documents relating to private ownership has prompted some researchers to reason that it was forbidden at the time. The organization and ownership use matched those of previous eras. According to the socioeconomic model favored by researchers of the Ur III period, the economic method operative in this empire centered on agricultural and industrial production in large palace and temple systems, and redistribution of the output to members of the court, office-holders, soldiers, and workers.[36]

Excavations have uncovered contracts, sale and rental documents, letters of guarantee, and other letters concerning personal property such as gardens, houses, and slaves.[37] People had the right to cultivate fields by virtue of their being workers of the king or the temple; the fields were leased to them in return for approximately one-third of the harvest.[38] As in the earlier era, they had no right to transfer the property to others, with the exception of a close family member, and that on condition that that individual would continue to hold the same position in the organization as had the transferor.[39]

Such arrangements were carried forward to ancient Babylon (second millennium BCE). In the Ḫammu-rapi era, for example, there was a method called *ilkum*

33 Postgate 1995, 96.
34 Van de Mieroop 1992; Steinkeller 2004, 91–111.
35 Postgate 1995, 186.
36 Steinkeller 2004, 91–111.
37 Lafont and Westbrook 2003, 185.
38 Renger 1995, 300; Lafont and Westbrook 2003, 205–6.
39 Waetzoldt 1987, 128–32; Van Driel 1998, 29–34.

in which public land was given to officeholders and soldiers, with a house, garden, and fields also provided so that the benefacted could generate supplemental income. The property could not be sold, but could be bequeathed. The arrangement was enshrined in Sections 26–31 and 36–41 of the Code of Ḫammu-rapi.[40]

No central lists of homeowners or plot owners in a given area have been uncovered in findings from third-millennium BCE Mesopotamia and Assyrian traders' documents. Also lacking are deeds affirming a given individual's rights to land. Holders of rights settled for documents of transfer of rights (sale) and marked properties with the help of officeholders in order to prove their entitlement to them. Transfers of rights (or sales agreements) were accompanied by written agreements and recording of transactions in the authorities' presence. The officeholder class included scribes who had acquired their literacy skills in special schools that also taught them how to draw up legal documents, such as bills of sale and leases, partnership agreements, leases of fields and plantations, and rental agreements for houses and livestock.[41] The principals in transfers of rights in Mesopotamia executed a contract in which they specified the type of property being transferred, its borders, their names, the location of the property and sometimes its size, and the price of the transfer of rights to it. The document was dated and witnesses swore to its veracity. Properties were measured and demarcated by surveyors or officeholders; scribes recorded the transaction. A copy of the document was kept in the palace or the temple if a party to the transaction belonged to either of these organizations.

Also found in the documents are arrangements for the transfer of rights under various forms of inheritance. They established which heir would receive rights and in what portion of the property.[42] Owners could let (*agārum*) the property under a rental agreement.[43] Some sales documents had clauses protecting buyers against measures that third parties claiming rights to the property might take; they imposed steep fines on sellers of others' rights.[44] The process of transferring rights was ceremonial.[45] Border stones were installed at the boundaries of the plot and stakes (*sikkatum*) were planted at houses; both carried inscriptions and seals noting the ownership of the rights. At the ceremony where the property was recorded, the stakes were anointed with oil.[46]

---

40 Edzard 1999, 114–7; Postgate 1995, 187.
41 Postgate 1995, 69.
42 Van de Mieroop 1992, 241*ff*; van de Mieroop 1999, 254–5; Charpin 1986, 121–40.
43 Veenhof 2003a, 473.
44 Ibid., 462–4.
45 Van de Mieroop 1999, 267–9.
46 Postgate 1995, 60–1.

Seals or stamps as proof of ownership have been known since the Neolithic era, from roughly the seventh millennium BCE. In the early fifth millennium BCE, seals began to be used for administrative purposes. They were made of stone with a handle and their impressions appear on properties and on bullae, or, in the case of goods, were attached with a strand to the goods and their packings. Cylindrical seals began to appear in southern Mesopotamia and southwestern Iran in the late fourth and early third millennia BCE. The cylindrical seal apparently came along with an inscription and served administrative purposes. It identified the individual who appeared as a party in the matter described in the inscription and specified whether the property belonged to an individual, the temple, or the palace. In the second quarter of the third millennium BCE, signatories began to appear by name and specified their personal rights to properties. Such seals appear on clay tablets and their envelopes.[47]

In Mesopotamia of the third millennium BCE and the Old Babylonian period, there was a judicial system that engaged, *inter alia*, in enforcing laws and customs and settling disputes and conflicts between individuals and groups. The judicial system rested on a system of statutes and case law that was published on steles, together with a sentencing system administered by local councils, courts, and rulers.[48] The litigation process included presenting witnesses, swearing to rulers and gods in order to validate testimonies or documents, and presenting the judges with documents confirming the arguments. The proceedings ended with a sentence handed down in writing and implemented by officeholders or prosecutors in the presence of witnesses.[49]

These laws and judicial processes included reference to proprietary rights to real estate, chattels, livestock, and slaves. Personal property rights were protected with the help of material and corporal punishments (including capital) imposed by those who had been wronged.[50] The system of statutes and enforcement viewed trespass with particular gravity. A property owner could deny entry to a stranger; thieves were severely punished, and restitution was made. In later periods, such as that of the Code of Ḫammu-rapi (the 18th century BCE), theft was a capital crime in

47 Edzard 1996, 109; Larsen 1977, 89–105; Nissen 1988, pp. 76–8.

48 As for the signficiance of the laws that have survived from that period on steles and clay, there is a debate among scholars. Some scholars believe that the kings published these documents simply to glorify themselves as men of justice and jurisprudence, without any corresponding judicial obligation. Nonetheless, there is no doubt that the laws that were published had a decisive influence on the customs and procedures of the period, and people could refer to them when writing contracts or when making inquiries.

49 Postgate 1995, 275–91.

50 Wilcke 2003, 141–429.

certain cases. The extent of one's rights was measured in terms of the probability of invoking the means of enforcement and affording their cost. Enforcement itself hinged on the authorities, informal social action, and current ethical and moral norms.

Sections 30–32 of the Code of Ur-Nammu (2112–2095 BCE) deal with the payment of damages for the infringement of field owners' property rights.[51] In the code of Lipit-Ištar (second half of the 20th century BCE), Sections 4–14 and 34–37 spell out penalties for infringing on the rights of the owners of assets such as oxen, boats, plantations, fields, and slaves.[52] In the Code of Nippur (17th century BCE), reference is made to property rights in oxen.[53] The Code of Ešnunna (first half of the 18th century BCE) protects lenders' property rights, but limits them by setting a maximum interest rate on loans in barley and silver (Sections 18–21); the code also sets limits on goods and services (Sections 1–11), thus effectively restraining property rights with respect to them as well.[54]

The Code of Ḫammu-rapi (mid-18th-century BCE) makes extensive reference to property rights.[55] The entitlements of the temple, the king, and ordinary individuals are defined and protected (Sections 6–49) with respect to the nature of ownership, restrictions on the right to benefit from and transfer assets, and the protection of assets (objects, livestock, slaves) against theft and home invasion. The code deals with matters related to rights in cases of loans and deposits and the status of pledges and guarantees (Sections 49–52, 113–119). Also noted are processes in which rights are established by means of witnesses and documents (e.g., Sections 7, 10–11). The judicial processes relating to rights before judges are spelled out (Sections 5, 9), and limitations of rights also appear. Ownership rights to a field, plantation, house, or livestock of a soldier, a fisher, and a state officeholder who received his property from the state could not be sold or bequeathed.[56] Other sections relate to credit, proscription of usury, and the property rights of traders and participants in commerce.[57]

According to contemporaneous evidence, people held documents attesting to their ownership of property[58] and relating to the sale of property, adoption and inheritance, the dowry for a bride, and court rulings that established property

51 Roth 1997, 20–1; Lafont and Westbrook 2003, 183–226.
52 Ibid., 73; Roth 1997, 26–8.
53 Ibid., 40–1.
54 Driver and Miles 1952, 111–57.
55 Ibid., 101; Roth 1997, 71–143, 176.
56 Driver and Miles 1952, 111–245.
57 Westbrook 2003, 361–430.
58 Veenhof 1987, 49–50.

rights. When these documents were lost, people could petition the courts for rulings to confirm title. Such legal proceedings included oaths and testimonies of the principals, including the authorities. The process was called *ṭuppam anniam uballiṭū*— "revive this document." Authorities defended property rights by maintaining an enforcement system that included registrars of rights, the judicial system before which disputes over rights were adjudicated, and a set of rules or a bureaucracy that engaged in enforcing contracts or court rulings.

* * *

In summary, societies and authorities in third-millennium BCE Mesopotamia recognized proprietary rights in many goods and services, both through outright ownership and in right of use enshrined in agreements and seals.[59] The institution of property rights appears to have been quite an ancient one, dating from the transition to permanent settlements and the accumulation of property by individuals and families. The structure of rights in southern Mesopotamia can be traced to the time when individuals came together in large organizations to build complex irrigation systems and cultivate the organization's lands. Most land rights were held by the organization and belonged to the ruler. Many land use rights were part of the system of remuneration reserved for workers who had senior managerial and professional status in the organization. Such rights were afforded for a lengthy term and could be bequeathed or transferred to another under certain conditions.

Third millennium BCE documents relating to the sale of privately-owned property address themselves to fields, plantations, water trenches, human beings, animals, houses, dates, gold, and more.[60] Rights in these assets could be let, sold, summoned, and bequeathed.[61] Some documents deal with the right to practice occupations such as fishing, reed-gathering, timber, and commerce. The palace, the temple, and individuals also held other property, such as jewelry, sculptures, furniture, equipment, and additional chattels that archaeologists have uncovered.

In the Old Babylonian period, the economy underwent restructuring. Large and small estates of private and institutional landowners, replaced the large systems of the temple and the palace that had typified production previously. The set of property rights available resembled that of the earlier system, but the ratio of palace and temple property to that held by private individuals changed, with the share of assets held by the latter having increased considerably.[62]

---

59 Steinkeller 2004; Wilcke 2003, 210–18.
60 Gelb et al. 1991.
61 Van de Mieroop 1999, 253–87.
62 Steinkeller 2004, 109–11.

Property Rights in the Old Assyrian Period

The trade institutions of the Old Assyrian period followed the pattern of similar institutions in earlier Mesopotamia. They were based on the social structure, customs, and culture of this region, in which private ownership was present. The documentation makes it clear that property rights were a highly important institution in the exchange of goods, services, and assets in Assyrian society. Their importance may be adduced from the protective system that accompanied them. The Assyrians used seals and stakes to affirm ownership of assets and installed a contractual system to protect their rights.

The existence of well-defined property rights and an enforcement system to support them were crucial in the conduct of Old Assyrian trade, facilitating individuals' access to the capital market and enabling the market to exist. There, the traders exchanged property rights in commercial commodities and also set their prices. Property rights to buildings encouraged traders to erect buildings and invest in them in order to make improvements in them. The rights allowed their holders to obtain loans for personal or investment purposes, and holders of rights could pledge them in return for a loan. Rights transferred as investments or loans were recognized and documented, obliging investees and creditors to repay them, together with profits and interest.

Property rights were especially important in long-term trade between Assyrian and Anatolian merchants, hailing from different cultures. Defining the rights and securing them by agreed upon customs, laws, and agreements with local leaders were crucial for the conduct of trade and mitigation of the risks arising from them.[63]

Assyrian traders' documents make frequent reference to property rights as part of the "private order," "the dictated rules," and the laws that governed their enforcement. Traders used terms that attest to their awareness of the importance of property rights, such as *šarûm* (wealthy), *išûm* (possess property), and *makkūrum* (owner of objects of value/property), as often recur in the documents. Traders possessed assets such as *luqūtum* (goods), *bābtum* (merchandise outstanding, or "accounts receivable"), and *be'ūlātum* (business capital). They had ways of enforcing their property rights. They could *ṣabātum* (seize, hold) debtors in an attempt to collect debts by means of witnesses; they could also file a *maḫārum* (present a claim) with a *dayyānum* (judge).

Below are quotations from traders' documents that attest to the rules of the "private order," the importance of property rights for individuals and society in

63 Demsetz 1966, 62; idem 2002, S653–72.

the Old Assyrian era, as well as that society's well-developed system of rights in real property and chattels. People who amassed property marked it, thereby protecting it from injury or interference by strangers. Property served as collateral for credit and was liable to lawsuit and confiscation pursuant to legal claims brought before the enforcement institutions. People bequeathed property rights, following agreed-upon procedures.

> The silver is guaranteed (lit. bound) by whatever they possess in the City (Assur)."[64]
>
> And his creditors have also taken whatever he owns.[65]
>
> I shall seize for you (lit. have your hand on) everything he possesses.[66]
>
> Why do you always store straw and wood in my house, do you not have any houses of your own?[67]
>
> Do you not know that the household property which they keep stealing is in fact my property?[68]

The Assyrian traders went about their business successfully and accumulated property; they also, of course, encountered financial hardships and difficult situations in which they lost assets. Their caravans encountered raiders or unforeseen expenses that inflicted losses. Political events, such as uprisings or wars between local kings, stymied trade and inflicted losses on the traders. Disruptions of trade often left borrowers unable to repay their debts, and debts that were in arrears triggered heavy interest costs. Proscribed commercial activity, such as smuggling, was met with fines and prison terms in Kanesh and Assur. Such situations plunged traders into financial straits and, at times, they suffered massive property losses. One example is reflected in a letter from the trader *Pūšu-kēn,*[69] in which he describes his plight and asks his children to help, and then in a later letter from his daughter, describing the situation after his death: "All of our father's wealth is lost."[70] Sometimes traders lost everything and were labelled "destitute." The manner of writing in this context may allude to the dim view that was taken toward this phenomenon, i.e., the propertied were more respected than the paupered.

64 KTH 19:22 ff., CAD I-J 290a.
65 BIN 6 195:25 ff., CAD I-J 290a.
66 CCT 2 13:30 ff., CAD I-J 290b.
67 BIN 6 119:21 ff., CAD D 22b.
68 TCL 17 53:8 ff., CAD $N/_2$ 335b.
69 BIN 4 32.
70 (*Prague* I 680), Veenhof 1999, 70.

> What is this extravagance(?) you keep writing me about? (if) there is not enough for us to eat, (how) could we keep living on lavish scale? what there was at my disposal I have already scraped together and sent, today I live in an empty house.[71]

> With regard to PN, about whom you wrote me, I did not get hold of him in the matter of the outstanding amounts because he is destitute and has been removed to Kanish.[72]

Wealth gave traders an important status in Assyrian society.[73] According to the documents, the traders' society was divided into *rabûm* ("big traders") and *ṣaḫḫurum* ("little traders"), apparently differentiated by the amount of property they owned.[74] The status of householders, in turn, was determined, *inter alia,* by the number of houses they owned in Assyria and its colonies, as well as their size. For example, Lamassī nags her husband, Pūšu-kēn, to build a house in Assyria because his friend had built houses before him; she seems jealous. Furthermore, she wants him to expand their real estate holdings in Assyria:[75] PN's wife complains about their house, while referring to her husband's associate, who has already twice "made" a house since PN's departure.[76]

The Assyrian traders' documents make no mention of fields and plantations, evidently because they did not wish to invest their wealth in such properties in Anatolia. Instead, such assets appear in documents of local Anatolian traders.[77] The Assyrian traders' property rights comprised for example the following: possession and sale of real property and chattels—such as slaves, livestock, offspring—that had been encumbered to foreigners; sale of merchandise for profit; encumbrance of assets for loans; bequeathing assets to kin; personal for-profit use of assets such as housing; and personal use of farm produce.[78]

As stated above, the Old Assyrian period saw abundant use of seals and stakes to demarcate ownership rights in assets. Seals were affixed to walls and apertures of structures to signify ownership. Stakes were driven into structures and stones were used to demarcate fields. Pieces of clay bullae were affixed to knots with ropes that tied sacks or were placed on the openings of containers. Clearly, stakes, stamps and cylindrical seals were used to assure property rights in a manner

71 CCT 3 24:32 ff., CAD E 320–1b&a.
72 TCL 19 5:26 ff., CAD E 321a.
73 Veenhof 1977, 116.
74 Dercksen 2004, 237–38.
75 Michel 1997, 285.
76 RA 59 (1965), 160, 30 ff. Veenhof 1977, p. 116.
77 Veenhof 2003a, 457; Dercksen 2008, 139–57.
78 On the shape and floor space of Assyrian houses, the manner of their construction, and other details in regard to them as reflected in the documents, see Michel 1996, 285–300.

much like the earlier Mesopotamian practices. Home thefts were punished by the traders' organizations and the authorities. Seals were carefully guarded and were bequeathed, as can be seen in the following:

> Seal the main building and the *durino* (part of the house) with your seals (...) they should keep the seals on the main house and the *durino* well watched.[79]

> Bring all furnishings which are in the house into the new house and seal the main building and our walls (with your seals).[80]

In one of the documents, a female member of the household, *Šāt-Aššur*, complains in a discussion concerning the estate of one of the traders about her exclusion from the deceased's property due to her youth.[81] She evidently lived in the house and took the opportunity to drive a cone into a wall as evidence of her right to the property.

> Why am I (considered) a child, that I cannot (get)? My father house and [...] my cone is in the wall.[82]

> Should this (sold) house be claimed, a cone (which serves as guarantee) has been driven (into his property) in his town and in the country?[83]

The Assyrians also used various methods to secure their rights in chattels, as well as their merchandise. They wrapped tin and silver bullion in special textiles for transport on donkeys' backs. Textiles were wrapped in sacks ahead of transport. After the merchandise was packed up by means of ropes and stakes, the owners stamped the knots to mark their ownership.[84] The packages were opened by breaking the seals; once opened, their contents were weighed in the presence of witnesses.[85]

> Seal the twelve sacks and the rope around the cones.[86]

Assyrian traders sold assets or bartered silver for assets, namely, they traded property rights in one asset (a building, for example) for rights to another asset (e.g.,

---

79 CCT 3, 14:10 ff., CAD D 191b.
80 CCT 3 14:7 ff., CAD B 283b.
81 Michel 1996, 285.
82 TTC 26, Michel 1986, p. 128; KTH 6, Hecker 1978, p. 411. CAD S 250b
83 MDP 23 236:12 CAD S 250b
84 Veenhof 1972, 41–4.
85 Ibid., 30–32.
86 ICK 1 135:13, CAD $N/_1$ 379b.

silver). Details of sales are reported in the documents in regard to chattels (e.g., merchandise) and houses. The traders' documents report real estate transactions including details about the properties, such as their prices in Kanesh and Assur.[87] Thus, we learn about differences between Assur and Kanesh in home prices, which appear to be higher in large cities.[88] The quotations below illuminate the traders' attitude toward the matter of rights to real estate and the letting of properties:

> For the house we paid four talents of copper, we gathered (that sum) partly from what (is due from) your agents, partly from (the price for) your barley, we paid out three talents, we borrowed one talent from a money lender on interest[89]

> We bought PN's house for you, they will measure three (*ṣubātums*), if there are more or less than three, adjust the payment accordingly.[90]

> Please, the very day you hear this letter you must offer sale the houses, both of your slave girls and both of your grinding girls and then send me the silver! Then you must rent a house and settle there.[91]

In addition to rights in properties, goods, and real estate, there were also property rights in human beings and livestock. The Old Assyrians used slaves intensively. They were part of the assets of the traders. The slaves were engaged in multiple jobs, doing the hard work in the homes. They served as cleaners, repairers, suppliers of wood for cooking and heat, movers and porters. Sometimes they were professionals who provided income to their owners, such as barbers.

People to whom property rights applied[92] were defined as *wardum* (he-slave) and *amtum* (she-slave). Slavery came in two forms: chattel slaves and debt slaves. The former was taken captive due to involvement in hostilities (for example) and were sold in the market to others for their labor.[93] The women were used for grinding cereals, cleaning, cooking, taking care of the children, and sometimes as sexual partners. Owners were liable for their slaves' sustenance. According to Old Babylonian documents, for example, a slave buyer had to obtain security from the seller to vouchsafe the unimpeachability of his ownership of the slave and the slave's good health.[94] The other kind of slavery was the result of the liquidation of

87 Veenhof 2003a, 457.
88 Michel 1997, 297–98.
89 KTH 9:16 and 20, CAD T 127b.
90 TC 14 11 6 ff, CAD Š/$_3$ 185a.
91 TC 3 88:10–21, Larsen 2002, p. 56.
92 Westbrook 2003, 380–85.
93 Wells 2005, 190–2.
94 Veenhof 1995, 1741.

human collateral for a loan after failure to meet the terms. Manumission from this kind of slavery could be arranged by repaying the debt;[95] in certain cases, however, a fine had to be paid for achieve this outcome. This form of slavery was time limited.[96] Chattel-slaves in Old Babylonia were marked in some way, probably with a special haircut. Manumission took place in a special process or through redemption by family members.

> PN has received 17 shekels of silver, the slave girl's price, PN_2 has bought (her).[97]
>
> For the price of 2/3 mana (forty shekels) of silver for the slave PN.[98]
>
> PN is "held fast" (as pledge) by the silver (owed) if he (the debtor) returns the silver, he may take away his son wherever he pleases.[99]

The usual manner of transferring rights to property in exchange was by oral or written contract in the presence of witnesses.[100] Such a contract specified actions that the parties were to take at certain times in view of the terms in effect at the time: usually delivery of goods, performance of services, or payment in silver. The terms covered dubious situations, the conduct incumbent on the parties when the contract was executed, and on an exchange of notices. These contracts were enforced by courts or other decision-making authorities, such as arbitrators and trade organizations' institutions.

Tablets on which credit agreements appeared were important assets that required special care in order to safeguard the rights written on them. Contracts, instruments of debt, and letters were placed in boxes or clay containers that were also sealed. Traders had special safe rooms in their homes where they kept documents dear to them. These rooms were also sealed. They could be opened by strangers, by court order, or in a process of liquidating a debt only by following a special procedure, in which the tablets were handed to the lenders.

> Take out all the objects from the house of PN—and not leave anything behind—and put (them) under seal in my house.[101]

---

95 According to the Code of Ḫammu-rapi (Section 117), a debt-slave is released after three years of servitude. Roth 1997, 103.
96 Veenhof 2003a, 449–50.
97 ICK 1 123:2, CAD $Š/_3$ 22a.
98 TCL 14 67:7, CAD $A/_2$ 244a.
99 KTH 22:8 ff., CAD T 249a.
100 Shavell 1998, 436–45.
101 BIN 6 182:5 ff., CAD $A/_2$ 377b.

> Open (pl.) the strongroom of PN which is under seal of his representatives, break the sealing, and let the three persons seal (it instead).[102]
>
> At the death of our father, our father's creditors entered (the strongroom), and our father's creditors entrusted to you twelve tablet containers, silver under seal, (all that was) in the strongroom sealed by our father.[103]
>
> (They entered the house of PN) and opened the strongroom of PN, whatever gold or silver or also tablets (in their) containers (there was) they entrusted to PN_2.[104]

Rights to assets were held by husbands and wives.[105] The status of rights held was determined in the marriage contract, as in the following:

> PN has married PN_2. The house [i.e., the property] [belongs] to both. If their wealth flees them or if they amass wealth in great amounts, all [will be] joint to them. If PN abandons PN_2, they will divide the house between them. When they depart from this world, PN_3 and PN_4 will receive the house.[106]

Transfer of rights by inheritance required a special procedure involving the writing of a will signed by witnesses.[107] Bills of inheritance were executed in Assur. According to the bylaws of that city, the deceased's debts were paid off in Anatolia and all of his property was taken to Assur, where the appropriate bills were drawn up and final documents for the apportionment of property after payment of debts were issued.[108]

> Sadly, our father has died. He did not speak his will. If it is good for you, then set out and come. Bring our father's house in order.[109]
>
> The rest (of the inheritance) they will divide in accordance with the disposition (i.e., will) of their father.[110]
>
> PN, brother of PN_2, PN_3 son of PN_2, PN_3, PN_4 the sons of PN_2 and their sister, the (consecrated) *gubabtum*, swore the oath of the City (of Assur). On the house in Kanesh, in which PN_3 is living, and the will of their father and anything else, PN shall not raise a claim against PN_2 and his (other) brothers (and sister), the children of PN_2. And the children of PN_2 shall not raise a

102 TCL 20 99:10 ff., CAD K 545b.
103 TTAED 4 7:7 ff., CAD T 110a.
104 TCL 21 270:19 ff., CAD M/1 337a.
105 Veenhof, 1998, 137–41.
106 KTS 2, 6 ff. Bilgiç 1951, 241.
107 Veenhof 2003a, 457–460, idem 1998, 119–58.
108 Idem 1995, 1726–7.
109 CCT 2, 33:2–6. Larsen 2007, p. 101.
110 TuM 1 22a:21, CAD Š/3 18b.

claim about anything against PN and his sons. The house plot next to the house PN_5, the son of PN_6, belong to them jointly.[111]

Assets held by traders could be summoned to guarantee a loan. Default on a loan triggered the possibility of a lawsuit and/or seizure of the collateral and/or other assets. Enforcement was carried out by traders' institutions or the authorities, and also by the parties harmed, in ways that varied in accordance with the society's laws and customs. The procedure included the possibility of entering the debtor's home, taking inventory, and seizing merchandise or tablets in a value sufficient to retire the debt. Holders of rights could lose them as the result of court rulings or rulers' decisions, punishments for acts of commission or omission, or breach of sales or credit agreements.

Take out all the objects from the house of PN—and not leave anything behind—and put (them) under seal in my house.[112]

(Inform me) whether you have paid the silver to the native Anatolian to whom I am indebted and who holds my pledges and (whether you have) obtain the release of my pledges.[113]

(They entered the house of PN) and opened the strongroom of PN, whatever gold or silver or also tablets (in their) containers (there was) they entrusted to PN_2.[114]

Ancient Assyrian society, like other societies in Mesopotamia, enacted laws and signed agreements with foreign rulers to defend rights. Thus, this society developed rules for the enforcement of rights by introducing customs and establishing judicial institutions.[115] Old Assyrian documents mention a set of statutes that existed in Assyria and its Anatolian colonies and that had been published on a *naruā'um* (stele).[116] The existence of this body of law and its related enforcement mechanism is mentioned both explicitly and implicitly. The documents include decisions of the Assur town council and the *Karum*[117] in Kanesh,[118] administrative directives of the ruler of Assur (the king), known as the *waklum* (the overseer, in-

111 Michel 2018 pp. 90–91.
112 BIN 6 182:5 ff., CAD A/$_2$ 377b.
113 BIN 6 68:26 ff., CAD K 509b.
114 TCL 21 270:19 ff., CAD M/$_1$ 337a.
115 Veenhof 2003a, 431–483.
116 The *naruā'um* (stele) was a pillar erected in a central place in town, on which the laws and regulations were written as adopted by the town institutions. See Veenhof 1995, 1717–1744.
117 *Kārum* is an Akkadian term that translates as "quay." Mesopotamians turned it into the name for a commercial district, a traders' residential district, and the traders' organization. On this organization and its duties, see the chapter on Enforcement, page 141.
118 The main Assyrian organization in Turkey.

spector), and documents relating to legal proceedings and private process: instruments of debt and absolution from debt, cancellation and transfer of claims of debt, and charges for the sale of property. Multiple kinds of contracts existed, such as those for services, haulage, deposit, consent, partnership, and *naruqqum* (joint investment).

Non-commercial contracts—marriages, divorces, wills, and undertakings to transfer ownership—existed as well.[119] The conduct with respect to property rights that is described in the traders' documents resembles that set forth in documents and statutes from elsewhere in Mesopotamia. In their agreements with local rulers, the traders defended their assets against confiscation by the same local ruler.[120] The discussion of enforcement appears in a separate chapter below.

* * *

The Old Assyrian trade documents emphasize the matter of traders' personal property rights. Assyrian society was influenced by the customs that prevailed in northern Mesopotamia and southern Syria and by ancient Mesopotamian customs from the fourth and third millennia BCE. Traders had "private order" customs that set forth individuals' norms of conduct, as well as arrangements dictated by the authorities in Assyria and the colonies and backed by an enforcement mechanism. They used seals and cones to demarcate their property rights. There were property rights to human beings, mainly as the result of their becoming enslaved after being used as collateral for debt. Rights were transferred via contracts written on tablets and sealed by the parties and by witnesses, with tablets kept in safe rooms. Disputes relating to contracts were settled by arbitrators and courts on the basis of an established procedure.

119 Veenhof 2003a, 432–4.
120 Veenhof 2008, 193.

Chapter 2
The Market and Means of Exchange (Money)

According to the generally accepted description, the field of economics essentially explains the allocation of scarce resources.[1] The market solves the basic problems of the economy by setting prices,[2] with resources allocated in a process of exchange. This exchange is crucial for the efficient use of resources, as it facilitates decentralization and specialization in production and consumption, and, at the same time, optimizes profit and utility for the parties involved.[3] The market is the place where exchange between potential buyers and sellers of goods, services and means of production occur; it is the medium by which exchange is implemented.[4] Exchange in the market may be natural (barter) or aided by a means of exchange (money). In a market economy, the use of money or credit makes it possible to establish terms of trade that are expressed in prices, which are determined when the exchange takes place. [5] The price of one good in exchange for another reflects the relative quantities of each at the time of the transaction. Thus, in a price system, prices rise when the quantity desired, or demand, is greater than the supply, and fall when the quantity offered, or supply, surpasses the demand. In a free competitive environment, the price system is based on independent decisions by autonomous individuals and not on coordinated control by institutions of authority. The price system derives its importance from its role as a mechanism for the distribution of a scarce goods and services among consumers, signaling to producers where they can make a profit and, consequently, what to produce.

At points of exchange in the market, property rights are exchanged among individuals. For this exchange to occur, property rights must be exclusive,[6] measurable, and enforceable. Price-setting in the market rests on a system in which costs are intrinsic.[7] The costs are the result of the need to measure both the volume of the goods to be exchanged and the scope of the services involved in the transaction, as well as the need to enforce the terms of exchange. The means of measurement and their acceptance by both sides of the transaction have been vital con-

1 Namely, the gap between people's desires and the resources available to them.
2 North 2003, 432–439.
3 Wilson 1987, 202.
4 Rutherford 1992, 286.
5 Vaggi 1987, 334.
6 This is not to say that property rights are unlimited. They may be limited by the sale price or the intended use of the property in question.
7 North 1981, 34–37.

https://doi.org/10.1515/9783111065533-005

ditions in economic history, given the importance of measurement in simplifying exchange and reducing the exchange costs between parties. Defining what is being exchanged, defining and supervising exclusivity, and negotiating and enforcing contracts for the transfer of rights all come with costs.

A third party, such as the state or an organization of traders, may lower transaction costs by developing a set of general rules and regulations that apply to transactions. Adherence to these external consensual rules lowers transaction costs for parties to exchange by sparing them the work of obtaining information about the process and its attendant negotiations. In addition to external limitations imposed on parties to an exchange, there are internal limits that the sides impose on themselves arising from consensual rules of social behavior ("private arrangements").[8] Information costs in a market are reduced with a large number of buyers and sellers. A price in an organized market represents information, which, if not available, would require significant research on the part of buyers and sellers to obtain it. The market also limits "opportunistic behavior'"[9] by accommodating competition among large numbers of participants and due to the personal nature of the exchanges involved.

Markets exist physically (in a marketplace) and virtually, wherever (and whenever) sellers and buyers meet.[10] The encounter may occur in a specific physical location, such as a trader's home, an organized city marketplace, or a virtual venue, like the internet.[11] Markets may exist on a street or a square, at a town gate, a designated location in the countryside, a geographic region, or more than one region. Each market has its own typical rules of conduct that vary according to the location of the market and the goods traded. Any economic unit (consumer or producer) can operate in several markets and assume the role of a buyer or a seller in any one of them. In sophisticated markets, interrelationships exist that allow quantities and prices to be set simultaneously. In each market, buyers and sellers negotiate arrangements for the purchase and sale of the goods traded there. When they conclude such an accord, it means that the quantities sought by the buyers are

---

8 See Chapter 4, Enforcement. Page 141.

9 When one party to a contract exploit the other by behaving after the agreement so as to breach it. Or, occurs where one party takes advantage of his superior knowledge, in order to further his/her interests, by failing to disclose such information to the other party.

10 Hill 1987, 332–334.

11 Historians and anthropologists define markets in a manner perceptibly different from the norm among economists. Economists relate to the market in the abstract; it exists wherever goods and services are exchanged. Historians and anthropologists stress the physical location of the exchange, say, a market place.

equal to those offered by the sellers at the price set. This situation is defined as a state of market equilibrium.

A free market is one in which supply and demand are not subject to control and regulation, apart from government policies that set the market institution's agreed rules of the game, such as property rights, weights and measures, and enforcement of contracts. The authorities regulate, guide, adjust, enact, supervise, and control the economic units' actions in the interests of economic efficiency, fairness, health, and safety. Approaches to supervision may be manifested in varying extents of intervention, as in control of prices, terms of employment, weights and measures, licensing of merchants and workshops, and so on. Supervision may be applied by passing laws, establishing supervisory agencies, or promoting the creation of self-supervising organizations (such as merchants' organizations).

The fundamental problems of the free (market) economy are solved by the market by means of prices set there. Some scholars insist that markets did not exist in antiquity, claiming that exchange in the primitive-substantives' economy of that time took place on a social basis and that prices were officially set rates of equivalences. Others see the market in antiquity as a place where exchange took place between buyers and sellers for economic motives of profit and utility. Exchange was either natural (barter), or aided by means of exchange (money), with prices set at the point of exchange.

* * *

In summary, in free markets, buyers and sellers avail themselves of the market mechanism to optimize their profit and utility. The market is an institution where activity is linked to costs occasioned by the need to measure goods and services being exchanged and to define rights to them. Markets exist wherever buyers and sellers meet. A free market is one where supply and demand are not subjected to control and manipulation, but are regulated by authorities supervising the extent of competition, weights and measures, the quality of means of exchange, fair conduct, health-related matters, and so on.

One of the most important matters in the evolution of exchange and of its venue, the market, is the determination of rules for units of weight and volume. The units must be clear and consensual and, in most cases, should be supervised by an element present in the market that can mediate disputes between the parties to a transaction. The weights and measures used in the market play this essential role.

Weights and Measures

Weights and measures appear to have developed in Mesopotamia during the Ubaid era (sixth millennium BCE), in which tokens wrapped in clay envelopes were used to document quantities and types of goods in a shipment. Units of measurement—of volume (quantities of barley) and of weight (copper)—are evidently associated with the agricultural revolution that took place 10,000 years ago and the first use of copper. Archaeological findings from the Ubaid civilization reveal parts of settlements across the Middle East that may allude to the existence of trade and of merchant colonies. It stands to reason that trade facilitators such as weights and measures were used in this culture.

While units of weight developed in different sizes in different places, research on the topic has found connections between units and specific sizes, which can be compared with the help of mathematical models. Over time, authorities began to supervise weights and measures and legislate standard units and models to which weight units in the market were compared.[12]

Table 1: Measures of Volume in the Ur III Era and Old Assyrian.

In Ancient Hebrew*	In Sumerian	In Akkadian	Volume**	No. of units	Notes
Shekel	Gin	*Šiqlum*[1]		180 barleycorns per Šiqlum	
Kav	Sila	*Qûm*	Liter	60 Šiqlum per *qûm* (sila)	1 *Qûm* of barley = 0.65 kg
Seah	Ban	*Sūtum*	10 liters	10 *qûm* (sila) per *sūtum*	
Kur	Gur	*Kurrum*	300 liters	30 *sūtum* per *kurrum*	

Source: Powell 1990, 95–118; Snell 1982, xx

* Volume in ancient Hebrew measures is somehow different from that in the table.

** According to Gelb 1982, 585–90. Weights and measures in the third millennium BCE varied at different times and places. The Qûm (sila), for example, was apparently 0.8 liter and the Kurrum 240 liters at certain times. Occasionally, kings such as Ur-Nammu and/or Šulgi (twenty-first century BCE) established standard weights and measures.

1 The name used by most researchers in the translation of documents is shekel.

12 Rahmstorf L. and Stratford E. 2019.

The Sumerians established a "base-60" system for weight units that are used to measure time and other measures to this day, evidently due to its mathematical convenience. Interestingly, the basis for calculating volume and weight was the barleycorn (180 corns per shekel of volume and of weight), possibly alluding to the importance of barley in the lives of people and the economy since antiquity.[13]

Since units of volume or weight were used for exchange, the sila and the shekel became units of means of exchange in which exchange prices were denominated. In effect, they became reflections of the money of the time.[14]

Table 2: Measures of Weights in the Ur III Era and Old Assyrian.

In Ancient Hebrew*	In Sumerian	In Akkadian	Weight**	No. of units
Barleycorns	Še	*Uṭṭatum*	0.046 gram	180 barleycorns in a shekel
Shekel	Gin	*šiqlum*	8.33 grams	60 shekels in a mina
Maneh	Mana	*Manûm*[1]	0.5 kg.	60 minas in a talent
Kikar	Gu(n)	*Biltum*[2]	30 kg.	

Source: Powell 1990, 95–118; Snell 1982, xix.

1 In Old Assyrian dialect *Manā'um*. In translation of Old Assyrian documents the researchers use mina. Some researchers use—(English) Pound (approximately the same weight)

2 *Biltum* is translated to talent.

* Weights in ancient Hebrew measures are somehow different from those in the table.

** The weight of the shekel differs between regions. Among Anatolians it was 11.7 grams, in the Levant —9.4 grams, in Syria 7.8 grams.[15]

In Mesopotamia, an agreed set of weights and measures was used to determine and control property rights. The authorities established as law official units of measure, kept standard units of measure, and supervised the measurement of assets and the weights that were used for the exchange of assets. The instruments of measurement, too—weights, scales, and volumes—were subject to inspection by the authorities. In an eponymous law book, King Ur-Nammu published standard weights and measures made of stone and copper.[16] The existence of an accepted system of weights and measures also facilitated the use of certain goods as agreed tender (money). Barley, for example, was an accepted means of exchange in the local market.

13 Perhaps since the agricultural revolution.

14 See Chapter Means of Exchange in Mesopotamia, page 78.

15 Massa and Palmisano 2017, 66.

16 Some attribute the code to his son, Šulgi (2047–2095 BCE).

The basic Sumerian unit of measure was the sila—liter—and subsequently the Akkadian *Qûm*. Measures of silver were used to establish the value of property and to keep records in large organizations and large-scale trading (especially interregional trade). The accepted units of measurement in silver were the shekel and mina. The existence of small units of weight (like barleycorn) suggests that people at the time had accurate scales.[17]

The Market in Mesopotamia

The question of the market and means of exchange in Mesopotamia has been the subject of academic debate for many years. One school of thought, arguing for a corollary of the primitive-substantive model, claims that there were neither markets nor means of exchange in late fourth millennium and third millennium BCE Mesopotamia.[18] For these scholars, society was primitive, engaging mainly in subsistence agriculture, with only a small number of products, such as metals and luxury goods, were traded interregional. Individuals arguably practiced natural exchange (barter) on the basis of exchange ratios (equivalencies) dictated by the authorities, with exchange driven by social considerations, reciprocity and status. Individuals' motives for exchange were not economic, based on profit and personal utility, but social and political. According to adherents of this school, there is no historical or archaeological evidence of the existence of markets, market-set prices, or universal means of exchange in the fourth and third millennia BCE. The term "markets" does not appear in the documents uncovered and no places that might be called markets have been found in the cities. According to proponents of the non-market model, the prices mentioned in the documents are values used by the palace and the temple for bookkeeping purposes that were predetermined and were not the outcomes of supply and demand. In their estimation, barley was used as food and for maintaining accounts of production and redistribution of subsistence rations; merchants and the palace used silver to keep their books of accounts, for ornamentation, or as a commodity exchanged in the market as a raw material. The traders were simply government clerks who carried out exchange on the basis of instructions. For these scholars, exchange was a social cus-

17 Powel 1978, 211–243.

18 For discussion of the various schools of thought, see Powel 1999, 5–23; Renger 2003, 15–127; Veenhof 1972, 348–357 and 389–400; Van de Mieroop, 2004, 54–64, and page 167.

tom meant to promote the situation and status of individuals, society, and the diplomatic and strategic exchanges of rulers with other rulers.[19]

Another group of scholars does find historical and archeological evidence of the existence of markets in the late fourth and the third millennia BCE. According to them, individuals belonged to households and the large organizational settings were economic creatures.[20] Individuals were employed by the systems as wage-earners (at various levels of freedom) and were compensated by means of a daily wage or a monthly salary. Skilled and senior workers of the organizations were compensated in the form of an allocation of land by long-term leases, allowing them the possibility of supplementing the salary they received from the organization. Wages and salaries were paid by the means of exchange (money) of the time, in agreed-upon units of measurement (volume) of barley and other commodities, such as wool, textiles, dates, and oil.[21] Barley was a means of exchange for daily business, and exchange ratios among goods were set in the markets. Market prices were expressed in units of barley for other goods and services such as meat, fish, salt, oil, reeds, beverages such as beer, and haulage.[22] Barley was also a means of measurement of loans and interest and in the organizations' bookkeeping. In the third millennium BCE, silver and copper were added to barley as a means of exchange for transactions in assets such as homes, fruit plantations, and slaves, and for interregional trade. Silver also appears as a medium in addition to barley for recording data in the palace and temple accounting systems, with a fixed exchange rate between barley and silver. These scholars find that in historical documents from the late third millennium BCE onward, the terms "market" (*maḫīrum*) and price (*šīmum*) appear.[23] Markets existed at city gates, on riverbanks (using a quay), on special city streets, and in traders' homes.

* * *

In sum, there is a debate between two schools of thought regarding the institution of the market in ancient Mesopotamia. Those of the primitive-substantive persuasion claim that Mesopotamia had no markets where prices were set, that individuals engaged in exchange on the basis of social interrelations, and that prices were equivalence ratios set by the authorities. The opposing school, the formal-modern

19 See Economic Models that Explain the Era Page 167.
20 Powell 1999, 5–23; Silver 1985; Silver 2004, 65–87.
21 The following researchers identify "rations" as employee salaries. The procedure of paying salaries in "rations"—*ba* in Sumerian and *kurummatum* in Akkadian—persisted until the first millennium BCE. See Gelb 1965. Waetzoldt 1987, 117–125. Jursa 2010, 669–672.
22 Van de Mieroop 1997, 144–145.
23 Veenhof 2003c, 106–111.

one, does identify the existence of markets where prices were determined, and notes the existence of means of exchange in units (volume and weight) of commodities. Authorities regulated these markets by supervising the weights and measures and assessing the quality of the means of exchange.

The Market in the Old Assyrian Period

Letters and documents of Assyrian traders demonstrate the existence and operation of supply and demand, exchange, universal means of exchange, prices, and market regulation as one would expect to find in economic models.[24] The Old Assyrians recognized, identified, and were very active in markets they called *maḫīrum*, by which they meant not only the physical marketplace, but also abstractions, such as a general location where exchange, trade, and market activities took place. According to **CAD** (Chicago Assyrian Dictionary), the term *maḫīrum* also included the idea of "business transaction; tariff, market price, and purchase and purchase price" which are terms associated with the market."[25]

> We will buy (a garment) in the market and send it to you.[26]
>
> There is no silver (to be had) on the market.[27]
>
> There is no business in the market.[28]
>
> Here (upon your order) PN borrowed one or two minas of gold at the Market Gate[29]

The market (*maḫīrum*) in which the traders operated was multidimensional—local, regional, and interregional. Economic players, acting as agents of supply and demand in chattels (commodities, livestock, and people) and real property (fields and homes), for consumer goods and raw materials, intermediates and services, met and carried out exchange in diverse locations: their homes, the institutions of the colonies (the Karum—*Kārum*), local rulers' palaces and courtyards, the gates of Assur city, various venues in Anatolia, cities en route to that province, and elsewhere. The following is an example culled from one of the traders' documents:

---

24 Veenhof 1972, 351–357; Veenhof 1988, 243–263.
25 **CAD** $M/_1$. 92–101; Dercksen 2014, 69 ff.
26 **TCL** 14 7:28 ff; **CAD** $M/_1$. 93_a
27 **CCT** 4 34c:8 ff; **CAD** $M/_1$. 93a.
28 **TCL** 20 111:15, **CAD** $M/_1$. 93a
29 **BIN** 4 38:5 ff; **CAD** $M/_1$, 98a.

The purchase will be made in our father's home (in our company).[30]

The Assyrian traders' commercial activity (including that in markets of assets such as homes and slaves) resembled that of traders of all generations. They made silver available for purchases (*ana šiamātim*), they offered goods for sale (*ana šīmim tadānum*), tendered price quotes (*ana šīmim*), and agreed on final prices (*ana šīmim gamrim*).[31] At the close of the transaction, the seller declared himself satisfied (*šabbū*) with the price and the deal.[32] Prices can be high up (*eliš*), and merchandise could be cheap (*batqum*) or could be given for sale cheaply or for a superior price (*batiq u watturum tadānum*). Traders provided their agents with minimum selling prices and terms beneath which they were not allowed to go, thereby indicating that negotiations among traders took place. Traders transferred (deposited) goods to their customers (*šakānum*)[33] for direct exchange payment (in direct exchange for silver, copper, or other commodity) (*ana itaṭlim tadānum*) or deposited on credit *(qīptum)*.

The Assyrian trade was subject to government supervision and regulation. The authorities implemented their system of enforcement of contracts and customs via traders' institutions. The authorities determined how market players should behave, inspected departing caravans for their contents, and set values that they calculated (not market values) for goods and the total value (*awītum*) of goods of different types in the caravan, evidently for the purpose of taxing them at a specified rate.

In certain places, local authorities gave Assyrian traders exclusive trade privileges and sheltered them from rival Akkadian merchants. The protective measures included turning captured Akkadian traders over to the Assyrian traders and allowing the Assyrians to execute their Akkadian rivals.[34] Weights, measures, and quality of silver and gold were under supervision, although traders used their own weights and there is evidence of differences in weighing when transactions were made. To eliminate doubt, traders sometimes used the weights of their organization, the *Karum.*[35]

The markets were prone to fitful activity due to security upheavals, shaky security situations (*sikkātum, nukurtum*), unrest, rebellions, or uprisings. In contrast, there are attestations of the cessation of a state of disorder—a peace agreement—

30 **TCL** 19 53:8 ff; **CAD** Š/$_1$ 357a.
31 Veenhof 1972, 358–388.
32 Veenhof 2003a, 462.
33 Veenhof 1972, 432–438.
34 Veenhof 2008, 186.
35 Veenhof 1972, 58–59.

and its effects on the markets.[36] These situations affected supply and demand for goods and their prices.[37]

> But after they had left the *sikkātum* went out (started) and the market is disturbed so we are not in a position to fulfil our promise given when the goods were commissioned. Silver is hard to get. Do not expect a lot of silver. Prices being low.[38]

> Here the king has fallen during/in the *sikkātum* and there is upheaval within the city and fear for our lives. There are enemies over a distance of one and a half hour and nobody dares to go out into the countryside. One even tries to make us set out together with him for doing battle! In the meantime, absolutely no contracts must be drawn up, lest we get indebted to our principles for no less than one talent of silver! When the country becomes peaceful again and the ruler will conclude an agreement with him, tablets can be sent somewhere.[39]

> As to the two minas of silver that you sent me, I did not send you (textiles for the silver) because the commerce in Akkadian (textiles) has been affected, I have not sent you any. If within ten days the trade in Akkadian textiles does not return to normal, I shall buy you tin and send it to you.[40]

> Concerning the purchase of the textiles of the Akkadians that you wrote about, since you left the Akkadians have not entered the city. Their country is in revolt, but if they arrive before winter, and if there will be profitable purchase for you, then we shall buy some for you.[41]

> Please my father, if approve of it, the 10 talents of copper which I have acquired ("made") here —I have it hearsay that there is upheaval in the country; I wish the country would at last go back to normal, [since] the copper has now become 'hungry' twice—if you agree let an instruction from you reach me that I may convert it right here into silver or gold, (but) do no look for an additional one or two minas.[42]

The Old Assyrians had a complex market system, trading freely in Assur and its Anatolian colonies. Nonetheless, the market was carefully organized to produce stability and mitigate conflicts among its participants and with the local environment. Central to the system were two organizations: "the City" in Assur and the Karum in Anatolia. These organizations were created to stabilize supply by buying goods (on deposit – *šipkātum*) at known prices and by buying and selling goods on the market. They also helped maintain stability among its traders by setting rules and introducing conflict resolution measures, such as arbitration and adjudication.

---

36 Veenhof 2008, 205–206.
37 Veenhof 2003c, 113–114.
38 CCT 4 10a, Larsen 2002, 63.
39 Kt 92/k 526:6–21, Veenhof 2008, 173.
40 TCL 4 11:11 ff; CAD Š/$_3$ 30a. Larsen 2002, 150–151.
41 VS 26, 17. Larsen 2015 199.
42 BIN 4, 34:6 ff. Veenhof 1987, 63.

The Old Assyrian traders acted in the manner of a modern cartel.[43] Their central organization controlled supply in the market through their directives regarding the structure of caravans to Anatolia (the ratio of tin and textiles in the cargo) and buying and selling goods in the markets in Assur and Anatolia.

The price system was complex.[44] They used a few measures of commodities as enumerators to describe units of exchange—prices. The commodities included gold, silver, tin, copper, wool and barley. The metals were measured by units of weight and the barley by units of volume. Silver and tin were used in the trade to and from Assur, and copper and wool in the internal trade in Anatolia. Barely was used for everyday local expenses.

The most important metal that served as a medium of exchange was silver. Its units were the weights of shekel (8.33 grams), mina (0.5 kilogram) and talent (30 kilograms). The preferred unit of account was a unit of refined silver (*ṣarrupum*). The silver weight units were used as a medium of exchange, a unit of account, a store of value, and a standard for different payments. These all represent the definitions of money. It is therefore clear that the Old Assyrians had a system of money based on silver weights.

> I refined the silver and from five minas (only) 3 1/3 minas came out (of the kiln).
>
> The balance of the silver of your caravan.[45]
>
> As to the five minas of tin which I gave you for converting into silver, send me the silver, the proceeds of the tin, under seal.[46]
>
> Whatever PN owes, whether silver or barley or anything else.[47]
>
> As interest on debt in silver: they will pay interest half in barley and half in wheat (?).[48]

* * *

In conclusion, the traders' documents indicate that market institutions existed and that market activity took place along modern lines, taking into account technological and cultural differences. There is evidence that various market situations emerged due to political disruptions that affected supply and demand. Trade

---

43 They were 'an association of traders who agree to fix common prices and output quotas in an oligopolistic market in order to limit competition'. Rutherford D. 2002.

44 Details on the prices in the trade see in Garelli 1963; Larsen 1967; Veenhof 1972; 1988.

45 CCT 2 6:25 ff; CAD K 247a.

46 CCT 2 12a:13 and 16, CAD A/$_2$ 247b.

47 CCT 1 26c:9 ff; CAD Š/$_2$ 351a.

48 ATHE 6 A:8 ff; CAD Š/$_2$ 351b.

was subject to official supervision and regulation, and merchants enjoyed exclusivity in certain locations.

Competition, Prices, and Market Power

In perfect markets, no player can affect competition or prices. Such markets are frequented by large numbers of buyers and sellers, none of whom can obtain market power as a result of the size of their activity, their organization, or an arrangement with the authorities or special exclusive information. Market power is defined as the extent to which an economic player can influence price or quantity in a given market. The more influence an economic player has on the quantity offered, and the more unbalanced is information about the market and the goods traded in it in favor of one side of the exchange, the more market power there is.[49] In such a case, a "market failure" occurs due to too few players, uncompetitive information, or misconduct by economic agents in the markets.[50] In Mesopotamia during the period of interest to us, there is evidence of market situations in which economic units exploited market power to set exorbitant prices for their goods or limit their quantity. These market conditions were occasioned by a dearth of competition brought on by the amassing of power by certain merchants or irregularities in the market itself, resulting from states of war, acute insecurity, natural disasters, or other disruptions of competition.

The authorities influenced commercial activity in the markets by setting statutory prices and publishing them. How and why, they did so is not known. There were likely two main reasons for this publication of established prices. The first was to determine the value of goods for making accounts with trade institutions in matters such as taxes or compulsory sale. The second was the motivation to intervene in the markets and help its players by providing information about (what the authorities considered) reasonable prices for goods. The authorities realized that lack of information and acute price volatility might trigger social disorder and riots. Yet another possible reason could have been the authorities' wish to show the public how successful their reign was by touting the reasonable level of prices of vital commodities. For example, Sections 1 and 2 of the Laws of Eshnunna (c. 1770 BCE) list the prices of grain, salt, potash, oil, copper, and tar. In Sections 3 and 4, prices of services, such as cart and boat rental, are shown.[51] In the

49 Scherer 1987, 342–345; Kaiser 2003, 439–442.
50 Ledyard 1987, 326–328.
51 Malul 2010, 82–83.

Code of Ḫammu-rapi (c. 1750 BCE), a price list for services such as medical care appears in Sections 215–223, veterinary services in Sections 224–225, rental of oxen in Sections 242, 243, and 271, and rental of boats in Sections 275–277.[52]

In the Old Assyrian trade period, the government evidently intervened in the markets to determine the quality of, and set reasonable prices for, metals such as tin, silver, and gold in municipal institutions' transactions. Traders used credit documents that contained expressions such as "tin of the market of City X" or "tin of the market of the City [of Assur]" and noted the standard price and quality in the locality mentioned.[53] There was also a set of agreed prices in which the value of wares in caravans were recorded for purposes of reckoning and paying duties by the Karum (the organization of traders in Kanesh—*Kaneš*) and the Anatolian authorities. There were also consensual values of purchases by the Karum for joint trading activities. According to Assyrian traders' documents, various market situations triggered price volatility.

The Assyrian traders favored silver as their principal means of exchange[54] and expressed this when they noted prices or exchange rates of goods:

> X pieces of cloth its price [its value in silver] (*kasapšu*) Y silver;
>
> X clay containers Y silver their price [their value in silver] (*kasapšunu*);
>
> Y silver are X [pieces] of cloth.
>
> When they wanted to specify the exchange rate between two goods, they used the distributive preposition TA, *ultu-*, i. e., "each":
>
> X minas of tin, at Y shekels each, its value/price in silver Z minas.[55]

The traders' documents report numerous prices of goods and assets that were sold in the market.[56] Most are expressed in units of silver, emphasizing the use of this metal as a universal means of exchange (money). The prices varied depending on the quality of the goods, the state of the market where the goods were sold, and the terms of the sale (direct exchange or credit). Different prices for the same goods prevailed in Assur, Kanesh, and various places in Anatolia. Barley prices in Anatolia were 6–15 silver shekels per Kurrum (300 liters), in contrast to roughly one sil-

52 Malul 2010, 158–167.
53 Veenhof 2003c, 111–112.
54 Veenhof 1972, 448–455; Veenhof 2008, 82–89. Dercksen 2014, 67–83.
55 Veenhof 1972, 448.
56 Veenhof 1988, 250–251; Veenhof 2008, 82–88. Dercksen 2014, 67–83.

ver shekel per Kurrum of barley in Babylonia.[57] Copper prices in Anatolia ranged from 60 to 120 copper shekels per silver shekel. Gold in Assur went for 7 and 1/3 to 8 5/6 silver shekels per shekel of gold. Woolen textiles (of different levels of quality), priced at 3.5–6.5 silver shekels per unit in Assur, were sold in Kanesh at 13.5–30 shekels per unit. The price of meteoric (natural) iron (*ašium; amūtum*) was forty times higher in Kanesh and Assur than the price of silver, or five times higher than that of gold.[58] Tin commanded 15–16 silver shekels in Assur and 7–8 shekels in Anatolia.

> Tin in an amount equivalent to 5/6 mina of silver (50 shekels) according to the rate of the City.[59]
>
> He must calculate for you the value of the tin in silver using the rate which is established by the enterprise, as for the donkey-driver, his wages have been paid for the stretch until GN [....] Entrust both the tin and the textiles, as many as are cleared (after taxes and forced selling) to PN and let him bring it to where there is even a single shekel of profit for me.[60]
>
> Tin for x silver at the exchange rate of the City (Assur).[61]

Examples of the state of prices in the market appear below. They pertain to goods, livestock, and houses. Traders needed information about market situations in order to plan sales or purchases. They regulated their supply and demand to forestall over supply effects on prices.[62]

> But today you want to sell/entrust me copper which is not even worth half a shekel (of silver) per mina (of copper).[63]
>
> They are offering me a poor (price) for the *amūtum* iron, I did not sell it.[64]
>
> I shall make purchases and send you, so they may be active for me. May every shekel of profit be realized for me, so I can make good my losses.[65]
>
> When you (plur.) sent me silver you said: "It should not lie idle."[66]

---

57 Seemingly, a windfall profit could have been made by selling barley from Mesopotamia in Anatolia. Due to the steep haulage expenses, however, the deal was not worth making. Much the same happened in trade in copper.
58 Of meteorite origin.
59 Hecker Giessen 9:8, CAD $M/_1$ 94a.
60 CCT 4 2b, Larsen 2002, 51.
61 MVAG 33 No. 183:8, CAD 127b.
62 Veenhof 2003c, 113–116.
63 Veenhof 1972, 450.
64 CCT 3 37b:18 ff; CAD B 166b.
65 TC 1, 29:20 ff; Larsen 2002, 27.
66 TC 1 29:28 ff; Larsen 2002, 27.

> As for the textiles you sent me, I have shown it couple of times. Since people offer a low price for it, your servant PN brings you the textile back, still under your seal.[67]

> Of whatever profit they make, PN will take two thirds, PN_2 will take one third.[68]

The traders offered their wares in the market on the basis of final cost (*šīmum gamrum*) plus markup.[69] Gross profit margins on textiles came to more than 200 percent.[70] For example, traders bought textiles in Assur for 3.5–6.5 silver shekels per unit and sold them for 13.5–30 shekels per unit. In tin, the gross profit rate was more than 100 percent: purchased in Assur at 15 shekels of tin per shekel of silver[71] and commonly sold in Anatolia for 7 shekels of tin per shekel of silver.[72]

Traders charged customers, partners, and investors for expenses and instructed their agents to sell goods at a price that would assure a small profit (*balāṭum*).[73] They sought profits in their dealings, either for their investment in a profitable transaction (*takšītum*) or for their investment in investment societies or funds (*naruqqum*). Warnings against spoilage, damage, shortfall, and loss (*ḫuluqqā'ūm; muṭā'ū; butuqqā'ū; bitiqtum*) were given as well.

An especially interesting letter that relates to the traders' motives was written by two Assyrian women who lived in Assur City and was sent to a trader in Kanesh. Written in an acute state of emotion, its authors complain about the trader's pursuit of profits, which has kept him away.

> Here (in *Aššur*), we ask(ed) female dream interpreters, female diviners, and spirits of the dead, the god *Aššur* gives you a serious warning. You love your silver and despise your life! (...)[74]

Elsewhere in their documents, traders note the importance of profits in doing business and the difficulties that losses caused. Profit was the traders' principal motive and was pursued in all possible ways in trading and in using money for loans. The profit appears to have sufficed only for making a livelihood (making a *balāṭum*).

67 AKT 6c, 592; Larsen 2015, 274.
68 ICK 2 60:2ff; CAD T 88a.
69 Veenhof (1972, 85) calculates expenses on hauling textiles from Assur to Anatolia at 30 percent of the market value of the goods.
70 Veenhof 1972, 82–85.
71 Within a price range of 12.5–16.5 shekels of tin per shekel of silver; Veenhof 1988, 250.
72 Larsen 1976, 104.
73 See CAD B 52a.
74 TC 1:5, Michel 2017, 99.

This is the origin of the expression "price with a small profit" (*šīmum ša balāṭika*).[75]

Scholars who study the traders' documents note how difficult it is to determine the general gross and net profit margins. Ostensibly, there are caravan documents that specify the expenses of hauling the goods from Assur to Anatolia. In contrast to these data, however, there are no exact figures relating to the additional expenses that traders incurred on account of the special loans (*be'ūlātum*) that they gave the caravan leaders and of the tax payments (*dātum*) that they made to their organization in Kanesh.[76] Neither are there data on the value of the goods sold. Merchandise was sold at various prices under different arrangements. Some was sold to the palace under special terms. Another portion was sold in the market immediately and in direct exchange. Yet another quantity was handed over on consignment and was sold in the market immediately and in direct exchange. Yet another quantity was handed over on consignment—with credit at a special price to the agent—and yet more was offered for sale by means of the Karum, the merchants' organization. Each form of sale commanded a different price.[77]

Nevertheless, the leading researcher Veenhof, attempts to estimates the caravan's net profit at around 50 percent of the value of the goods transported. In his estimation, based partly on traders' documents, a trader's net profit was roughly 100 percent per year over the value of the two caravans that the trader led to Kanesh during the year.[78]

In Jan Grit Dercksen's estimation, Assyrian traders' profit on commercial shipment of tin and textiles from Assur to Kanesh was around 50 percent. Given that the Assyrians' sales turnover was comprised of two rounds of shipment between Assur and Kanesh, Anatolia each year, the presumed annual profit was 100 percent (or twice the size of the investment). This presumed profit was based on purchase prices of tin and textiles in Assur and the sale price of these commodities in Anatolia net of taxes in Assur, taxes and expenses in towns and crossings en route, and taxes in Anatolia.[79]

Examples of how the subject of profit appears in the traders' documents follow:

---

75 Veenhof 1987, 56–58.

76 Veenhof 1972, 279*ff.*

77 Veenhof 1988, 248.

78 Veenhof 1988, 249.

79 Dercksen 2014, 84*ff.*

In accordance with the policy of the City, any Assyrian will go where it is profitable for him. You went where it was profitable for you, and I as well went where it was profitable for me in accordance with the policy of my city. Accordingly, you are not my partner.[80]

Send me the two talents of tin belonging to our father so that I can invest them wherever I can make a small profit.[81]

Take the tin and the textiles en bloc and sell the goods (on credit) either on short terms or on long ones, as long as a profit can be assured. Sell it as best as you can, and then inform me in a letter about the price in silver and the terms.[82]

I shall make purchases and send you, so they may be active for me. May every shekel of profit be realized for me, so I can make good my losses[83]

When you (plur.) sent me silver you said: "It should not lie idle."[84]

Since the day you came to GN and we met each other, I have always collected ("torn out") a purchase price which exceeded the double (of the price I paid) and the rate of exchange of 60:1 (for copper). Could I, as the copper always returned in time three-fold, have suffered a loss of 100 talents of copper? *Aššur* himself and your god have rejected the gentleman; but as for me, silver fell into my hands, so that up till this very day you have been able to satisfy yourself financially.[85]

As for the textiles you sent me, I have shown it couple of times. Since people offer a low price for it, your servant PN brings you the textile back, still under your seal.[86]

Of whatever profit they make, PN will take two thirds, PN_2 will take one third.[87]

The traders were knowledgeable in determining the quality of commodities such as raw materials and consumer goods. They set prices commensurate with quality. They were also conscious of customers' tastes and demand for different types of goods in the market. Evidence of this is the wide variety of textiles and traders' comments about the kind of weaving that satisfies customers in Anatolia.[88] There were differences in the quality and weight of wool woven, the density of the weave, the size of the cloth, the type of processing, and color. Simple textiles were used for packaging and delicate ones for clothing.[89]

---

80 AKT 6b, 493; Larsen 2015, 272.
81 CCT 4 21c:17, cf., CAD B 52a.
82 TC 3, 21. Larsen 2015, 182.
83 TC 1, 29:20 ff, Larsen 2002, 27.
84 TC 1 29:28 ff, Larsen 2002, 27.
85 CCT 3, 16b, Veenhof 1972, 451–452.
86 AKT 6c, 592; Larsen 2015, 274
87 ICK 2 60:2 ff., CAD T 88a.
88 Veenhof 1972, 104–105.
89 Veenhof 1972, 89–128.

Researchers identify several levels of textile quality: excellent (*watrum*), good (*damqun*), average (*qablīum*), damaged, and poor *(maṭium).*[90]

> For two shekels buy wool from GN, soft long-staple (wool), of good and superior quality.[91]
>
> When you perform the buying, do not buy a brightly colored cloth or a *šinītum* (cloth).[92]
>
> Let them comb the surface of the garment once but not teasel it, its weave should be close. On each one adds one more mina of wool than on the first garment which you sent me so that it may be fine (i.e., closely woven), they should comb the second side ...., and if it still shows (loose) wool, they should teasel it as (one does) a *kutānum* garment.[93]

There was also acute sensitivity to the quality of raw materials traded, such as wool, copper, gold, and silver.[94] The traders were experts in metal quality and used local smiths (*nappāḫum*) to improve it by refining. Refinement was immensely important in setting prices. The purer the metal, the more it could command in trade. For example, the 1:8 ratio of silver to pure gold shifted to 1:4 when the target was gold alloy.[95] The purity of metal was determined mainly by its external form, color, and additional characteristics, such as softness (mainly in gold). Metal purity is a complex topic and few documents about it have survived. In Assur and Kanesh, specific bureaucrats specialized in determining metal purity, particularly in gold and silver.[96]

> There is good (*pašallum)* (gold) in the market.[97]
>
> There is no market for either tin or refined copper.... but if the tin is of bad quality, get rid of it (even) at a loss.[98]
>
> If your tin is corroded, they are mutually responsible (for the damages incurred).[99]
>
> Buy me either good tin or pure small (?) *amūtum* iron.[100]

90 Veenhof 1972, 191–202.
91 TCL 19 65:18 ff; CAD Š/$_3$ 61b.
92 TC 3:69, Larsen 1967, 75.
93 TCL 19 17:11–16, CAD Ṣ 222b.
94 Veenhof 2003c, 112.
95 This ratio persisted for centuries during the period investigated.
96 Dercksen 2004, 76.
97 CCT 1 12a:3 ff; CAD M/$_1$ 93b.
98 BIN 4 15:17 ff; CAD A/$_2$ 127b.
99 TuM 1 19b:21 ff; CAD A/$_2$ 127b.
100 CCT 4 34c:16 ff; CAD Z 24b.

I shall exchange your copper against refined (copper).[101]

* * *

In conclusion, buyers and sellers in perfect markets cannot influence competition and prices because they are too numerous. In certain markets, traders may amass market power by the sheer scale of their activity, unique information they hold about the state of the market, competition-crimping organization, and arrangements with the authorities. In our context, the authorities intervened in the markets by advertising prices of goods in order to support price stability. Assyrian traders used weight units of high-quality silver to express the prices of goods and assets. They gathered information about the state of supply and demand and price levels in the markets and priced their wares on a cost-plus basis. The traders pursued profits in silver wherever they could extract them. Their profits in the trade with Anatolia amounted to about 50 % per caravan cargo and 100 % per year assuming two caravans per year. They knew a great deal about how to determine the quality of commodities such as raw materials and were aware of market tastes in textiles in Anatolia.

The Markets in Assur and Anatolia

Assur city sat at an east–west and north–south crossroads. Caravans of traders came through from the mountainous area to the east and southeast, where tin and precious stones were sourced, to the plains to the west and northwest. They also crossed from the mountains in Anatolia, where silver and copper originated, to southern Mesopotamia and the Persian Gulf, where textiles, copper, gold, and precious stones were sourced.

The tin in which the Assyrians traded reached Assyria from today's Iran as well as from, evidently, today's Afghanistan and beyond East. Textiles arrived from southeastern Iraq (Babylonia) and silver from northeastern or southwestern Anatolia. Assyrian traders operated in the area between Assur and Anatolia and in Anatolia itself. There is evidence of activity of Akkadian (Babylonian) traders in textiles in Assur and Anatolia and among Eblaites trading in copper and silver in Anatolia. Assyrians were not active in Mesopotamian trade in the copper that reached the area through the efforts of other merchants to the south (apparently Magan, today's Oman). Copper also seems to have originated north of northern Syria—eastern Turkey—or northwest (Cyprus). The distance between Assur and

101 CCT 4 47a:5 ff; CAD E 321b.

Kanesh, the central trading town of the Assyrians in Anatolia, was approximately 1,000 kilometers.

Several main routes connected the two points, with traders travelling on donkeys. Assuming an average of 25–30 kilometers in travel distance per day, it took them approximately forty days or six weeks to cross the trading area.[102] Trade was suspended in the winter due to harsh weather conditions in the mountainous part of Anatolia. To transport goods, traders had to invest in donkeys and their gear, hire caravan leaders, donkey drivers, and guards, and meet expenses associated with life on the road,[103] chiefly food and lodging for the travelers and their animals and passage taxes in cities and at river crossings. In Anatolia, the Assyrians participated in regional trade, mainly in silver, wool, and copper. An account of trade in Anatolia indicates the existence of salient commercial centers that specialized in trading in certain goods.[104]

Kanesh, in central Anatolia, was the hub of Assyrian traders' activity in Anatolia. Durḫumit, in northern Anatolia, was the center of trading in copper and wool; Purušḫaddum, in western Anatolia, played this role in trade in silver, copper, and wool.[105] There is evidence of participation of merchants in other areas, such as Eblaites, in trading in copper and silver in Anatolia[106] and Akkadians in the textile trade in eastern Anatolia.[107]

One of the most interesting questions is how the large price differentials between the markets persisted for centuries despite the extensive commercial activity of Assyrian and other traders. The differentials endured throughout the trading era even though there was a continual flow of goods from low-price areas to high-price ones, meaning that a price-leveling process of arbitrage should have taken place.[108] After all, arbitrage occurs as long as price differentials exist. When buying takes place, expenses for transport and care of the goods as far as point of sale should be borne in mind, as should the risk originating in the possibility of a change in price during the time between purchase and sale. Price discrimination—the existence of different prices in efficient markets—cannot occur when

102 Some shorten the time needed to complete the trip from Assur to Kaneš to thirty days by calculating 35 kilometers per day by donkey and a shorter distance. This doubles the number of trips between the cities and, commensurably, the volume of trade and enabled quick delivery of mail and documents sent in special caravans. (Stratford 2010).
103 Larsen 1967, 140–172.
104 Barjamovic 2008, 87–100.
105 Veenhof 2008, 147–152.
106 Veenhof 2003, 114.
107 Veenhof 2008, 98.
108 Huberman 1987, 106–109.

the possibility of arbitrage exists; only when markets are inefficient does profiting from ongoing arbitrage become possible. In inefficient markets, buyers incur high transaction costs to obtain information about prices and quality, put their knowledge to use, and raise prices. The traders' documents reveal vigorous activity in obtaining market power by controlling information and limiting competition. Traders organized to influence prices or available quantity.[109]

Assyrians maintained a presence in the trading centers in Anatolia and the important cities along the trade routes, obtained information about market conditions, and disseminated information about the markets by means of a well-appointed communication network.[110]

They established traders' institutions in Assur and in the colonies in Anatolia. Their organization—the Karum—engaged largely, if not exclusively, in helping merchants obtain rights and status in the markets of Anatolia and the cities along the trade route and establishing and enforcing ground rules for trading and credit. The institutions fixed the quantity of goods offered in the markets by limiting offered quantities of Assyrian tin in Anatolia, for example, and restraining trade in locally produced textiles in that province. Traders secured local rulers' cooperation by signing documents to regulate trade, paying taxes, and delivering goods at reduced prices.

There are indications that the traders themselves were aware of the state of the market and limited quantities or set prices in accordance with market developments. This proves that individual traders had considerable market power that they exploited to boost their profits or maintain price levels that would keep their profits healthy. This market power originated in the scope of activity in the local markets and to the traders' abundant knowledge of market conditions.

As their documents make clear, they shared information with each other over a well-developed communication network[111] based on the presence of their agents in the markets and on written correspondence among them. Local traders were less able to amass information due to their limited presence in the markets and their lack of a sophisticated communication system.

To manage supply for the purpose of keeping prices high, information about the state of the market was needed. Traders describe market situations of cessation of trading, inactive market, shortage of merchandise, difficulty in obtaining mer-

---

109 Veenhof 2003c, 111–116.

110 Documents moved quickly between Assur and Kaneš, reaching their destination in an estimated fifteen days (Stratford 2010).

111 Veenhof 1988, 260.

chandise (*batqum*), and glut (*mādum*).[112] There are reports about the effect of gluts on prices.

> There is no business in the market.[113]
>
> There is no silver (to be had) on the market.[114]
>
> Do you not know that (the value of) silver is high?[115]
>
> Do you not hear from all sides that silver is high (in price) and so there is no market for textiles?[116]
>
> There is no silver on the market, and one had to make enormous stocks of copper.[117]
>
> I did not send you (textiles for the silver) because the commerce in Akkadian (textiles) has been affected.[118]
>
> The price of the *pirikānum* textiles is low here [and] the market at kanesh is not high enough.[119]
>
> There is no gold available as payment.[120]
>
> Your tin which you have acquired is (still kept) here, nobody wants to buy it.[121]
>
> Write me whether there is any *ašium*-iron available anywhere.[122]
>
> All the merchandise which his brother has left behind, either textiles or tin or wool or donkeys, he has dispatched ahead (but) the man should not sell his merchandise at any price (*batiq watturum*).[123]

The combination of agreements with the authorities that controlled the markets and the traders' own actions helped to perpetuate price differentials that were created by special market conditions in both markets. The traders exploited accords that they signed with rulers in the trading areas to keep rivals at arm's length. Rulers exploited their control of the political system to subject traders to binding rules

---

112 Veenhof 1972, 376–378, 389–400.
113 TCL 20 111:15; CAD M/$_1$ 93a.
114 CCT 4 34c:8; CAD M/$_1$ 93a.
115 BIN 4 220:24 ff; CAD K 247a.
116 KTS 18:23 ff; CAD Š/$_3$ 30a.
117 CCT 4, 34c, 8 ff; Veenhof 1972, 391.
118 TCL 4 11:11 ff; CAD Š/$_3$ 30a.
119 Pa 29 L 29–588:18–20, Gwaltney 1983, p 80.
120 KTS 18:27 ff; CAD Š/$_3$ 30a.
121 TCL 14 42:11 ff; CAD B 146a.
122 BIN 4 45:12 ff; CAD B 146a.
123 TCL 14 27:5 ff; CAD L 253b.

that limited quantities offered in the markets and maintained price levels as they wished.

Special conditions in both markets that affected demand for and supply of traded commodities also helped to create different price ratios. One presumes that the price of silver in Assur and other areas in Mesopotamia was higher because this metal was much in demand due to its being a means of exchange, a commodity that retained its value, an important ingredient in jewelry and tools in Mesopotamia, and an item in limited supply due to trade with distant areas. In contrast, silver was cheaper in Anatolia because it was in greater supply due to its origin in mines in Asia Minor, and because demand for silver as a means of exchange was weaker in Anatolia due to the area's lower level of development.

One reason for stability in the price of gold was that the Assyrians accumulated it in their temples and palaces for religious and strategic reasons and as a means of saving for public and personal needs. Tin prices were lower in Assur than in Anatolia due to the supply of this metal from Iran and Afghanistan, to which the Assyrians evidently acquired rights, and the high demand due to the activity of the Anatolian bronze industry, which relied on large copper mines in the north.

Something similar happened in the market for an industrial commodity, textiles. The textiles of Assur and southern Mesopotamia (Akkad) were more diverse and of higher quality than were those from Anatolia[124] and, as a result, in greater demand. Also, large factories of the palaces and temples in Babylonia turned out textiles in massive quantities. The strong demand for Assyrian textiles in Anatolia, combined with the limited supply, boosted textile prices there to over three times their level in Assur. The superb textiles that the Assyrians delivered were of a quality that local producers could not match. Assyrian traders also restricted competition with locally produced Anatolian textiles (which were of poorer quality) via their trade organization (the Karum), which forbade them to do business with the locals. They also successfully crimped competition with other local producers by making arrangements with the authorities.

* * *

In summary, the Assyrian traders used their communication system and their information to manage local trade in wool and copper even within Anatolia. They bartered wool for copper in places where wool was in greater supply and sold it in other places where its price in terms of copper was higher. They also bought copper of different levels of quality, sent it out for refining, and then sold it for silver

124 Veenhof 1972, 181–213.

elsewhere. The wool and copper traded in the local market in Anatolia was of large volume and was bought and sold in large quantities. To transport these commodities, the traders used carts.[125]

Assur sat on a crossroads from east to west and north to south. Caravans passed through from the east, where tin and precious stones were sourced, to high-demand areas in the west, and from the sources of textiles in the south to those of silver and demand for tin in the north. Within Anatolia, traders participated in regional trade in copper, wool, and silver. They gathered information on activities in the markets by means of their literacy and their well-developed communication system. They controlled the supply of goods in the market by exploiting the special status that they secured by making arrangements with local rulers and by setting up a special organization that regulated terms of trade. With the help of their status in the market, they took advantage of the supply of inexpensive tin from northern Iran, the strong demand for tin in the Anatolian bronze industry, the supply of cheap silver from the Anatolian highlands, the supply of high-quality textiles in Babylonia, and the brisk demand for silver in Mesopotamia, to make large profits from their trading activity.

The Old Assyrian Trade Policy

The Assyrian trade policy was mercantilist and typically manifested in two main fields: monetary and commercial.[126] The policy favored the accumulation of precious metals (silver and gold) by maintaining a positive trade balance (more exports than imports). The goal was attained by promoting trade, supporting exports, and limiting imports.[127] At the outset, there is evidence of official intervention in Assur to develop trade. In 2000 BCE or so, King Ilušuma announced[128] that he was giving the Akkadian (Babylonian) traders carte blanche to operate in Assur, especially in copper. Erišum (1974–1935 BCE), Ilušuma's successor, declared[129] freedom of trade, including tax cuts, on a series of commodities, such as silver, gold, tin, cop-

125 Veenhof 1972, 130–132, 137–139.

126 Contemporary mercantile economists mention a third field: the social one, as in promoting industrial activity, educating against overconsumption, encouraging population growth, and imposing wage limits. To discuss these spheres, special research is needed.

127 Brezis 2003, 482–485; Allen 1987, 445–449.

128 RIMA I, 18.

129 RIMA I, 22.

per, wool, and barley—all to lure traders from southern Mesopotamia and bolster Assur's standing as a trade center.[130]

Afterwards, much as in much later mercantilist policies in Europe, the Assyrians concluded "oath-agreements" (*māmītum*)[131] with foreign rulers in Anatolia and along the roads leading to it and established colonies in trade centers. The Assyrians promised these rulers tax revenues and the right to buy some of their merchandise at reduced prices. In return, they received the right to settle and maintain security in their colony, extraterritorial rights to manage and judge the colony's residents, protection of caravans that moved along the byways of Anatolia against piracy and assault, and payment of compensation for damage.[132] The rulers prevented Babylonian (Akkadian) merchants from entering.[133] A draft of a treaty (*māmītum)* with a ruler of unknown small town:

> There shall be no loss of (property) belonging to an Assyrian in your country—rope, cone or anything at all. If a loss occurs in your country you shall search for (what was lost) and then return it to us. If bloodshed occurs in your country, you shall hand over the killers to us, so we may kill them. You may not let Akkadians come here. If they do travel to your country, you must give them to us so we may kill them. You shall not demand anything from us. Like your father you may take 12 shekels per donkey-load in caravans going up (to Anatolia). You may—like your father—use 1 1/4-shekel silver per donkey-load on the way down. You cannot take anything more. If no caravan is coming because of warfare, they will send you 5 minas of tin from Hahhum.[134]

The Assyrian traders also created systems that protected their markets in Assur and the colonies. The authorities in Assur imposed restrictions on trading in inexpensive Anatolian textiles in order to weaken competition with the textiles from Assyria.[135] The restraints came with heavy fines for transgressors.[136] A restraint of a different kind was applied to the proportions of tin and textiles in caravans destined for Kanesh. By decision of the city, traders at a given time could send tin to Kanesh at up to one-third of the freight in a donkey caravan and no more. With the help of such restrictions, the authorities could affect the quantities and prices of tin and textiles offered in the market in Anatolia.[137]

130 Veenhof 2003c, 83–85. Larsen 2015, 146–7.
131 See Chapter 4 (Enforcement), page 141.
132 Veenhof 2003c, 85–89.
133 Veenhof 2008, 186; 2003a, 478.
134 Kt n/k 794. Larsen 2015, 152–53.
135 Veenhof 2003, 89–90.
136 VAT 9290, Veenhof 1972, 126–128; Larsen 1976, pp.172–173; Veenhof 1995, 1733.
137 Veenhof 2003, 91–93.

The merchants were aware of the need to make adjustments in view of the dual set of prices that had evolved in Assyria and Anatolia. A weight unit of silver in Anatolia was equal to twice the quantity of tin in Assyria, making silver dearer in terms of tin in the latter country than in the former. Similarly, the calculation in Assur of the value of gold in an investment "sack" was sometimes given at a special rate vis-à-vis silver. Therefore, they determined that in matters related to the investment fund—the "sack"—special long-term loans would be given and management of funds for final settlement would be bequeathable in Assur but not in Anatolia, all of which to take into account the special prices of gold and the higher value of silver in Assur.[138]

> If anyone has given PN in Anatolia (lit. "the countryside") a capital investment "sack" (*naruqqum)* or *ebuṭṭum*—special long-term loan, he shall take it (or: it shall be taken) back, together with [his] other investors, by means of his witnesses in the City. If he has promised any silver in Anatolia, in accordance with the words of the stele, when it is confirmed by his witnesses, he shall take it (or: it shall be taken) back only there. Nobody shall touch the silver; it shall be brought together in the City.[139]

The sentence that follows, appearing in one of the letters, explains another aspect of market behavior as set by the traders' institutions. Purchase transactions could not be carried out in Assur, for example, by persons present in Anatolia and vice versa. Transactions were limited to markets where traders took turns meeting. One reason for this might have been an instruction relating to the use of gold in commercial transactions. In Assur, it was forbidden to use gold in trade with foreigners; the situation in Anatolia was different. Another reason might have been an injunction against trading in certain goods:

> The order of the City (of Assur), (namely), one should buy (the goods) of the Province (Anatolia) in the Province. (But) one must buy (the goods) of the City in the City.[140]

The Anatolian and Assyrian authorities in Kanesh also restrained trade in meteoric iron (*ašium; amuttum*) and lapis lazuli (*ḫusârum*),[141] which were very expensive (several times more so than gold).

> If the *amuttum*-metal which you took from PN is still there with you, go and send me the *amuttum*-metal here, (but) the Karum should not know. Here the generals from GN and

138 Veenhof 1995, 1725–1726.
139 Kt a/k 394, Veenhof 1995, 1725.
140 Pa 16 L 29–571:34–37, Gwaltney 1983, 47.
141 Veenhof 2008, 213.

GN², are threatening me with a lawsuit, saying "should there be any *amūtum*-metal anywhere, write!"[142]

The authorities in Assur also imposed restraints on trading in gold in order to accumulate more of it in the city.[143] Traders could use gold to pay for purchases from other traders in the city or for investment, but were enjoined[144] against selling it to foreigners.[145]

Thus (said) the ruler, speak to the Kanesh colony: the tablet with the verdict of the City, which concerns gold, which sent to you, that tablet has been canceled. We have not fixed any (new) rule concerning gold. The earlier rule concerning gold still prevails. Assyrians may sell gold among each other, [but] in accordance with the words of the stele, no Assyrian whatever shall give gold to Akkadian, Amorite, or Subaraean. Whoever does so shall not remain alive.[146]

* * *

The authorities in Assur, like other rulers in the ancient world, thought the well-being and might of Assur depended on amassing gold and silver. The gold was evidently deposited in the temple of Assur—in sun-shaped disks for ritual use or in ingots—or was stored loose in sacks in the temple warehouses. Traders invested gold in a commercial investment fund—a "sack"—but used the accumulated contents of the "sack" after converting it into silver.

In sum, the Assyrian trade policy was indeed mercantilist. In the monetary sense, it was typified by accumulating silver and gold by maintaining a positive trade balance. The Assyrian authorities encouraged trade, supported exports, and restrained imports. They concluded accords with other authorities on trade routes and established colonies in major cities. They placed limits on quantities available in the markets and forbade trading in gold with foreigners in their capital.

Means of Exchange—Money

An exchange economy is one that progresses beyond the point at which each household produces goods for its own use.[147] People engage in exchange by barter-

142 BIN 4 45:11 ff; CAD A/$_2$ 441a&b. Veenhof 2008, 213.
143 Veenhof 2003, 95–96.
144 See above, page 72, on the Assyrians' mercantilist policies.
145 Dercksen 2004, 81–83; Veenhof 2008, 88–89.
146 Kt 79/k 101, Veenhof 1995, 1733.
147 Wilson 1987, 202–206.

ing—swapping one product for another—or by using a consensual means of exchange, money, that is accepted as payment in exchange transactions and for multiple products. Barter makes exchange difficult because it requires a double coincidence: a seller interested in a specific good and a buyer who owns it and wants what the seller wishes to sell, in the quantities supplied and demanded.[148] An accepted means of exchange—money—simplifies the swap because it allows people to avoid having to calculate multiple price ratios between goods that they encounter or need. Today's definition of the institution of money is "anything which is generally accepted as payment for goods and services or discharge of debts."[149] When a consensual means of exchange is available, exchange operations can take place at different times and in different places: present or future, in a domestic market or a faraway one.

Institutional Economics explains the importance of money in that it lowers transaction costs in the market.[150] Efficient markets rely on accepted and available means of exchange. Money is an institution that people created to simplify exchange and help manage their resources. Once a means of exchange is created, the advantages of specialization (division of labor) and scale economies can be realized.

Researchers disagree about the meaning of money. Some stress the abstract sense of the concept.[151] For them, "money" describes (or denotes) an abstract medium that reflects a price or a debt. Others stress money as something physical (commodity money) that is used for exchange transactions and payment of debts; it also has social significance.[152] Economists emphasize the abstract meaning of money and its utility in economic research; anthropologists and some researchers in the social sciences accent the physical aspect of money and the way society relates to it. Economists accept any commodity or unit of measurement that serves as money, whereas anthropologists distinguish between "primitive money," a commodity that primitive tribes and ancient societies created for social and economic needs, and modern money, used in modern economies—sometimes in virtual forms. They also differentiate between social uses of money, such as gifts, doweries, tributes to rulers and gods, fines, and compensation, emphasizing these uses. Some researchers with a socially-oriented worldview argue that money aggravates social inequality by being amassed by specific individuals; therefore, they argue, natural exchange and government-set price ratios should be used.

148 Also called "the double co-incidence of wants."
149 Foley 1987, 519–525.
150 Coase 1992, 713–719.
151 Keynes 1935, 3–5.
152 Einzig 1949, 322–326.

Researchers agree about the roles of money. As noted above, money serves as a unit of measurement of value and a means of exchange. It is also used to retain value over time and to allow production, acquisition, and consumption to be temporarily separated. Additionally, it operates as a standard of measurement and, as such, a standard for deferral of contractual payments associated with future debts.[153] Money alleviates ignorance about terms of trade and increases the volume of trade.[154] To use money, experts in means of exchange must be available to serve as intermediators. For a given commodity to function as money, it must be in demand by the entire population and it and its quality must be identifiable at no expense and with no need for great expertise. Commodities of stable value are preferable for retention of value and as a means of exchange for exchange.

Researchers of primitive money established tests that commodities must meet to qualify as money in the ancient world (and in primitive societies). The commodity must be useful and valuable to the user. It should be portable, homogeneously structured, divisible into separate units, stable in value, and easily identifiable. The tests need not be absolute; a commodity's price may exhibit short-term volatility but remain stable over time. The units of measurement of commodities that serve as means of exchange must be small enough to allow transport in reasonable quantities over short distances for the requisites of exchange in daily life.[155]

Agreed means of exchange may be of diverse kinds—paper money, plastic credit cards, or other commodities such as beads, seashells, barley, dates, wool, silver, gold, tin, and so on. Several commodities may serve as means of exchange concurrently. At first glance, this would seem inefficient. However, if there is a fixed and known exchange rate among them, they can function as one unit of money.[156] In the second half of the third millennium BCE, for example, when barley and silver were means of exchange and there was a fixed and known rate of 300 sila of barley per shekel of silver, both "currencies" functioned as one unit of payment—the money of that era.

With different commodities, measured in different ways, being used as money in Mesopotamia, the Akkadian used different verbs to express the act of paying. When payment was made in barley, it was called measuring (*madādum*); when silver was used, it was called weighing (*šaqālum*- LÁ). To circumvent the problem of the form of payment, the expression "to satisfy the payment recipient's wish" (*apālum*) was used to denote payment.[157]

153 Kindleberger 1993, 19–20.
154 Alchian 1977, 133–134, 138–139.
155 Einzig 1949, 330–335.
156 Kindleberger 1993, 20.
157 Von Soden 1994, 123–124.

It is conjectured[158] that accepted means of exchange can be dated back to prehistory. In excavations at ancient sites, numerous beads and seashells of specific types appear in defined sizes in large areas far from the sea.[159] Absent supportive testimonies, their use as a means of exchange or as jewelry or as ritual objects cannot be verified. However, the fact that they were found in graves allows one to hypothesize that people attributed importance and value to them. The distance from the places where shells were discovered to their presumed marine origin implies that they were obtained via exchange with people from elsewhere. In the modern era, primitive societies still use shells as means of exchange. It is even believed that animals served this purpose. In some African societies, this still occurs, for example, in doweries and accumulation of property.

* * *

In conclusion, people exchange things either naturally, by bartering, or by using an accepted means of exchange (money). Means of exchange simplify exchange transactions. Their use allows for advantages of specialization and scale economies to be realized. Economists consider money an abstract instrument used to express prices, book values, or debts. According to anthropologists, money is a physical device that has social meaning. To serve as money, a commodity must be useful, portable, rare, homogeneously structured, divisible, stable in value, and easily identifiable. Several commodities may serve as means of exchange, provided there is a fixed and known exchange rate among them.

Means of Exchange—Money in Mesopotamia

There are two schools of thought about the use of money—an accepted means of exchange—in Mesopotamia in the fourth and third millennia BCE. One posits that[160] the large organizations were composed of extended families that managed production and redistribution systems based on shared ownership of means of production and redistribution of subsistence rations to organization members.[161] The exchange rates that appear in contemporaneous sources pertain to barter and non-commercial exchange using money. Exchange was part of social activity

158 Quiggen 1949, 1–10.

159 Shells also served as primitive money in underdeveloped societies in the modern era in Oceania and Africa.

160 See summaries in Robertson 1995 and Yoffee 1995, and Economic Models that Explain the Period page 167.

161 Gelb 1965, 230–243.

that centered on reciprocity and status-building.[162] Authorities used units of silver and barley, for example, to record economic activity within the framework of the temple and palace organizations.[163] There were no markets in which these commodities were exchanged and there was no price-setting as a consequence of market supply and demand, driven by economic motives of profit and personal utility and facilitated by means of exchange.

According to the other school, the Mesopotamian economy operated with economic institutions along modern lines, with the necessary changes with respect of the culture, technology, and social structure of its era.[164] According to this theory, barley served in the late fourth millennium and the third millennium BCE as a universal means of exchange (money) for transactions in the local market. People who visited the markets paid in volume units of barley for means of production, goods, and services. Barley qualified as money in the following senses: widespread use, utility and value to the user; standard structure; divisibility of relatively stable price due to governmental involvement in setting its quality and price in the market; and easy identifiability by one and all. Its use was inhibited neither by high transport expenses due to large volume nor by steep storage costs. Evidently, too, barley was a common means of exchange because it was used to recompense its workers, issue loans, pay field lease fees, and record the activities of the temple and the palace.[165]

The use of barley as money in the local market evidently started in the Uruk period (or even before), a time of urbanization and grouping of population in large organizational units of the temple and the palace for large-scale irrigation projects in southern Mesopotamia. Having put people to work, these organizations had to recompense and maintain them by paying them wages (rations). The second half of the fourth millennium BCE saw the first written documents of the Uruk that contain data on the economic organizations' bookkeeping system.

The data relate to quantities (volumes) of barley and other commodities produced, labor inputs, and goods redistributed (or paid) to members of the organization. The data appear to describe the recording of inventory, the movement of goods in and out, and the use of labor by the economic or social organizations.[166]

162 Dalton 1965, 47–48.
163 Barley is še in Sumerian and *še'um* in Akkadian.
164 See summaries in Powell 1999, 5–23; von Soden 1994; Silver 1985; Silver 2004, 65–87.
165 Grains were used as money in the modern era, too. In nineteenth-century Myanmar (Burma), for example, standard measures of rice served this purpose. Einzig 1949, 409.
166 Englund 2004, 21–25.

The records use volume units of barley to translate data on other products into a single numerator for addition purposes.[167]

The organizations employed people in agriculture, crafts, and services. Their workers grew barley and other crops, such as dates and legumes, and produced beer and textiles. Workers were recorded by sex and age.[168] They were recompensed for their labor by wages (ba—rations, according to certain scholars) expressed in Silas (unit of measurement—liter) and differentiated by age, sex, and, apparently, status in the organization.[169]

Reinforcing the hypothesis about the importance of the measurement unit—the sila—as a means of exchange (money) in Mesopotamians' daily lives at this time is the discovery of thousands of standard beveled-rim bowls, each with a capacity of roughly one liter (a sila), in excavations of Uruk strata.[170] The bowls were means of measurement that the population used when it made payments (like weights and scales for payment in weight units of silver). It stands to reason that every household owned such a bowl and used it to measure quantities of barley in exchange. According to another hypothesis, the sila bowls were standard implements for use in eating the daily ration. There is no general consensus on the topic because the very question of barley as a means of exchange is disputed due to its broad significance in the socioeconomic model that explains the contemporaneous structure of the Mesopotamian economy. The bowl is also mentioned in palace reports from the time of Sargon as an item manufactured in large numbers.[171]

In palace and temple documents from the Ur III period, workers are reported as being paid 60 sila per month,[172] children aged 5–10–15 sila per month, and women 30. Professionals were paid 500 and even 900 sila per month and managers received 1,200–5,000. Wages were paid in means of exchange that accorded with commodities that were available for this purpose, usually barley, wool, textiles, oil, and dates. Barley predominated.[173]

It is conjectured that an adult's subsistence ratio comprised about one liter of barley (approx. 650 grams) per day[174] or thirty liters (approx. 20 kilograms) per

---

167 Englund 2004, 37, 180–181.

168 Englund 2004, 41–42.

169 Englund 1998, 184–188.

170 Englund 1998, 180–181; Nissen 1988, 83–85.

171 Gelb 1982, 589.

172 Weitzoldt 1987, 117–141.

173 Researchers disagree about the volume of a sila. Some set it at 0.8 liter, making the Kurrum 240 liters. In his study on sila bowls, Gelb sets the measure of a sila at one liter. Gelb 1982, 585–590. The sila may have been differently sized in different periods.

174 Providing roughly 2,600 calories.

month.[175] Hence, what remained of the thirty-liter barley wage was exchanged in the market for other commodities that met workers' needs, such as legumes, oil, lard, dried fish, and salt, and products such as ceramic and copper implements and textiles and wool.[176] In the Ur III period, a sila of legumes went for 0.6 sila of barley and a mina of wool (approx. half a kilogram) for 30 sila of barley.[177] A sila of lard cost twenty silas of barley and a sila of oil (evidently sesame) went for twenty-five silas of barley.[178] In sales of assets (e.g., houses, plantations, and slaves), silver and copper were main means of exchange (in weight units). In inter-regional trade, silver was the universal currency.

In addition to their wages, high-status members of the organizations received parcels of land to cultivate.[179] Parcel size was determined commensurate with the worker's status in the organization. The land was received by lease. Lease rights in land were bought and sold, *inter alia,* using units of barley as means of exchange. Loans were given and repaid the same way.

The use of barley as money also appears in the laws of the time. In statutes not attributed to any particular king in 2050–1800 BCE, labor wages of seventy, twenty, and six silas of barley are cited. The term of employment and the employee's identity are specified, but from other sources, one may surmise that these were the monthly wages of a man, a boy, and a little boy, respectively. A loan of one Kurrum of barley (300 silas) earned 100 silas in interest.[180] According to the Laws of Eshnunna (c. 1750 BCE),[181] the price of one silver shekel (8.33 grams) was 300 sila (Gur—*Kurrum*) of barley. Six hundred silas of salt cost one silver shekel.

Barley remained in use as a means of exchange into the second millennium BCE and appears in the laws of Eshnunna and Ḫammu-rapi. In the former code (Section 15), traders and innkeepers are enjoined against accepting payment from slaves in the currency of the time:

---

175 See discusson of the matter in Englund 1998, 179. According to Englund, the daily ration redistributed to a woman in the Ur III and Uruk periods was a subsistence quantity of one liter. Support for this hypothesis appears in a marriage contract from Sippar, 1820 BCE, in which a secondary wife must grind a liter of barley per day as a daily ration for the primary wife (Westbrook 1988, 116–117). A subsistence ration for a six-person household was roughly 85 sila per month in the Ur III period (Potts 1997, 81).

176 Heimple 2009, 117–141; Powell 1999, 5–23; Waetzoldt 1987, 117–141; Cripps 2007.

177 The amount of wool needed to weave cloth for a tunic was four minas (priced at 120 liters of barley—two months' pay). The economic organizations distributed wool and textiles as wages/rations.

178 Waetzoldt 1987, 134.

179 Waetzoldt 1987, 128–132.

180 Roth 1997, 38.

181 Roth 1997, 59.

> A merchant or a woman innkeeper will not accept silver, grain, wool, oil (means of exchange), or anything else from a male or female slave (Laws of Eshnunna).[182]

Multiple sections in the Laws of Ḫammu-rapi concern themselves with loans and the interest rates applying to them.[183] Loans given in barley and silver are mentioned. The means of exchange in which the loan is given are equal in status from the standpoint of the law but the interest rate varies: 100 sila per Kurrum (300 sila) or 33 percent for a loan given in barley, thirty-six barleycorns per silver shekel (180 barleycorns in a silver shekel) or 20 percent for a loan given in silver:

> If a merchant gives grain or silver as an interest-bearing loan, he shall take 100 silas of grain per Kurrum (300 silas) as interest (33 %); if he gives silver as an interest-bearing loan, he shall take 36 barleycorns per shekel (180 barleycorns) of silver as interest (20 %) (Laws of Ḫammu-rapi).[184]

Evidence of problems in using barley as a means of exchange appears in Section 108 of the Code of Ḫammu-rapi, which expounds on an innkeeper's wife who refuses to accept barley in payment for beer and demands silver instead:

> If a woman innkeeper should refuse to accept grain for the price of beer but accept silver measured by large weight (compared with the official weight—i. e., cheating), they shall charge and convict that woman innkeeper and they cast her into the water. (Laws of Ḫammu-rapi).[185]

The legacy of barley as a means of exchange—money—appears in the system of concepts in Mesopotamia. Barleycorns (še- *uṭṭatum*) were used to measure weights smaller than a shekel. A shekel weighed about eight grams, equal to 180 barleycorns.

For large transactions—involving land purchase or interregional trade, for example—the principal means of exchange was a metal such as copper or silver. Copper had been reaching Mesopotamia since the fifth millennium BCE from the Persian Gulf (Oman). Silver first appeared in the fourth millennium[186] and is mentioned in the writings of Sargon of Akkadia and Gudea in the second half of the third millennium BCE.[187] The sources of silver were today's Iran and perhaps

182 Roth 1997, 61.
183 Roth 1997, 97–99.
184 Roth 1997, 97.
185 Roth 1997, 101.
186 Moorey 1994, 232–239.
187 Leemans 1960, 117.

Afghanistan, as well as and northeastern and southwestern Anatolia. At first it was used for the production of tools and jewelry. When it came into wider use, it also served as the main means of exchange for traders in Mesopotamia on the basis of agreed-upon weight units. In the fourth and third millennium BCE, several rulers introduced official weights and measures that developed throughout the region afterward.[188]

The weights and measures were determined and supervised by the authorities. Punishments were set for using them misleadingly. The consensual units of weight found expression in the form of weights (stone or bronze) used to measure on two-pan scales. The weights were sometimes objects in an agreed shape, such as a duck. The traders were expert in identifying the types and quality of silver.

The authorities hired experts to help determine silver quality. In archaeological excavations, scale pans were found next to weight stones and documents were discovered that refer to both. Evidently, different kinds of scales were used to weigh different sizes. Traders who used silver brought along packets/cases/sacks (*kīsum; naruqqum*) containing pieces of silver (*šibirtum*). They weighed the pieces on the scales (by using variously sized weights that they carried in another sack) at point of exchange. In various places, attempts were made to establish different shapes for standard weights of means of exchange (silver, copper, bronze) in order to simplify weighing and exchange (silver rings and coils, bronze axe heads, ducks and spear heads).[189]

The next revolution in the use of metals as money came 2,000 years later, with the advent of coins in Asia Minor in the late seventh century BCE. The coins were weight units of metal of a specific quality and form, minted with inscriptions and depictions by the authorities. Even after coins came into use, however, traders continued to weigh out quantities of metals that they received in exchange in the fear that the weights of the coins were compromised or inaccurate.

* * *

In summary, researchers are not of one mind about the institution of means of exchange in ancient Mesopotamia. Those of the primitive-substantive school claim that there were no means of exchange in the markets of Mesopotamia. The economy, they say, was based on subsistence production; the limited trading that took place was socially grounded. In lieu of means of exchange, natural exchange took place at rates set by the authorities. The second view, the formal-modern, asserts

188 The most salient of these rulers were Ur-Nammu and his son Shulgi (2094–2047 BCE) from the Ur III dynasty. Steinkeller 1987, 21.
189 Snell 1995, 1488–1489; Powell 1978, 211–243.

the existence of means of exchange such as units of volume (barley) and of weight (copper and, later, silver). People traded in the markets and used measurement units of barley for bookkeeping, credit, paying wages, rents, and interest on loans. The standard unit of measurement was the sila of barley and containers of exactly this size existed. There is documentation of "exchange rates" of barley volume for other goods, interest rates, and payment of rents. Silver weight units came into use in the middle of the third millennium BCE.

Means of Exchange—Money in the Old Assyrian Trade

Assyrian traders used different means of exchange for different kinds of transactions in different places. When dealing in daily necessities such as small quantities of food, personal loans, services, or wages of local workers, they used barley. Barley and wheat appear in many debt documents, both personal and commercial. Local (Anatolian) debtors are recorded in most of them,[190] probably suggesting that barley served as a means of exchange in the local market much as it did in coeval Mesopotamia.

> They (the debtors) will pay interest half in barley and half in wheat (?).[191]

Silver was the Assyrian traders' principal means of exchange (money). Trade transactions between different regions in Anatolia were also consummated with copper and wool as the means of exchange. Trade in Assyria with Babylonians and Elamites apparently took place in silver. Traders quoted prices of assets such as houses and slaves and executed credit agreements in units of silver. Reckoning between traders and their central institution, the Karum, and among each other as well, was carried out in silver. When gold was used in investment agreements, it was converted (literally or for reckoning purposes) into units of silver.[192] In caravans to Kanesh, a standard value for the merchandise in the caravan was calculated in weight units of tin, and en route from Kanesh to Assur, the value was expressed in silver.

Traders themselves related to silver (*kaspum*) differently than they did to ordinary commodities (*luqūtum*). Silver was the purpose of the trade and its starting point as well. They used the expression "Turn the merchandise into silver" (*luqū-*

190 Veenhof 2008, pp. 87–88.
191 ATHE 6 A:8 ff; CAD Š/$_2$ 351b.
192 Veenhof 1972, 450.

tam ana kaspim tu'ārum)[193] or "Turn my tin into silver" in instructions to their agents.[194]

They also expressed the importance of silver in trading by ordering their agents "not to let silver get hungry," meaning that silver should be quickly exchanged for goods that could be sold at a profit, thus quenching its "appetite."[195] They also ordered their agents to convert merchandise in their possession into silver and gold or to collect debts in silver.

> You sent me silver saying: "It must not get hungry."[196]
>
> Until the tin and the textiles are converted into silver.[197]
>
> Turn (them) into silver, whether they are (promissory notes on) case-enclosed tablets stemming from transactions of agents or from natives, or (whether they are) stores (of barley).[198]
>
> The merchandise was converted into gold.[199]

Gold had a special status in Assyria. Assyrian society evidently saw it as magical or as a way to increase national wealth; they accumulated it mainly in the temples. Traders gave the temples gold disks as gift-offerings or accumulated them in sacks that they placed in the temples. The use of gold in Assur was limited to exchange among Assyrians only and was forbidden (on pain of death) for use in trade with Akkadians, Amorites (*amurrū*), and Subarians (*subartū*).[200] Gold served as a unit of measurement for deposits in investment funds (*naruqqum*) and for long-term credit. It was also amassed by individuals and rulers for use in jewelry, tools, and sundry objects. Another reason for its accumulation, apart from the cultural and social effect, was long-term savings, as in the following:

> Keep a close watch on the bracelets and rings (of gold) that are there, they should be available to provide you with food.'[201]

* * *

193 Veenhof 1987, 44.
194 Veenhof 1972, 351, 365.
195 Traders also used the word "hungry" in reference to other means of exchange such as tin and copper.
196 TC 1,29:27 ff; Veenhof 1987, 62.
197 CCT 4 15c:15 ff; CAD T 260b.
198 BIN 6 59:23 ff; CAD T 141a.
199 BIN 4 104:24 ff; CAD T 260–1b&a.
200 Veenhof 1999, 55.
201 CCT 3 24:5 ff; CAD B 146a&b.

In conclusion, silver weights were used as a principal means of exchange in Old Assyrian trade. Accumulation of silver and gold was the very purpose of the traders' activity. Other substances, such as copper and tin, also served as means of exchange. Gold was limited in use as a means of exchange; it was reserved mainly for financial requisites such as calculating investment funds ("sacks") and savings/accrual in the temples of Assur.

Chapter 3
Organization and Finance

In this chapter this writer investigates the institutional aspects of organization and finance of the Old Assyrian trade. He begins by explaining how the traders organized for long-term commerce with Anatolia, starting with the theoretical aspect of the economic structures and the reasons for their use, and continuing with the traders' organizations. He then addresses two aspects related to the topic of finance: Institutional Economics, associated with the institution of exchange involving credit; and financial institutions relating to finance and credit. To elucidate these matters, the writer will use terms from the fields of modern accounting and finance.

One of the most vigorous debates in economic matters relating to the third millennium BCE concerns credit and interest.[1] Those who subscribe to the primitive-subsistence model hold that a system of subsistence production did not use credit; instead, credit balances were maintained for record-keeping purposes and interest was charged as a penalty for tardiness in paying the authorities. In this type of system, individuals' private credit was an exchange of goods and repayment of favors for social reasons, and interest represented a payment of gratitude.

In contrast, another view posits that organizational and financial institutions existed in Old Assyrian trade along the lines of similar institutions that were maintained in the third millennium BCE.[2] These institutions met the needs of the economic organizations of the palace and the temple, paying salaries that workers could exchange in markets for other commodities. There were private property rights in fields for leasing, and ownership rights in houses, personal property, fruit plantations, and slaves. Agricultural and commercial credit was given with barley and silver as means of exchange. Very high agricultural productivity, generous profit margins in trade, and daunting political, security, and natural risks led to high interest rates. There were also private traders who operated for profit motives, foremost in interregional trade.

What different scholars do agree about is that the structure of the Mesopotamian economy and society underwent a dramatic change the early second millennium BCE.[3] As the dominance of the palace-and-temple economy waned perceptibly, private sector activity grew. Various activities, once the purview of the palace

1 Hudson 2002, 7–37.

2 Veenhof 2003a, 431–483.

3 Van de Mieroop 2002, 69–72.

https://doi.org/10.1515/9783111065533-006

and temple organizations, such as collecting taxes and leasing fees, were privatized. Private property rights expanded and credit organizations evolved into those familiar to us today. Archaeological excavations have unearthed thousands of credit documents from this period. In the opinion of certain researchers, there were especially high interest rates on debts, which was indeed noted now and then by some kings. According to their view, the credit system and the steep interest were among the factors that brought down the Mesopotamian economy and society in the middle of the second millennium BCE.

The Assyrian economic organizations lowered commercial transaction costs and risks, thus increasing traders' profits. The institutions and entities appearing in traders' documents from this period recur throughout history where interregional trade is concerned. These included organizations such as the "lone trader" (*tamkārum*), who operated within the framework of the family—the "house" (*bētum*); partnerships among traders (usually grounded in contracts—*tappā'utum*); and the limited partnership—the "sack" (*naruqqum*). Additional short-term partnerships took shape in caravans (*ellatum*) and transactions under the umbrella of the joint organization in Assur City—the "City House" (*bēt ālim*) and its counterpart in Anatolia, the Karum. Commercial activity took place in individual transactions under his control or "shipments" (*šēpum*). The concept of the "house" was invoked in discussions regarding the property of the head of the family, inheritances or inclusive debts, and unspecified joint transactions.

Traders operated as individuals who owned the assets and were personally liable for them. One of the things they valued the most was reputation, measured in three respects: the scale of their activity, the relative importance of their activity (e.g., number of transactions per year), and the trader's credibility. A trader's reputation determined his ability to raise money from investors to finance his trade, receive goods as an agent for other traders, obtain credit (and at what interest rate), and maintain his status vis-à-vis the political organizations ("the City" and the Karum). Reputation also influenced those who operated as part of a "house," in concert with a reputable family leader.

Traders sent agents to transport their wares to the target markets, sell them there, and manage their business in the markets there. The agents received goods on consignment and had to pay for them by a given deadline. Failure to pay on time resulted in an interest charge. The Assyrian traders, mindful of the principal–agent dilemma, gave their agents an incentive in the form of a below-market price, allowing the agents to profit from the sale. The agents were thus incentivized to realize this profit by choosing reliable buyers who paid on time.

Old Assyrian society enjoyed sophisticated credit institutions that included consumer credit to acquire and maintain long-term assets and commercial credit and other available instruments to help operate the trading system. These institutions resembled those used in credit and investment markets to this day. Even then, there were long-term financing instruments, such as long-term loans (*ebuṭṭum*) and long-term investments in limited partnerships—the aforementioned (*naruqqum*) "sack." Short-term commercial credit was used for matters such as depositing goods on consignment, which were recorded by their recipient (and the recipient of the credit) as goods deposited ("accounts payable"—*qīptum*).[4] These goods were recorded with the depositing trader (the lender) as "accounts receivable" (*bābtum*).[5] In addition to commercial credit, a regular credit system (*ḫubullum*) of interest-bearing loans was operative. Much like a bank-credit system, it issued credit, usually on the basis of an agreed loan contact supported by witnesses, guarantors, and additional collateral. The institution of interest was well developed; it was invoked as a penalty for arrears in debt repayment and served as an instrument for pricing borrower risk.

Traders ran a private accounting system to finance and operate their activity, recording memorandum of balances (*taḫsistum*) on large tablets. They also maintained a system of periodic settling of accounts (*nikkassum šasā'um*) with other traders and with the institutions, in which they recorded outstanding debits and credits in their commercial relations.

Organization

In a society that operates on the basis of a market economy, resources are held and moved about by nongovernmental organizations, such as households and companies. Holders of rights in resources boost productivity by specializing on a cooperative basis. The need to cooperate creates demand for economic organizations that can facilitate cooperation. The theory of economic organizations tries to explain the conditions that determine whether the advantages of specialization and cooperation can be attained within the organization or in the markets; it also attempts to explain the structure of the organizations in question.[6] There are two aspects to the business activity of an organization: first, the organization as an instrument

4 CAD defines *qīptum* as a quantity of a commodity (in silver value) that is deposited with an agent for sale on consignment, on which no interest is charged for a predetermined time. In modern bookkeeping, this form of commercial credit is called "accounts payable" in the books of the agent who receives the credit.

5 CAD defines *bābtum* as outstanding goods not in the possession of the trader who expects to receive them, or their proceeds, in the near term. In modern bookkeeping, this form of commercial credit is called "accounts receivable" on the lending trader's books.

6 Alchian and Demsetz 1972, 777.

that helps to solve the problem of exchange; and second, the organization as the entity that raises sources of funding for its activity. The latter aspect is discussed in the section on Finance, below.

The economic organization is known by the general term "the company" (the firm). According to a theory first presented by Coase (1937), "the company" is created as an instrument that helps to solve exchange problems and lower transaction costs.[7] The company sets its own operating rules, including the organization of its operating system and its manager–agent or employer–employee relations. This entail determining the responsibility for carrying out the requisite work and paying wages for labor services.[8] Exchange in the market involves a series of activities that incur expenses called "transaction costs." Repeated activity in the market includes investing in hiring workers, obtaining information about the state of the market, negotiating prices, and enforcing contracts, among other things, which can result in the accumulation of heavy transaction costs. Establishing an organization dedicated to these purposes reduces transaction costs by making a series of internal decisions about resource allocation based on long-term contracts that govern its internal conduct instead of short-term contracts and market behavior. In lieu of exchange transactions between buyer and seller, in which the sides spend resources on information and ensuring that the transaction will take place, exchange is consummated by transferring goods and means of production among workers within the organization. The cost of "in-house" management of the transfer of sources and the contractual system are lower and joint production is more efficient; also, the cost of information within the company is lower than that obtained in the market.[9]

Organizing within the framework of a company has additional advantages. For example, a company develops knowledge that is its alone, such as organizing production and maintaining a business culture that attain greater efficiency than that of its competitors. The formation of companies and the construction of a system of exchange relations within them, however, also entail costs that climb as the organization grows and the efficiency of its structure changes. Organizations compete with each other in the market, and with the competition comes adjustments to the state of the market in the transaction costs within the company. In imperfect markets, resource allocation within companies has an advantage over using the market.

7 Coase 1937, 386–405; Demsetz 1988, 141–161.
8 Coase 1992, 713–719.
9 Alchian and Demsetz 1972, 794–795.

A company may also be an individual who runs his or her other business alone and obtains resources from other individuals. The responsibility for running such a business and the property rights associated with it are neither corporate nor familial, but personal. In this case, individuals may maintain complex relations with their family or society, using them to identify and consummate transactions and conclude agreements with agents to carry out tasks for them in the course of their economic activity.

A business may be an organization headed by a partnership among several people. Economic organizations with multiple partners, as in a limited partnership or a share company, are possible as well. These forms of organization mitigate transaction costs because the companies they create have lower transaction costs. In addition, they allow permanent arrangements to form, becoming responsible for: the long-term regulation of relations among partners; division of risk and profit among partners in a way that generates a return on equity, initiative, and risk-taking; and savings on the expenses that would amass if relations had to be determined for each transaction.[10]

Researchers debate the status of the trader in the third millennium BCE.[11] Some, particularly those who deny the existence of a market economy and insist that commerce was organized solely by the authorities, reject the view that the traders had independent status. Traders, they argue, were clerks who managed trade as part of the social system of palace and temple production and redistribution. Most interregional trade took place among rulers and in special commercial zones ("trading ports") on the basis of agreed-upon price ratios. Traders had a special title (*tamkārum*) and were part of an organization that posted managers over them. According to this line of scholarship, the traders did not receive a return in the form of a profit for their commercial endeavors, but, instead, received land from the authorities and used it to generate income. Traders also engaged in commerce due to the special social status that this vocation awarded.

A different line of scholarship maintains that traders in Mesopotamia at that time had independent status and conducted commerce for profit purposes in a market economy.[12] The noun "trader" (*tamkārum*) denoted a profession, like a blacksmith (*nappāḫum*), and was in use among traders and those who oversaw them. Traders also issued credit to the public via interest-bearing loans. Regardless of the details, scholars do not dispute the special role and status of traders in Mesopotamian society of the early second millennium BCE.

---

10 Ribstein 1998, 10–13.
11 Gledhill and Larsen 1982, 197–229; Dercksen 2000, 135–151.
12 Powell 1977, 23–29.

The Old Assyrian Organization

The writer decided to open this part of the chapter by presenting one of the letters of an important Old Assyrian trader that includes some clues about the organization of trade and its operation. It describes a father who heads a "family firm" (*bit abini*) and high-handedly manages his representatives or agents (his sons) and his personal capital and money affairs. Each participant in the system manages his own financial system of investment, income, and debt. There is no recognition of family ownership of resources. Each person owns all the asset at stake or a share in the assets. When he dies, his assets are transferred to Assur, converted into silver (money), and then divided to his heirs according to the will as supervised by the City (Assur). This system of personal ownership of property rights was a major weakness of the Old Assyrian economic and social system. It probably posed a major obstacle to the transfer of assets and the intergenerational ownership and functioning of economic activities, disrupting the operation and development of the lucrative trade between Assur and Anatolia at a specific point: the death of the old heads of the family.[13]

The trader used the solidarity among family members and the fear of losing credibility ("name" or "face") to manage the participants in the "firm" in such an autocratic manner. Honor, good business relations, and exchanging "favors" were highly valued.[14]

In the following letter, the father, *Aššur-idi*, complains about his fate as a father and trader with problems with his sons as agents and representatives active in the trade in Anatolia. The letter describes many aspects of a trader's life. It exudes anger, anxiety, and sarcasm:

> You left four years ago, but so far, have any goods (money-silver) left (Kanesh to me in Assur)? PN (one of my debtors) has paid you in full for the (with) interest on my goods (and you are withholding my money). Why is it that caravans arrived (from Anatolia) at least twice, but you have not sent me any silver?
>
> (In addition to the problems with you) against the will of God, your brother has caused (me) the loss of some 30 minas (a large sum of money) of my silver. Instead of giving me encouragement (help me) you withhold the silver yourself! Indeed, get hold of some (silver from any source) and send (me) at least 30 minas of silver, and if you say: "I am out of funds (I do not have any money)"—so, two shekels may be deducted for you (sarcastic comment—petty sum). But clear the rest of my silver and send it with the first transport, then I shall make purchases and send (the goods), so they be active for me (be part of my turnover and yours and we can

13 Larsen 2015, 72*ff.*

14 Dercksen 2014, 61.

make profits on them). May every shekel of profit be realized for me, so I can make good my losses (be compensated for my losses).

If you are truly my brother (a form of speaking of a father—want to be very nice to me), then take care to send me the (much needed) silver (money).

(I want to remind you that) when you (plur.) sent me silver (to buy tin in the past) you said: 'It (the silver) should not lie idle.' Because of your orders (sarcastic remark of the father) I bought tin when it was in short supply (and very expensive), and if fact that (tin) has been lying idle there! (in fact, you made me buy expensive tin that was not needed). Today tin is available at the rate of 16:1 (15:1 is considered the right rate for tin to silver) or even higher! (lower price for tin). The tin can be sold in Anatolia for 6 or 7:1 silver. (The father is enticing the son to send silver to buy tin and make a large profit for both). Send me at least 30 minas of silver (that you accumulated) from what has been entrusted to you (for sale in Anatolia by other traders—my colleagues). Then I shall buy goods for you. Purchases (of tin) are available.[15]

Pay on my behalf at the time of the accounting (a periodic settlement of accounts procedure in the Karum in Anatolia) Why have you written to me about converting it into goods? (not paying silver?).

From where should the silver come to me? (I am swamped with expenses in silver). I have paid 16 minas of silver on behalf of PN to the City Hall (an accounting balance in Assur). As to the house of PN_2 (which I bought), to buy it and (to) make (ready) it (invest in it) cost 15 minas (silver).[16]

The Assyrian traders' basic organizational unit was, as stated, the individual trader,[17] who was personally responsible for his business and held property rights to his assets. The reputation and status that he acquired were based on the scale of his activity and assets and his business and personal conduct. Reputation and status affected one's ability to do business. Well-regarded traders could raise capital from investors more easily and close sales on commission from other traders. Such traders also had superior political and social status and held political posts in Assyrian society. Traders relied on a supportive social system that helped to create business structures, such as partnerships and joint transactions, and overcame business crises by helping each other.

The traders belonged to family organizations—the "house" (*bētum*) or "our father's house" (*bēt abini*)—that were instruments for cooperation and mutual aid.[18] The family head of such an organization created a socio-familial structure that activated men and women as members, employees/servants/ "boys" (*ṣuḫāru*) or

15 TC 1, 29, Larsen 2002, 26–27.
16 TC 1, 29, Larsen 2002, 26–27.
17 Larsen 2007; Stratford 2010.
18 Larsen 1977a, 119–124.

agents (*šamallā'ūm*) in Assur and Anatolia. The family was not an economic unit that owned its assets and concluded transactions under joint proprietorship; assets and transactions belonged to individual traders who were members of the family. The head of the family strove to guide family members' development and persuade them to carry out assignments for him (e.g., creating partnerships, collecting debts, or making purchases under preferential terms) by invoking accepted family norms, his reputation, and his economic and political power. The reputation of the head of the family, as stated, influenced economic matters, such as attracting investments (the "sack"), obtaining suppliers' credit and merchandise on a commission basis, receiving a preferential interest rate, securing assistance from others, when necessary, particularly at times of crisis, and recruiting suitable people for complex tasks of haulage and sales. The reputation of the trader and the "house" were also important for traders' status in society, the political system, and their own integration into the organizational and social structure. Women were part of the commercial system and coordinated their moves as traders and producers with their husbands. They enjoyed a share in the property according to the marriage agreement and according to what was customary in inheritance agreements.

The "house" structure rested on social norms and was backed by sanctions that the head of the family could apply. It was meant to maximize cooperation within the family, streamline the process of exchange among family members, and mitigate the risk inherent in exchange by making market processes "in-house." In this "family company," relations among members were based mainly on family traditions and general values (the so-called "private arrangement") and less on the judicial system. The enforcement system within the "house" was grounded in the expectation of behavior in accordance with accepted rules of meeting conditions and maintaining reputation. Penalties for breaching the conditions included ostracism, loss of trading opportunities, and a lawsuit. Management was based on generational hierarchy within the family. Family members who engaged in trade directly (that is, not as subordinates as the head of the family) based their relationship within the family on a formal set of agreements and contracts. Loans to offspring who went into the trading business were repaid with interest; their property belonged to them and not to the "house." Interpersonal relations in the family had no economic significance associated with commercial activity and debt. The head of family wielded his authority over family members' behavior and members could expect him to help them in advocacy, making connections, and personal loans for subsistence needs. When the head of family died, all of his property was handed over to Assur city and was redistributed between his wife and their children on the basis of the will and on permanent procedures.[19]

> I shall do my duty for your firm and you so that nobody will do damage to your (pl.) firm.[20]
>
> One or two evil persons are set to cause confusion in our firm.[21]
>
> Write me as to how much gold either your or your firm's share (in the partnership) amounts to, so that I can take your tablet and direct exchange in as much as I can.[22]
>
> If PN has a share in the silver, let his son stand at your side and pay strict attention to the tablet listing the purchases and sell (them) and seal half the silver and send (it) to me. Establish witnesses of the shipping (of) the silver so that he may not prosecute (lit., seize for oath) you some day. If his son (should say): "Give me the goods. I agree with the words of my father's house." Why has he opened up the matter with you? Then you (shall say), "Whatever he should take in your father's house from my account, I shall take from your account." Validate your tablet and your witnesses! Release the merchandise![23]

Family members, women included, usually handled the trade and, where necessary, were involved in producing textiles in Assur or selling them in Anatolia. Relationships within the extended family—the "house"—were complex. In some cases, traders used family members or close friends as standing for or agents of the head of the family (*muzzizum*), who did his bidding. This status, institutionalized in the expression "like me"/ "like you" (*ša kīma yâti*; *kuāti*), spared the traders from having to conclude agreements; it also mitigated risks. As stated, agents were recompensed in the form of goods that were consigned to them at a sub-market price; they could sell these goods in the market at a higher price and pocket the difference.

> Whether PN acted as the agent of PN_2, or whether PN_2 acted as the agent of PN.[24]
>
> Your father acted as agent of my father.[25]
>
> Send your strict instructions to your representatives and me in GN in writing, and we will indeed have your silver paid in GN.[26]

---

19 Larsen 2 007, 93–106.
20 KTS 1b:28 and 30, CAD $A/_1$ 75a.
21 CCT 2 33:10 ff, CAD $A/_1$ 75a.
22 CCT 4 9a:6 ff, CAD $A/_1$ 96a.
23 Pa 14, L 29–568, Gwaltney 1983, 42, 17–40.
24 ATHE 24B:17 ff, CAD $Š/_2$ 245b.
25 CCT 5 11a:4 ff, CAD $Š/_2$ 245b.
26 TCL 14 27:19 ff, CAD $Š/_2$ 245–6b&a.

> If it suits him, I shall instruct my representatives that they should give him ten fine *kutānu*-garments on the arrival of my caravan (from Assur).[27]

As stated, the traders sent agents to vend their wares in the destination markets. The agents accomplished this either by hiring caravan leaders to deliver goods to the destinations or by consigning merchandise to agents traveling to a number of destinations. Both methods created principal–agent and agency-dilemma problems. That is, how could the principal ensure that the agent would promote the principal's interests and not the agents? The problem arose then, as now, when information asymmetry existed between the principal and the agent as to the transactions that the agent performed.[28] To resolve the dilemma, a set of incentives needed to be created that would reward the agent or harm him in the same way in which the principal might be harmed.

The Assyrian traders created an instrument by which the caravan leaders were rewarded: *be'ūlātum*, translated as "capital" by some researchers and "working capital" by others.[29] They gave caravan leaders goods at a submarket price for the term of the caravan's journey, effectively lending it to them and thus committing them to their role as caravan leader. When the caravan reached its destination, the leaders could sell the goods and use the proceeds to pay back the loan and keep the difference. The very acceptance of the goods, which belonged to the caravan but were assets in their own right, made the caravan leaders partners in the caravan and gave them an interest similar to that of the other partners.

The traders posted a representative of the family (usually a son) to Kanesh. This representative was responsible for receiving the merchandise from Assur, clearing it through the palace (customs) in Kanesh, and forwarding it in the caravans that commuted between Kanesh and Assur. He was also in charge of consigning goods to agents for sale in other Anatolian cities and responsible for collecting debts. The representative, acting on behalf of the house, traded in wool and copper within Anatolia, where the goods were sold using agents who received them on time-limited and interest-free suppliers' credit (*qīptum*). Interest was charged on proceeds not remitted on time. The system was formal and accompanied by signed (sealed) agreements (notes).

27 CCT 2 27:10 ff, CAD I-J 83b.
28 Stiglitz 1987, 966–967.
29 In existing studies and CAD, *be'ūlātum* is defined as "working capital." This term is unsuitable because it is defined financially as capital needed for the ongoing operation of a commercial venture, i.e., the investment that is needed to hold cash and maintain an inventory of goods. A better definition would be "capital" only. See discussion below of the meaning of *be'ūlātum* as an instrument of finance.

Traders (or trading houses in the head of the family's name) also organized in partnerships or as part of a joint agency (*šazzuztum tappā'utum*) in which both sides presented themselves as representatives/partners (*kīma yâti; ša kīma; šazzuzti*). In this case, liability and apportionment of the profits from the transaction were mutual.[30] The two sides co-managed the commercial venture, were liable for the partnership's undertakings, could represent each other in claims, collected joint debts, and entered into joint contracts. The commercial property and the profits and losses were divided equally among them. These Assyrian partnerships resembled commercial partnerships not unlike the Greco-Roman *societas,* the medieval *compagnia,* and arrangements that appear in relevant legislation in contemporary industrialized states.[31] The traders' partnership in Assyrian commerce trade consisted of an investment in or deposit of goods or means of exchange (usually silver) in another trader's venture or in a joint venture among several traders. There were explicit agreements about the division of obligations among the partners and the apportionment of the profits. The investment was recorded in a partnership agreement or was based on an oral accord made in the presence of witnesses. The partners could take loans jointly and repay them singly or severally.[32] By organizing in partnerships, traders could also mobilize more resources, including capital and experience. Like other companies, the partnership internalized transactions and thus saved on expenses and risks in the partners' interrelations.

> If PN's share is a (separate) share and PN_2's share is a (separate) share (i.e., they are not jointly responsible), if PN's share is not (separate) share, they are jointly responsible for the silver.[33]

> They placed the responsibility for the silver upon whoever among us is solvent and I paid it.[34]

> He will swear that they did not establish a partnership and (he will) pay him the silver.[35]

> The price for the copper which I have paid to the Amorite is recorded together with my partners in a list.[36]

> You have written on my tablet concerning one talent of copper, that I will enjoy half of any profit and be responsible for half of any losses.[37]

30 Larsen 1976, 95–102; idem 1977a, 123; Veenhof 1997, 345–346; idem 2003a, 474–475.
31 Ribstein 1998, 10–13.
32 Veenhof 2001, 148–152.
33 Kültepe c/k 680:16*ff* & 25*ff*, CAD Q 195b.
34 CCT 5 45a, CAD R 101b.
35 HUCA 39 3 L29–553:19, CAD T 160b.
36 CCT 4 1b:24*ff*, CAD T 185a.
37 TCL 20 110:20*ff*, CAD L 86b.

(The heirs) seized us by mutual agreement (as arbiters) and swore the oath of the City, and we brought an end to their dispute: Irrespective of whether PN has functioned as the agent of PN_2 or PN_2 has functioned as the agent of PN whether one of them has send *maskattum*-deposits to the other; whether one of them has collected current debts on behalf of the other, either (on the basis of) certified tablets bearing their own seals or witnessed documents; Whether one of them has made *sipkatum*-deposits for the other, be it in the City or abroad—The sons of PN, the daughter of PN (who is) a priestess (*gubabtum*), will raise no claims against each other regarding anything.[38]

Traders organized for joint ventures, such as intercity caravans (*ella/utum*) or joint purchases of wool in Anatolia.[39] The caravan partnership was a unique type that lasted briefly only.[40] It was established for the purpose of hauling goods and tablets from place to place. Each caravan was organized by a different large-scale trader; other traders deposited their shipments in the caravan in the hands of the caravan leaders whom the principal trader appointed.

The caravan massed at city gates under the supervision of the authorities, the traders, and the investors. Employing donkey drivers and guards, the caravan leaders were responsible for the integrity of the shipments and a reasonable level of expenses during the journey, apart from unforeseen factors beyond their control, such as robbery or security disruptions. Caravan leaders were paid for their services in the form of goods on credit (capital—*be'ūlātum*) and "free tin" (tin was a means of exchange for travel expenses) to fund the caravan's expenditures. Their job was to steer the caravan to the courtyard of the Karum in the traders' colony. After arrival, a caravan report was drawn up. Caravan leaders had to report their actual expenditures; each caravan had a tablet on which the calculated values (*zamārum*) of each participating trader's goods were recorded. The total value of the caravan was called the *awītum*. Values of goods were recorded in units of tin in passenger caravans to Anatolia and in units of silver in caravans to Assur.

The common denominator for the value of goods was the joint investment (*mišit ellitim*) of the partners in the caravan. When the caravan reached the Karum in Kanesh, it was charged the Karum tax at the calculated value of the caravan; then the caravan leader was sent to the palace for payment of customs duties and exercise of the palace's purchase rights. These expenses were subtracted from the value of the caravan, after which its net value and the profit derived from it were divided among the partners in an accounting that took place at the Karum

38 AThE 24 A 13–37, Larsen 1976, 100–101.
39 Veenhof 2003a, 475.
40 Dercksen 2004, 148–180.

offices. In cases where robbery caused losses, the participants had to bear the damage.[41]

> The silver from here, the goods from there will travel overland in the name of the trader.[42]
>
> Two minas of tin (loose tin) either for guards, or for lodgings or for feed for the donkey.[43]
>
> The (calculated) losses and expenses the trip.[44]
>
> 36 *kutānū*-garments belonging to PN's caravan, which PN_2 led out (from Assur) have been lost in the mountains of GN—inform me whether he (the caravan leader PN_2) did or did not compensate the enterprise.[45]
>
> They are jointly responsible for their expenditure and their taxes (of the caravan) according to their assets.[46]
>
> I shall take x shekels as my one-third (share) of the enterprise of PN (profits) from the office of the Karum and x shekels from the storehouse (?) of the enterprises.[47]

The Old Assyrian traders created a new form of partnership, the "sack" (*naruqqum*). A trader or a group of investors initiated a joint venture in which the parties approached the City (Assur) to organize it. The venture included a trader (*tāmkārum*—tractator) who needed money to invest in merchandise and trade and a group of investors (*ummiānum*) who were looking for profitable use of their capital. Other investors could buy into the venture. The trader in many cases was also an investor in the venture. To be a trader backed by investors, he needed to have experience in trading, well developed connections, and a good reputation.

The trader withdrew the capital from the "sack" (the venture) and used it in his trading activities. Any debt obligation created during these activities was not passed on to the investors. The investors were entitled to inspect the trading activities that took place in the City, and there were periodic meetings of the partners (an investment accounting—*nikkassum)* in which the trader gave an account of the use of the resources of the partnership and the resulting profits (if any) were divided one-third to the trader and the rest to the investors. Usually, the profits were reinvested in the venture.

41 A clause that deals with such losses apparently appears on a stele from Kanesh. Veenhof 1995, 1730–1731.
42 KTH 24:11*ff*, CAD T 126a.
43 TCL 20 165:1*ff*, CAD $A/_2$ 128a.
44 BIN 6 212:19*ff*, CAD Ḫ 110a.
45 CCT 2 11a:19 ff, CAD I-J 83b.
46 TCL 21 247 A:20 ff, CAD $N/_2$ 270b.
47 CCT 1 38b:15 ff, CAD I-J 84a.

The *naruqqum* was not only a form of business organization, but also a very important financial instrument that was used to finance large-scale operations. Its financial aspects are discussed below in the subchapter on long-term finance.

> People less important than you administer *naruqqum* (an investment venture—limited partnership) and people less important than me have invested ten minas of gold. Come and take over an investment venture and only then leave.[48]

The limited partnership lowered the traders' transaction costs by mitigating the need to raise capital and sign frequent agreements with investors. The investors, in turn, were given the option of investing in the "sack" and spreading their risks by investing in multiple "sacks."[49] Similar organizational structures of limited partnerships are known in the Roman and Medieval eras, especially in maritime commerce: the Roman *commenda*[50] and an organization of the same name in the medieval and modern eras.[51] The conspicuous difference between the "sack" and the Roman partnership concerns the duration of the contract. In the Roman partnership, the agreement was drawn up for the purpose of a specific maritime voyage to a specific market; the "sack," in contrast, was meant for multiple overland journeys and for a term of up to twelve years. In both types of accords, the investors received most of the profit and the traveling trader received one-fourth of the income (in the Middle Ages) or one-third (in Assyrian trading) for his risks and labors. In both types of arrangements, a trader might also be an investor, in which case, he received an investor's share in the earnings. Traders' shares in profit and risk varied in different periods, as did the extent of the investor's influence on the conduct of trade. In the Roman era, the authorities recognized another form of organization: the public partnership (*societates publicanorum*), a limited partnership of investors who entered into a long-term economic venture. In this case, one or more of the partners had unlimited liability and the liability of the numerous other partners was limited to their investment in the venture. It should be noted that the Roman authorities recognized the *societates publicanorum* only for the purposes of investing in and operating mines, receiving public works or tax-collection contracts. Some claim that the Romans disallowed a similar structure for other private economic activity—commerce, industry, or agriculture—because they wished to reserve it for raising large-scale capital for public activity.

48 CCT 4 2a, Larsen, 2002, 31.

49 Veenhof 2003a, 475–476.

50 Similar organizational forms existed in Byzantium (the *chreokoinōnia*) and in the Islamicate (*qirād–mudaraba*).

51 Prior 1977, 5–37; De Lara 2003, 480–483; Hejeebu 2003, 315–318.

Another short-term Assyrian partnership was a joint transaction under the umbrella of the joint organization in Assur city—the "City House" (*bēt ālim*)—and its counterparts in Anatolia, the "Karum House" (*bēt kārim*) and the *wabartum*. Traders who participated in these organizations made joint purchases of large quantities of tin and textiles in Assur and of wool and copper in Anatolia. The management of these arrangements were evidently similar to that of the caravan partnerships, but their accounting (investment, expenditure, sales, and profits) was centralized within the joint organization. The institutions also kept the traders' books and issued credit.[52]

Another institution that took part in the trading system was the temple. Many details about temple economic activity are unknown. The Old Assyrian community had a tradition of allocating a votive offering (*ikribū*) to their gods from their income.[53] The offering was probably institutionalized as an asset of the religious establishment. The exact operational structure of the *ikribū* is not clear.[54] Dercksen analyzes how the temple received (and used?) votive offerings and participated in trade by making the funds (called *ikribū*) available as long-term investment loans to traders.[55] CAD defines *ikribū* as "money and goods pledged by a vow to a deity." The writer preferences lean to this more general definition provided by CAD. According to tradition, one aspect of traders' conduct involved making vows.[56] Once such a pledge was made, the goods pledged were labeled (and recorded) as *ikribū*. The pledged goods could be gold, silver, tin, copper, textiles, or even utensils. They were stored and labeled as votive offerings that had been made. The traders and anyone who held a votive offering (which the trader allocated to him) could use it until the day it was shipped to the temple. Dercksen correctly describes an *ikribū* in a person's possession as a loan from the temple—an asset belonging to the deity that the holder is using. The writer thinks, however, that it is likely that the *ikribū* is more like a stored deposit (labeled merchandise) created by the trader that can be used for different purposes until it is handed to the priests in the temple. The loans recorded as *ikribū* funds may be lent by using *ikribū*-labeled resources.[57] They were used as small loans at special interest or as *tadmiqtum* loans.

52 Dercksen 2004, 14–39.

53 Veenhof 1987, 61; Dercksen, 2004, 77–81; idem 1998, 75–100.

54 There may have been a connection among the authorities' involvement in managing the "sack," deposits of gold at the temple, the ban on using gold in transactions with foreigners, and the use of deposited gold for investments.

55 Veenhof 2008, 104. Dercksen 1998, 75–100.

56 Like the Jewish tithe and the Islamic *zakat*.

57 Dercksen 1998.

The owner of an *ikribū* could send it to the temple as he or she wished. To encourage the delivery of the offering to the temple, priests circulated rumors to the effect that those who failed to remit them quickly would suffer deadly diseases. The people who used *ikribū* in trade (and made profits in so doing) were sometimes protected from taxation or forced buying (when they are part of a caravan cargo) on them. Dercksen finds many instances in which taxes and duties were levied on *ikribū* goods. The authorities may have been aware of the practice of using labeled goods as *ikribū* for regular trade and therefore taxed them as such.[58]

When the holder of an offering was ready to transfer it to the temple, it was converted into silver or gold and sent by caravan to Assur. In Assur, it was converted into gold (unless it had already been sent as gold) for deposit in the temple. Sometimes the owner of such an offering could make golden sun-disks of equal value and send them to the temple.

It is not clear what happened when votive offerings were brought into the temple. In one letter, a trader gives instructions on how to deposit the goods in the temple. He says that they may be added to existing sacks in the temple, with his name appended. The use of the offerings and the purpose of their accumulation in the temple is not clear. There are some indications that they were used in trade and that the "'sack"' system, the *naruqqum*, was associated with the gold in the temple (or the City). It is possible that the votive offering (the gold) in the sacks marked with the traders' names sat in the "hall" (a storage room in the temple, the palace, or the City hall) and was managed by officials who answered to the king. In a different corner of the hall, new sacks were created. Gold invested in the sacks moved from investors' sacks to new sacks bearing the traders' names. The gold probably never left the storage area.[59] The traders received silver from the sacks for use in their trading activity, with the priests providing them with the silver needed. The accounting (*nikkasum*) of movements (withdrawal and deposit) in the investment funds and of profits in the sack took place in the temple/the City, where traders, investors, and officials or priests met periodically to account for the movement of funds in the "sack" (*nikkasum*).

The accumulation of gold in temple storage was considered part of the growth of wealth and power of the city/state.[60] Unanswered questions about the votive offerings and the gold and silver that were stored in the temple remain. Primary among them is how the depositing system worked and what role the authorities played in managing it. Another question concerns the connection between the vo-

58 See Dercksen 1998, 82–83, for examples of *ikribū* goods taxed.

59 Like gold that moved from one location to another in Fort Knox when the world was on the gold standard.

60 This was a common practice in the city/states and empires of the period and later.

tive-offering system and the ban on trading in gold with foreigners, and between the "sack" investment system and the sacks in which gold was accumulated in the temple. In this context, several hypotheses have been broached. Perhaps the deposits had something to do with the special attitude toward gold in religious faith, or Assur's mercantilist policies, or the imperial treasury that was earmarked for special public and emergency expenditures:

> Seal one mina of silver for me as my votive offering.[61]
>
> Four linen garments from among the votive offerings pledged to Assur, two linen garments from the votive offerings pledged to Ishtar.[62]
>
> Buy tin with the gold of the *ikribū* funds I have been entrusted with.[63]
>
> In your home in GN there was silver, gold or cups belonging to my pledged votive offering.[64]
>
> PN is bringing one mina of *pašallum*-gold, its excise is added, under my seals, votive offering of divine *Aššur*, to you. My dear fathers and lords, on the day that PN arrives (and) you hear my message—they should not open the seals of the bundles—take its (i.e., the gold's) excise and deposit it together with the silver of the merchants. And my relatives must not know (it). If, in accordance with my order which I sent you. PN_2 has left ahead of PN, you must bring the sealed bundle with gold into *Aššur* temple. Ask the priest (*kumrum*) for the sack which is where the bundles carrying my sealings are, check my sealings and remove them, then place the bundle with gold on the upper. Seal it and indicate my name on the sealings.[65]
>
> Since the silver represents our pledged votive offering, it will, of course, not be subject to (lit. it will not learn) toll when under way.[66]
>
> Why do you retain the pledged votive offering? Take care to make (of it) the sun disk! (And send it to the temple).[67]
>
> Concerning the merchandise amounting to thirty minas silver, the temple's investment *(ikribū)* entrusted to PN, whoever seized it will release it and return what he took, whoever has not released it or returned it, it will be taken away from him.[68]
>
> The girl PN fell sick here on account of the silver pledged as votive offering.[69]

61 TCL 14 4:20 ff, CAD I-J 64a.
62 TCL 4 80:20 and 22, CAD I-J 64b.
63 CCT 2 32a:22 ff, CAD Š/1 351a.
64 TCL 21 271:7 ff, CAD I-J 64b.
65 TC 3 68, Dercksen 1996, 86–87.
66 KTS 27b:13 ff, CAD I-J 64a.
67 BIN 6 30:20 ff, CAD I-J 64a.
68 TCL 4 3:15 ff, CAD Š/2 56b.
69 KTS 24:4, CAD I-J, 64a.

> Why did you not sent the silver of our father's *ikribū* of *Aššur*, and so failed to encourage me and save us?[70]

In addition to the occupation/class of trader, we encounter the investor class (*ummiānum*).[71] Investors supplied traders with sources, either directly as partners or as limited partners in an investment fund, the "sack" (*naruqqum*). Investors and members of their families (*mer'ū ummiānē*) were active in trading and supervising traders' activity; they were financial players but, like traders who lent money to others, they also engaged in trading or in other capacities such as temple priests, City officials, or even kings.

* * *

In summary, the organization of Assyrian trade in family firms, partnerships, and investment companies lowered transaction costs by internalizing transactions and mitigating the need for lengthy and expensive processes. They also lowered individual traders' risks. Second, the organization of trade in joint houses/warehouses in Assur and the colonies contributed to stability in the markets, allowed safe storage of goods, and encouraged stable relations with local rulers in the colonies. Third, the division of the funding structure into investors and traders, both active in trading, and the formation of limited partnerships enhanced the efficiency of the financing system by mitigating risks to investors on the one hand, and giving traders commercial maneuvering room on the other. The structure lowered transaction costs in a society that featured very high interest (30 percent), steep trading risks, and long-distance interregional trade that required strong maneuverability. Finally, the matter of the gold votive offerings and their centralized placement in the temple (or in special halls) is not clear. The nature of the discussion suggests that gold commanded a special place in Assyrian society at the time. How the system operated, however, remains vague.

Credit and Finance

Credit and finance are two sides of one coin in a market where dates of receipt and payment are exchanged. The institution of credit allows consumption and payments to be made earlier than otherwise; financing institutions, in turn, are the accepted instruments by which these actions are taken. When credit is issued

70 Kt n/k 516, Dercksen 1998, 86.
71 Dercksen 1999, 86–87.

and a permanent liability is created and recorded, a liability may become an asset and, in turn, a means of exchange or an instrument for the financing of economic operations. The credit and financing institutions created in the past were diverse and designed to meet the needs of those who had created the credit and financial arrangements and of those who used them. The main differences between the two groups concerned the types of uses to which these instruments were put, the term of the credit, the risks, the collateral, and how the use of the credit or the investment would be paid for. The institution of credit is immensely important in a market economy. Together with money, it allows low-cost exchange to take place and introduces the dimension of time into transactions. The meaning of "issuing credit" is the contractual surrender of property rights to something (say, a sum of money) in return for claim to something (e.g., a given sum of money) at a specified future time. In other words, it denotes the exchange of goods, service, or money for a written or verbal undertaking to give the provider of the goods or the service a return on a later date.[72]

Several institutions deal with the matter of exchange, credit, and their attendant problems. The first is the contract, in which the form of the exchange, the terms, and other relevant particulars may be laid down. "Contract" is a general term for financial and other contracts, notes, and agreements that help to create funding instruments and govern their use. According to theory, the institution of funding is created when a loan is given in a value and under terms that are recorded in order to assure the repayment of the loan. The document created, which is legally binding on the borrower, may itself change hands.[73]

Contracting and financing institutions in antiquity had special enforcement institutions. There was a system of laws and procedures for adjudication of disputes arising from the use and documentation of financial instruments. The system-imposed sanctions, such as expropriation and revocation of personal freedom, including enslavement, on those who evaded the web of laws and procedures. The judicial system, resting on select members of the community, was independent and effective. A bureaucracy engaged in enforcement and had the power to punish those who failed to keep their word. Research into these institutions includes examinations of the systematic management of the judiciary, the presentation and identification of penalties attending to breach of contract, agreements about how to apply the penalties, which penalties to invoke, and explaining why offenders did not flee to evade punishment.

72 Baltensperger 1987, 715–717.

73 Chick 1987, 322.

In the modern era, credit falls into three distinct categories: consumer credit—received by consumers; business credit—given by merchants to other merchants, producers, or business customers; and bank credit—issued to consumers and for business purposes by banks. Consumer credit is extended to individuals so that they can consume now and pay later. Business (commercial) credit is extended by one commercial firm to another or by one individual to another for investment in a business; it is also created by delaying the receipt of sums due or payments for service rendered on the basis of invoices presented to the debtor. Bank credit is usually backed by collateral, including the possibility of a mortgage—an encumbrance (lien)—the pledge of specific assets (including human beings), or an agreement with guarantors that assures timely payment. An encumbrance is created via a legal agreement that describes conditional ownership of assets as security for a loan; the conditional ownership is revoked when the loan is paid back. In the event of default, guarantors are liable for the debt.

The use of credit and interest evidently traces back to earliest antiquity and is associated with surpluses that ancient societies created when specialization and exchange allowed them to advance from subsistence agriculture to farming. The use of these surpluses was related to exchange and trade; they were given to others who paid for them after selling or trading them for other goods. Informal customs pertaining to credit are also ancient; they arose when individual members of a society wished to consume at an earlier time or to invest in for-profit agricultural, commercial, or productive ventures. Additionally, credit was crucial for the ancient agrarian economy because it introduced the element of time into a transaction. One party in the exchange could not always immediately pay for goods received, Farmers, in particular, had to plough before seeding and seed before reaping, and were vulnerable to the seasons and the ravages of nature. Therefore, they needed credit to launch the growing cycle and to weather unforeseen events. Societies adopted the ritual of giving credit for a specified time, with or without an agreed-upon payment for it (interest) in the presence of witnesses. The debtor had to repay the loan in a timely manner on pain of social pressure backed by sanctions.

There are also other views about credit in antiquity.[74] They are associated with the socioeconomic model that describes Mesopotamian society in the third millennium BCE as one organized within large frameworks of extended families that were known as the palace and the temple—a society that had no market means of exchange and exchange but rather exchange among individuals on a social basis with agreed equivalencies.

74 Hudson 2000, 132–161; Hudson 2002, 7–58.

The socio-anthropological theory behind these hypotheses holds that the gifts (or, alternatively, the loans) were part of a preexisting mutual-aid network that helped to strengthen social connections. Interest was a surplus that the giver was given as an expression of the recipient's appreciation. Recipients repaid their gifts or loans not only to avoid becoming habituated to them, but also to avoid social pressure and shaming. The institutions (palace and temple) gave loans (gifts with surpluses) and engaged in trade in order to generate surpluses for the satisfaction of social needs such as religious rituals and care for widows and orphans.

Another opinion about the origin of credit flows from the Marxist view of credit as a tool in the class struggle that allows owners of wealth to amass property.[75] According to this approach, loans are given at usurious rates that debtors cannot afford, allowing the lender to seize the collateral.[76] Thus viewed, lending constituted not a transfer of wealth in order to make a profit (the interest), but an instrument in a social struggle in which interest is used to accumulate property. According to this worldview, Old Babylonia tumbled into a grave economic crisis due to private sector activity related to credit. Lenders charged exorbitant interest; borrowers could not afford it and, as a result, lost their property. Kings occasionally issued debt-amnesty edicts in order to protect borrowers.[77] It is arguable that a credit crisis was one of the reasons for the collapse of Mesopotamian society in the late seventeenth century BCE.[78]

The first text that mentions an interest-bearing loan is a royal inscription from the king of Lagaš, Ennmetena, in the year 2400 BCE.[79] War broke out between the city-empires of Lagaš and Umma, the monarch explains, due to nonpayment of an interest-bearing loan. Until the Old Akkadian Empire era (2350 – 2150 BCE), no credit and debt documents in the form we know today were found. Many documents from Lagaš, however, note that the way arrears in payment to palaces and temples were dealt with[80] was via a penalty (interest). In documents from that time, delinquency in payment was called *ḫubullum* in ancient Akkadian, a term that usually

75 Steinkeller 2001, 47 – 49.

76 At issue here are agricultural and consumer credit in the main, as opposed to commercial credit.

77 Other explanations of the debt forgiveness orders were economic hardships occasioned by excessive demands from the authorities for taxes and forced labor, social disorder and wars, or climate changes and natural disasters.

78 Van de Meiroop 2004a, 88 – 89.

79 Hudson 2002, 7. Bulgarelli 2011, 37.

80 Van de Mieroop 2002, 63.

denotes a loan given at interest.[81] For the next two thousand years, the term would remain in use in the context of loans throughout Mesopotamia.

Numerous documents from the Ur III period (2150–2025 BCE) deal with loans, but their meaning is vigorously debated.[82] Some claim that the economy was dominated by the palace and the temple at this time, meaning that at issue are arrears and penalties and not loans and interest. This era also evidently saw the institutionalization of commercial credit and the formation of written contracts. The contents of these contracts or deeds were inscribed with the consent of the lender, the recorder of the agreement, the borrower, and the witnesses to the transaction, and these parties signed the documents as well. The deed was placed in an envelope on which the agreement was inscribed and signed by all parties to the accord. The deed, secure in its envelope, was kept in the lender's archive until the loan was repaid or until something related to the agreement was clarified in court. At the time of the inquiry, the agreement was opened in the presence of witnesses and the judges. When repaying the debt, they broke open the envelope and the agreement tablet. A tablet without an envelope was invalid.

In addition to the written contracts, the institution of king's justice took shape; it supported the credit institution and formalized the socially consensual level of interest and the institution of justiciability based on universally accepted jurisprudence. The topic of credit appears in the codes of Old Babylonian kings (Eshnunna and Babylon) in the first half of the second millennium BCE. The statutes related, *inter alia*, to setting interest rates on loans denominated in barley and silver. Some claim to have found differences between southern Mesopotamia and northern Mesopotamia in lending procedures.[83] Procedures in the south pertained mainly to public-sector activity, whereas those in the north centered on the commercial doings of private traders.

Relations between traders and their agents, as adduced from the Assyrian traders' documents, appear later on in Sections 100–107 of the Code of Hammurapi.[84] The law required agents to repay supplier's credit along with interest. If the commercial venture foundered, the agent had to pay twice the principal. If a trader gave an agent a "favor" loan (an interest-free loan, a *tadmiqtum*) and the commercial venture failed, the agent had to repay the principal only. If the agent was robbed en route and affirmed this by swearing to the gods, he was absolved of having to return the silver. If the agent received goods for sale, he had to

81 Some doubt that the term was used in a similar sense in the third millennium BCE; Van de Mieroop 2002, 65.

82 Garfinkle 2004, 1–30; Steinkeller 2002, 109–137, Bulgarelli 2011, 37–53.

83 Skaist 194, 238–239.

84 Melul 2010, 129–130.

return the silver to the trader and receive a sealed tablet as proof of payment. Absent the tablet, the silver was not considered repaid at the time of accounting. If the agent took silver but afterwards denied having received it, and the trader presented a claim before the gods (by oath) and produced witnesses against the agent, the agent had to repay the loan threefold. If the lender denied that the borrower had repaid the loan and the borrower proved under oath and with witnesses that he had paid, the lender had to compensate him in a sum six times greater than the loan.[85] In Section 112, cases are given in which a recipient of credit (or a deposit) in the form of silver or goods failed to deliver them to the destination; his penalty for this was set at five times the value of the goods.[86]

* * *

The institution of credit allows people to consume earlier than they could otherwise and to carry out exchange on the basis of deferred payment. The institution of finance, in turn, comprises the accepted instruments in which deferred payments can be made. Both institutions, credit and finance, are immensely important in a market economy because, together with money, they facilitate exchange at a low cost and invest transactions with the dimension of time. The institution of the contract (written or verbal) accompanies that of credit. The contract makes it possible to determine the form of the exchange, the terms, and other particulars associated with carrying out the agreement. The contract is defended by consensual enforcement. Enforcement mechanisms include laws and procedures for the conduct and adjudication of conflicts that originate in the institutions of credit and financing and determine the places where said adjudication will take place and by whom.

The institutions of credit and financing in ancient Mesopotamia are topics of debate among researchers. One school, basing itself on the primitive-substantive model, claims that such institutions did not exist in the third millennium BCE. Trade took place on a social basis and involved neither credit nor money; loans were gifts to strengthen social relations; credit on the palace books was issued for record-keeping purposes and for the imposition of penalties in the event of late repayment (interest). The other school speaks of credit and financing institutions (including interest) that were documented in agreements and backed by enforcement arrangements.

---

85 Roth 1997, 101.
86 Roth 1997, 102.

The Assyrian Financial Institutions

The institution of credit in the era of the Assyrian traders saw the continuation of customs and rules that had evolved several centuries earlier. Broader use of credit was facilitated by the refinement of writing, the institutionalization of ritual granting and receiving of credit, and the use of devices, such as the small inscription tablet, the envelope, and the cylindrical seal and regular seal. The credit institution was supported by agreed jurisprudence and a judiciary. Credit was central in the development of trade, enabling traders to raise capital and invest in developing networks of agents who distributed tin and textiles all across Anatolia and received silver and gold in return. The extent and intensity of this trade caused credit activity to grow in sophistication and led to the initial creation of a capital market, where traders who had silver offered it under limited liability in return for interest or a share of the profits to traders who wished to put this metal to for-profit use.

It appears that, in the Old Assyrian world, supply of and demand for finance in the traders' pursuit of business activity existed, as did interest and profit mechanisms that maintained equilibrium in the financial markets. The Assyrians used agreed means of exchange (money)—weight units of silver—to record investment transactions and loans and documented their transactions in written and oral agreements. The traders were aware of the monetary significance of the time factor and made sure that their money would be "at work," namely, that their savings would be invested in loans and commerce and would earn interest and profits. In another indicator of their awareness of the dimension of time and interest, they charged compound interest. Interest was not only a penalty for tardy repayment, but also a price for the use of silver over time. The interest on credit extended was associated with trading and borrower risks, on the one hand, and with profits from the trade in which the silver was invested, on the other.

In the Old Assyrian era, traders moved resources about in all kinds of ways. Temporary transfers of merchandise took place as personal aid to the recipient (*tadmiqtum*) and all types of credit—consumer credit, business credit, and bank credit—were in use.[87] Consumer credit provided means for personal exigencies, such as ongoing necessities and housing. Business credit came in many forms, including long- and short-term.

87 The writer speaks of "sources" because he cannot speak of "money." The things that passed from hand to hand was commodities such as silver, cotton, copper, or wool. However, as stated in Chapter 2 with regard to means of exchange, silver was widely used in contracts and agreements among individuals.

Traders obtained resources from relatives and close associates in the form of a "favor" (*gimillum*) that they had to be paid back (*gimillam liḫḫiblam*).[88] This was not formal credit, but, rather, financial assistance among partners, friends, or family members. Sometimes traders received monetary (or in kind) assistance (*tadmiqtum*) via a temporary transfer of resources from family or friends. One trader, for example, described his request for an advance: "Allow the silver to get out of your control for a few months."[89] Such transactions required neither a written agreement nor payment of interest. Aid or transfers (*tadmiqtum*) for personal use (consumption) were temporary and the resources received were not allowed to be used for business activity.

> Before you left you asked from me a textile. In front of PN you said: "Give me a *kutānum* and as soon as I arrive (in Kanesh) I will send you the equivalent out of my own money, and I will do you a favor." You have not sent me the equivalent out of your own money. If you are my brother, do me a favor! I am a man of favor(s), I will do you a favor (in return). Send me my *tadmiqtum* with the very first envoy! I bought a house. (It will be) as if you made me a present.[90]

> Send me our *tadmiqtum*, it is not for you to do trading (with it), but still, you do trade with our *tadmiqtum*.[91]

> PN owes PN_2 x silver, should PN_2 say, "He did not give me the *tadmiqtum*," he (PN) will pay the silver on the return of PN_3, he will not request an oath from PN_2.[92]

> PN and PN_2's son as representative of PN_2 settled accounts with PN_2 and put their affair before us, and we settled all their affair, be it that he had given him tin for an *ebuṭṭum*-loan, lent him even one shekel of silver, had given him a *tadmiqtum*, or there were (payments for) votive offering.[93]

Traders and members of their households did not settle for sources that relatives and close friends transferred to them for personal use; they also borrowed from merchants who doubled as bankers when they needed to endure periods of shortages or to purchase or build houses. To obtain these loans, they encumbered slaves, relatives, and assets such as houses and chattels.

A system of business finance and credit coexisted with private consumer credit. Traders raised capital to finance their commercial investments, as in commer-

88 Veenhof 1999, 57–58.
89 Veenhof 1972, 409.
90 TTC 18. Dercksen 2014, 60.
91 KTH 9:29, 31 ff, CAD $M/_1$ 127a.
92 ICK 2 70:5 ff, CAD T 36a.
93 ICK 2 113:9 ff, CAD T 36–7a, b.

cial buildings,[94] inventories of goods for trading, and suppliers' credit. Commercial buildings were storage facilities, safe rooms, and courtyards where trading took place and livestock was kept. Traders lived there, too. They also used capital on hand to maintain inventories for customer credit, give interest-bearing loans, invest in joint ventures, and keep positive balances with the institutions. Bank credit was manifested in the transfer of resources (usually silver) from a trader to someone in need of a loan. Here the trader acted as a credit-granting institution as would a bank, receiving collateral in the form of real estate or chattels such as human beings—usually male or female slaves—and enlisting guarantors to assure timely return of the loan. The recipient was personally liable for repayment. In the event of default, the borrower risked his encumbrance to the lender and repaid the loan by working for the lender. He might also encumber his wife and children, who repaid the debt by providing the lender with labor services.

Capital was classified not only in accordance with the type of credit from which it was created, but also in keeping with its owner: advance payments from family and partners, capital on hand, temple capital, and capital originating in organizations in Assur City and in the Karum. It was also classified by the type of funds in which they were deposited (joint, trust, investment [the "sack"]). That this was done indicates the existence of a well-developed accounting system, in which capital available to traders was classified by sources and uses.[95] The traders were aware of the advantages and drawbacks of each source of capital.

* * *

The Assyrian traders were also aware of the various types of credit and instruments of finance. They based their commercial activity on profit and charged interest for the sale of credit. There was one system of credit for personal use—consumption—and another for commercial purposes. Credit was given for long and short periods. In addition to the credit system, there was a capital investment system for joint ventures. A complex accounting system operated parallel to the system of credit and financial instruments.

94 See Chapter 1, Property Rights, page 27.
95 See the section on record-keeping and settling of accounts, page 136.

Long-Term Financial Instruments

The traders were cognizant of the concept of financial resources (*be'ūlātum*—capital) with which they could do business.[96] Included in this rubric were goods held by the traders as a result of the original capital that they owned, capital transferred to them from various sources (e.g., investment capital or transfers of capital from a trader for the management of a caravan), and profits from trading, including investment and interest income. Traders also recognized resources freely available on hand in traders' possession (*šalṭum*), including commodities for exchange. A typical reference to the matter of capital (resources) appears in the following letter, written by a senior trader to his investors in Assur:

> Speak to the *ummiānum* (my financiers), PN, and my representatives, thus (said) PN_2: I requested a term of three years from the god (=the City Assembly?), saying "I shall recover my *be'ūlātum*-capital, and I shall put it, be it little or a lot, before (my financiers—*ummiānum*)." PN promised me a term of five years, and you yourselves agree to that. I shall apply to him and say "I cannot wait five years. I will go the length of the term I requested from the god and recover my *be'ūlātum*-capital. Two or three of my *tamkāru*'s, on whom I am dependent, were foolish so that I was deprived of a lot of silver. This is not the right moment to disclose their names to you. I thought however:" As soon as they go the *tamkārum*-trader will release to them every shekel of silver (he owes them) and then they will bring to me as much as they can. "By *Aššur* (the god) and by your (pl.) god! I have been deprived of some two talents of silver. That is enough! My dear lords, if you please, consider how many *nisḫātum* can be levied at the house of my *ummiānum*; draw up a certified document stating that my *maškattum* (account) go for three years and that the silver cannot be claimed (by another). Write me something friendly which my servant can communicate to me. I shall collect some silver of my *be'ūlātum*-capital (already) at harvest time (and send it to you)."[97]

Other examples appear in traders' letters and agreements:

> The cold weather caught with us, and consequently the *be'ūlātum*-capital that I was expecting reverted to outstanding claims.[98]
>
> If you have not received anything yet from my outstanding claims (*bābtum*), then let a colleague send me the silver, let me then either pay interest as one colleague pays to another, or let me become indebted to him with *be'ūlātum*-capital.[99]

---

96 Veenhof 1972, 407–412; Dercksen 1999, 87–88; Kienast 1989, 87–95. The concept of *be'ūlātum* captures both equity and capital given to another for the other's use under terms that entailed an undertaking to carry out various actions for the issuer of the capital and sanctions in the event of nonperformance.

97 BIN 4, 32, 1–38, Dercksen 1999, 85–86.

98 CCT 3, 7a, 8 ff, Larsen 2002, 73.

99 KTS 1, 12, Larsen 2002, 89–90, 29*ff.*

I do not have any silver available-*šalṭum.*[100]

The proceeds of their sale should be available for *šalṭum*-disposition.[101]

Whether he owns deliveries still outstanding or whether he has *šalṭum*-merchandise on hand, seize it.[102]

The term "capital" (*be'ūlātum*) also denoted a financial instrument. Traders hired caravan leaders and others under capital transfer or loan agreements in return for labor services. Goods were given to caravan leaders and traders on credit and were recorded by the recipient as capital. The caravan leaders managed the caravans, the donkey drivers, and the guards. They managed the caravan in return for a capital transfer as a loan (*be'ūlātum*). When it reached its destination, they sold their merchandise at a profit and, repaid the loan, and retained the profit. Some define this loan or deposit as "working capital" given to the caravan leaders. In the traders' documents, the debtors are described as "held" (*uktâl*) in the creditor's hands and, therefore, obliged to perform service for him. They also had to return the capital deposited without interest after a certain period of time. Failing this, in some instances, they had to pay interest as a penalty.[103]

In special cases, traders received capital (*be'ūlātum*) from another trader/investor for special purposes. The arrangement for the giving of this capital resembled that in which caravan leaders received capital. The debtor was "held" as a provider of labor services to the creditor. For his labor, he received an income from others or a profit from the sale of the goods that he had obtained with the help of the capital that he had received. According to Veenhof, such deposits were given to traders who were facing difficulties in order to help them repay debts. The trader received the silver in Assur, used it to buy merchandise, hauled the merchandise to Anatolia, sold it at a profit, and used the receipts to repay the original sum.[104]

The cold weather caught with us, and consequently the *be'ulātum*-capital that I was expecting reverted to outstanding claims.[105]

100 KTB 18 r. 20 ff, CAD Š/1 270a.
101 CCT 2 22:9 ff, CAD $Š/_1$ 270b.
102 CCT 4 5a:24 ff, CAD $Š/_1$ 270b.
103 Kienast 1989, 87–95.
104 Veenhof 1999, 69–74.
105 CCT 3, 7a, 8 ff, Larsen 2002, 73.

If you have not received anything yet from my outstanding claims (*bābtum*), then let a colleague send me the silver, let me then either pay interest as one colleague pays to another, or let me become indebted to him *be'ūlātum*- capital.[106]

PN has no claim to any *be'ulātum*-capital, he already has the *be'ulātum*-capital due him and will travel for three months (for his employer), should he not return after three months, the tablet concerning his *be'ulātum*-capital will still be valid against him and he will pay half a mina of silver above (the amount stated in) this tablet concerning his *be'ulātum*-capital.[107]

PN_2 took thirty shekels of silver belonging to PN (the creditor) as *be'ulātum*-capital for his son PN_3, PN_3 is under obligation with regard to the silver, should he (PN_2 return the silver, then he may take his son (PN_3) wherever he pleases.[108]

PN_2 (the creditor) has given twenty shekels of silver at *be'ūlātum*-capital of PN, he (PN) is under obligation with respect to (this amount of) silver, his father PN_3 has taken the silver (PN is to serve PN_2 for five years and to pay two minas if he leaves PN_2 before that time).[109]

PN owes 4 1/2 minas of *litu*-silver to PN_2, PN is held (in employment) by PN_2. Whatever income he may achieve, PN_2 will take two-thirds, and PN will take one-third. If he goes into hiding from PN_2, he will add interest at the rate 6 shekels per mina per month (10 %). If without PN_2 permission he takes up work for hire, it will be taken away from him. He may enter and leave PN_2's house. Without PN_2's permission, he must not take up work for hire.[110]

One of the instruments of long-term finance was the interest-free, long-term standing loan (*ebuṭṭum*).[111] Such a loan was apparently an arrangement of participation in profits in the manner of an investment in an investment fund, i. e., the limited partnership, the "sack." The Assur City directives concerning such loans resemble those regarding "sack" investments and the repayment of these loans was affected much as were "sack" investments. When the loan was given, a tablet was prepared but witnesses' signatures were not affixed. In **CAD**, it is surmised that this happened among traders who cooperated in the market for a lengthy period of time and who created this arrangement to divide the profits associated with this kind of loan.[112]

He has been keeping twenty minas of (…) as an *ebuṭṭum* for twenty years.[113]

106 KTS 1, 12, Larsen 2002, 89–90, 29 ff.
107 BIN 4 211:1, 4, 11 and 13, CAD B 215b.
108 KTH 22:3, CAD B 215b
109 AAA 1 68 No. 14a:2 ff, CAD B 215a and b.
110 ICK 1, 83 and ICK 2, 60, Larsen 2002, 232.
111 Dercksen 1999, 97–99.
112 See discussion of this matter in Veenhof 1995; see also CAD E 21 a–b—*ebuṭṭu*.
113 KTS 40:42 ff, CAD E 21a.

> The City (Assur) has passed the following verdict: "If anyone has given PN in Anatolia (lit. "the countryside") a *naruqqum*—capital investment or *ebuṭṭum*— *(long term)* loans, he shall take it (or: it shall be taken) back, together with his (other) investors, by means of his witnesses, in the City. If he has promised any silver in Anatolia, in accordance with the words of the stela, when it is confirmed by his witnesses, he shall take it (or: it shall be taken) back only there. Nobody shall touch the silver; it shall be brought together in the City.[114]

There was also other long-term credit (ten years or more) that bore interest. The difference between it and the standing loan is not clear.

> Two minas of refined silver and the interest on it for ten years.[115]

> For thirteen years the silver has been accumulating interest with you.[116]

The third form of long-term finance was investments/deposits (*šipkātum*) by investors (*ummiānum*) in a limited (or joint-stock as it is called by others) partnership in a specific investor's investment account.[117] The term "sack" (*naruqqum*) aptly describes such a fund because those investing in it deposited and withdrew silver to and from the account as they would with the personal sack that they used to conduct commercial transactions.[118] The investment was deposited in an account (*maškattum*) that was registered with "the City" (Assur) for the purpose of managing a commercial venture (*makārum*) by the trader. The trader who received the silver used it to purchase textiles and tin for trading (and recorded the expenditure). The income from the transaction was recorded to the investment account. Exactly how investors' shares in the profits that were paid out is unclear; the question is whether payment was made on each transaction or whether profits of all transactions during a period were distributed cumulatively. [119]

The new partnership structure, probably an Assyrian invention, enabled these traders to operate on a larger scale than before on the basis of a sizable investment by a large group of investors. Being a trader with a joint-stock/limited partnership investment was considered an important honor among the Assyrian community.

---

114 Kt a/k 394, Veenhof 1995, 1725.

115 OIP 27 62:27 ff, CAD Ṣ 158b.

116 CCT 4 9b:7 ff, CAD Ṣ 159a.

117 Veenhof 2003a, 475–476; Larsen 1977a, 124–145; Dercksen 1999, 85–99; Dercksen 2004, 83–95.

118 Larsen 1977a, 124–145; Dercksen 1999, 92–97.

119 The reason for this is not clear. Dercksen suggests that it had to do with the designation of gold as a unit of value in Assur and the city authorities' involvement in the "sack" (Dercksen 2004, 83). In my opinion, the reason is something deeper, relating to the injunction against trading in gold with foreigners and the accumulation of gold in sacks in the temple. To create uses for the gold that accumulated in the sacks, the authorities allowed it to be invested in trade and transferred from one sack to another in the temple for a return calculated in silver.

According to a detailed study of the hundred documents that deal with this investment structure, they were mainly conducted in a period of some forty years (1903–1863 BCE) and fifty to one hundred Assyrian families were involved.[120]

The following investment contract was found in Kanesh:

> In all: 30 minas of gold, the *naruqqum* of PN. Reckoned from the eponymy PN_2, he will conduct trade for twelve years. Of the profit he will enjoy (lit., "eat") one-third. He will be responsible (lit., "stand") for one third. He who receive his money back before the completion of his terms must take the silver (back) at the exchange-rate 4:1 for gold and silver. He will not receive any profits.[121]
>
> After this part, a list of seven witnesses follows, the first being the *laputā'um*, an official of "the City" (Assur).

Investments in the venture were calculated in units of measure of gold, but the investment transactions were conducted in silver. The initial investment in the venture was calculated at the ratio of four units of silver to one gold. Upon the dissolution of the venture at the end of its term (10–12 years) all investors in the venture were expected to reclaim their investment in gold at the rate of eight units of silver to one gold (a 100 percent profit). The venture was formalized by an agreement (tablet) signed by the parties and by witnesses (including officials of the City). The investors' share in the venture could be sold, transferred, withheld, or inherited. Partners could withdraw from the venture; in which case they could obtain only a 4:1 ratio of silver to gold.

The structure of the organization is reminiscent of today's limited partnership.[122] The trader was the general partner who held unlimited liability for debt created by investment funds withdrawn from the "sack" (his trading venture); the investment partners' liability was limited to their investment. The general partner also oversaw and ran the business. Some Assyriologists describe the organization as a joint-stock company because the investor received a tablet (possibly company stock) that he could pass on to someone else. However, the responsibility of the trader (the general partner) for the operation of the venture and his larger share in the profit are more suggestive of the modern limited partnership.

Movement of silver (and gold) of the investment fund (the "sack") was recorded in three places: with the provider of the silver (the investor), with the institution

---

120 Larsen 2015, 223.

121 TTAED 4/3 20 No. 3:17, CAD $N/_1$ 381a. Larsen 1977a, 125.

122 Limited partnership—a general partner who manages the business and has unlimited liability, and limited partners with no personal liability. *Routledge Dictionary of Economics*, D. Rutherford, ed., London & New York, 2002.

where the partnership or the investment fund was registered ("the City") in the name of the benefactor of the investment, and with one who received silver. In each of these places, a tablet was kept in which the movements in the account —silver received and silver withdrawn—were recorded.

The limited partnership (i.e., the investment fund—the "sack") was the most important instrument of long-term finance of the traders. It enabled them to raise a large stable capital for the long term from colleagues and from the city institutions. Unlike other credit the price of this capital was contingent on the success of the commercial venture. In contrast to other researchers' assessment, The writer does not believe that this instrument resembled share equity or transformed the venture into a stock company. This instrument did not control the activity of the trader in the venture and the value of the investment in the instrument was constant, in line with the original agreement. The instrument more closely resembles a limited partnership, in which the trader is the general partner and the investors are the limited partners.

In return for investing in the investment fund—the "sack"—the investors, in addition to a multiple of their investment upon the liquidation of the partnership, received a share of the profits of the venture that had been financed by means of the fund. The share of profits to which they were entitled was commensurate with their share in the total investment. The earnings from the trading activity (*nēmulum; šēlū'utum; šalšātum*)[123] were divided between the investors and the trader, such that the trader's share in the profit was called a "third" (*šalšātum*) and the remainder was recorded in favor of the partners in the form of profits deposited in the investors' names.[124]

Investments in the "sack" were transferable by inheritance and could be bought and sold at an agreed price (a ratio of gold to silver).[125] Investors were protected against misconduct on the part of traders in whom the fund had invested by officials in Assur who investigated whenever the fund showed no records of profit. Investments in the fund could be "seized" and confiscated in the event of noncompliance with obligations.

> Let us discard your three tablets and write a single tablet concerning your *naruqqum*-business (investment) interest.[126]

> Let him sell the goods for direct exchange on delivery, and send the silver here! He must not release it (on credit). Please, sell the goods for direct exchange on delivery and send me his

123 Dercksen 1999, 94.
124 Larsen 1977a, 137–128.
125 Larsen 1977a, 132.
126 KTS 1 34a:4 ff, CAD Ţ 138a.

half of the silver raised. Do not listen to anything else! Do not use the man's silver as a joint-stock (limited partnership) investment. Even if they are ready to give it as a gift, you must not take any![127]

You wrote as follows to me: "The investors of PN have realized on their gold (investment) each two minas of silver for every mina of gold." If you can see that he can give you more than two minas—say, 3 minas—for each (mina invested gold), then make a deal with him. If he does not offer (?) more than two minas, then write so I can charge him for his *šalšātum* here and make a binding agreement in the City.[128]

When PN settles accounts with his shareholders (investors, partners—*ummiānum*) in *Aššur.*[129]

We took your exit dues of 15 minas out of (your investment in) PN's *naruqqum*-venture.[130]

I have to make my payments to my shareholders (limited partners) in the month of GN. Have PN seal 20 minas of silver for me. PN_2 has entered under PN's name two minas od gold as an investment in PN's *naruqqum*-venture; (in addition) he will enter under PN's name (another) two minas of gold as investment in the *naruqqun*-venture of PN3, his (PN_2's) brother.[131]

Our father left us a record saying that your father was entering two minas of gold in his *naruqqum*-venture under our father's name in the City (bring evidence) about whether he entered our father's name in his *naruqqum*-contract or whether our father has been paid in full.[132]

PN_3 will give PN_2's representatives the tablet concerning PN's and PN_2's *naruqqum*-capital and if (the tablet stipulates that) there is joint liability for the *naruqqum*-capital and that they take over one-third of the profit (and guarantee one-third).[133]

Be present (pl.) together with his investors so that they register me (as shareholder-partner) for two minas of gold when they draw up his *naruqqum*—contract.[134]

Our father left us a record saying that your father was entering two minas gold in his *naruqqum* venture under our father's name in the City; (bring evidence) about whether he entered our father's name in his *naruqqum*-contract or whether our father has been paid in full.[135]

I tried to seize the silver from PN's *naruqqum*-venture.[136]

When PN settles accounts with his shareholders (investors, partners—*ummiānum*) in *Aššur.*[137]

---

127 Pa 14 (L 29–568):6–16, Larsen 2002, 16.
128 VAT 13458, Larsen 1977a, 138.
129 KTH 19:14 ff, CAD $N/_2$ 224a–b.
130 KTH 9:4, CAD $N/_1$ 382a.
131 TCL 21 244a:2 & 7, CAD $N/_1$ 381a.
132 CCT 4 10a:32 ff, CAD $N/_1$ 381a-b.
133 MVAG 35/3 No. 328:14 and 17, Larsen 1976, 95*ff*, CAD $N/_1$ 381b.
134 TCL 19 54:23 ff, CAD $N_{/1}$ 381b.
135 CCT 4 10a:32 ff, CAD $N/_1$ 381a&b.
136 KTH 7:3 ff, CAD $N/_1$ 382a.
137 KTH 19:14 ff, CAD $N/_2$ 224a–b.

> Of this silver I received four minas from PN, and he has a certified tablet bearing my seal, stating that we have been paid in full for one mina of gold which was booked in PN_2 *naruqqum*, and that we shall raise no claim against him.[138]

> If I were dead, you would carry away my *naruqqum*-investment.[139]

> X gold invested by PN2 in PN *naruqqum*, and x gold, PN's investment share, reverted to that of the paternal estate.[140]

> The City (Assur) has passed the following verdict: 'If anyone has given PN in Anatolia (lit. 'the countryside') a *naruqqum*—capital investment or *ebuṭṭum— (long term)* loans, he shall take it (or: it shall be taken) back, together with his (other) investors, by means of his witnesses, in the City. If he has promised any silver in Anatolia, in accordance with the words of the stela, when it is confirmed by his witnesses, he shall take it (or: it shall be taken) back only there. Nobody shall touch the silver; it shall be brought together in the City.[141]

* * *

The traders were familiar with the concept of capital (equity) (*be'ūlātum*), which included goods in the trader's possession. They used this concept as an instrument of finance for caravan leaders and credit arrangements to labor service providers. In return for the capital transferred (on credit), the service provider was obligated to provide services to the trader. Investment arrangements existed in the form of special long-term loans with terms of participation in profits and limited-partnership-type investments in the "sack" that could be bequeathed or sold to others.

Commercial and Private Credit

Credit could be created when receipts for goods delivered were delayed. Traders preferred to sell by direct exchange (*ana itaṭlim nadānum*) for other goods available to the buyer inventories (*šalṭum*) when market conditions and the buyer's ability were suitable.[142] If goods could not be sold in this manner, traders gave them over on credit in the form of a consignment deposit (an account payable). Sales by direct exchange were made at a low price and sales on long-term credit at a

---

138 CCT 4:10aff, Larsen 1977a, 140.

139 TCL 19 32:30 ff, CAD $N/_1$ 382a.

140 ICK 1 20b:5 ff, CAD $Š/_3$ 69b.

141 Kt a/k 394, Veenhof 1995, 1725.

142 By "direct exchange," the writer means goods for goods, e.g., silver or copper for textiles, in a manner that resembles barter. CAD translates *itaṭlim* as cash—a problematic translation because money did not exist at the time and various commodities served as means of exchange. "Direct exchange" is a more successful translation from the standpoint of economics.

higher price.[143] Thus, textiles were sold for 10 – 20 silver shekels per unit by direct exchange and for 50 percent more—13.5 – 30 shekels per unit on credit.[144] This credit was interest free. However, if the credit was not repaid on time, interest started to pile up.

> Let him sell the goods for direct exchange on delivery, and send the silver here! He must not release it (on credit). Please, sell the goods for direct exchange on delivery and send me his half of the silver raised. Do not listen to anything else! Do not use the man's silver as a limited partnership (joint stock) investment. Even if they are ready to give it as a gift, you must not take any![145]

> Do not release (to a *tamkāru*) or sell on commission the tin and the textiles, sell the tin and textiles for direct exchange only, and receive the silver.[146]

> Sell (the tin and textiles) either for direct exchange or on long term or short term (credit).[147]

When goods for payment by direct exchange (cash) were unavailable, other goods were handed over to the trader on credit to an extended term of several months ("open days"—*ana ūmē patiūtim*) or to a short term several weeks long ("close days"—*ana ūmē qurbūtim*). The transfer was called a deposit on consignment (an account payable).[148] Goods were sold or transferred on credit in various ways depending on the type of recipient, the risk, the collateral, and the terms of payment. When credit was issued, like other economic operations described above, tablets were written in the presence of witnesses upon the consummation of the transaction and these documents were handed to both parties. Creditors kept records of debtors and stored accounting tablets or agreements with them in marked crates or clay containers in the safe room of their home. Debtors paid interest only in the event of arrears in repayment, at a rate that varied with the creditor's identity. When the credit was paid back, the debt tablets were broken.

> Give ten minas of silver's (worth) of merchandise on consignment and give me likewise ten minas of silver on the same terms on which you gave the consignment to the *tamkāru*. Immediately after you give me the consignment, I will give your representative in GN ten talents of refined copper, and the copper should enter GN_2, and send however much silver they agree on to the City (i.e., Assur), (with it) they should make purchases for me in your firm to be my

143 Veenhof 1999, 61.
144 Larsen 1976, 104.
145 Gwaltaney 1983, 40 – 43, Pa 14 L 29 – 568:6 – 16, Larsen 2002, 16.
146 ICK 1 189:30 ff, CAD N/$_2$ 127b.
147 CCT 2 34:20 ff, CAD N/$_2$ 127b.
148 Dercksen 1999, 92.

> *qīptum* (consignment). Never mind! Give me your cooperation in this matter and for every shekel of silver that I realize abroad, as long as you stay there, I will use only my *qīptum* for my food expenses in GN_3.[149]

> PN is on the way to you with twenty minas of silver belonging partly to my (entrusted goods—accounts payable) *qīptum*, partly to my business capital (*naruqqum)*, and partly to (the proceeds from selling) my merchandise (*luqutum*).[150]

> You are my father; you are my lord! One mina of silver which PN has brought to you, plus all the which PN_2 has sent to you—dispatch (that) with the first (caravan), and let the goods reach me here for inspection (?), and let me receive them from the caravan so that it can be heard, and the owner of my trust at my departure will not demand a warrantor from me, and I shall (consequently) not be humiliated. If the goods have not left and it will (therefore) not be heard here-then who will sign as my warrantor for all the silver. Thus, they (will say):" Go to your father!" (But) whether the father is as good as his name."[151]

> In all thirty minas of silver in PN's (entrusted goods)—*qīptum*. I have first claim on the silver.[152]

The date of payment for a deposit or consignment ("accounts payable") varied from one transaction to the next. The terms included the due date, expressed in weeks.[153] In the Assyrian ruling system in Kanesh, selected officials—eponyms—served during the term of one *hamuštum*[154]—a week. In the records, the periods are named after a chosen official. The term of credit was extended term of several months ("open days"—*ana ūmē patiūtim*) or to a short term several weeks long ("close days"—*ana ūmē qurbūtim*)—and the price of the product (and its markup, i.e., the profit) was greater.

> Draw up a certified tablet concerning his debt to run for 25 weeks. If he does not agree with you, then draw it up to 30 or 35 weeks. Certify his tablet and entrust it to PN.[155]

> If he will not pay in a year, 1 1/2-shekel (per mina) every one (every month) interest according to the order of the Karum (he pays).[156]

149 VAT 9301:33–47, CAD Q 261–2b–a.
150 RT 31 55:4 ff, CAD Q 261a.
151 CCT 3 8b:40 ff, Larsen 1967, 163–164, CAD Q 263a.
152 BIN 6 31:12 ff, CAD Q 261b.
153 Veenhof 1996, 5–26.
154 The term *ḫamuštum* denotes a period of several days—a week. CAD defines it as five days but the matter is not totally clear (CAD Ḫ 74b–75a). Von Soden sets it at six days and Veenhof at seven (Veenhof 1996, 5–26; 2008, 77).
155 TC 3, 95:13 ff, Larsen, 2002, 10.
156 BIN 6 51:8 ff, CAD Ṣ 159a.

If they have not paid, they must add interest at the rate of one shekel (per mina) per month (20 % per year). They are jointly responsible for the silver.[157]

If they have not paid within their completed term, they will add interest at the rate 3 shekels per month per mina (60 % per year). They are jointly responsible for the silver.[158]

To manage the commercial credit that they issued, traders used the concept of outstanding deliveries due to them. This form of "accounts receivable" (*bābtum*) was a general concept for goods (a means of exchange) owed (debts) under agreements. Some construe the concept as outstanding shipments and others as outstanding debt.[159] In today's terminology, it would appear on the "accounts receivable" line in the creditor's books.[160] Records of outstanding credit that include debts or monetary rights of various kinds, discovered among the traders' documents, reinforce this claim.[161]

The record of the outstanding deliveries (*bābtum*) which you have left in your home.[162]

Make people pay whatever is outstanding (*bābatum*) to him and convert your father's merchandise into direct exchange.[163]

If you cannot take (the silver) from my delivery outstanding (*bābtum*), take it for me on interest.[164]

Although traders preferred to sell their goods by direct exchange (*itaṭlim*) with agents, they transferred merchandise on credit as well ("accounts payable"—*qīptum*) for varying periods of time. Prices of goods and terms of credit varied in accordance with payment dates and types of customers, risks, and collateral. Transactions were recorded on tablets in the presence of witnesses. Since the tablets had to be presented for repayment by those who held them, they were kept in a safe room. Records of outstanding credit balances (*bābtum*) were kept as well.

157 CCT 5, 23c, Larsen 2002, 201.
158 BIN 4, 170, Larsen 2002, p.198.
159 Veenhof 1987, 42.
160 CAD B 14b, for example, notes that the exact interpretation is contested.
161 See CCT 2:8 and ICK 1:119 in Larsen 1982, 233–236.
162 CCT 3 19b:4 ff, CAD B 12a.
163 KTS 1b:15 ff, CAD B 12a.
164 TCL 19 31:31 ff, CAD B 12a.

Loans (Banking Credit)

When they had to, traders could turn to a "house" of other traders (*bēt tamkārim*) (Assyrian and even Anatolian) and take a loan at interest (bank credit—*ḫubullum; kaspam ana ṣibtim laqā'um*)[165] for business or personal exigencies or for any other need, such as repaying debts, buying houses, or even basic sustenance. Regarding repayment, the terms principal (*šīmtum*) and interest (*ṣibtum*) were used. The loans were taken in (or calculated in terms of) refined silver (*kaspam ṣarrupum*).

> For the merchandise (*luqūtum*) which we contracted (as a loan; verb *šasā'um*) at a merchant's house, you only sent us the capital sum (*šīmat kaspim*); because we also had to add interest and had to refine the silver (you sent), the merchant still has a claim on us of one mina and 22 1/3 shekels of silver and he retained our promissory note. (To pay it) we borrowed the silver at interest and interest accrues since the eleventh month.[166]

> I did not give you merchandise (*šīmam*) nor did I give you a consignment (*qīptum*—accounts payable), I gave you refined silver (as loan).[167]

> When we bought the tin, we borrowed four minas of silver at interest; let the interest on the silver not get (too) much![168]

* * *

Traders also served as lenders at interest. They lent for any purpose, personal or business. The loans were denominated in refined metal. When loans were given, the particulars of the guarantors, the collateral, and witnesses to the transaction were recorded.

Interest

In modern times, interest is a sum of money paid per unit of time and expressed as a portion or percent of a sum lent.[169] It is the price a borrower pays for the use of someone else's money for a given period of time and the lender's return on deferring his or her use of the money. Interest rates are explained in two ways, non-monetary and monetary. The former emphasizes two determinants of an interest rate. One is the productivity of capital, by which people who save and invest can

---

165 Veenhof 1999, 62–69.
166 CCT 4 32b:15, Veenhof 1999, 63.
167 BIN 6 38:11*ff*, CAD Q 262a.
168 BIN 6 117:15*ff*, Veenhof 1999, 62–63.
169 Panico 1987, 877–879; Homer and Sylla 1963, 17–65; Syla 2003, 113–115.

receive a return on their investment and enjoy greater future consumption. The second is time preference. Given that people would rather consume today than consume tomorrow, they need an incentive for deferring consumption, which interest can provide. The monetary way, in contrast, stresses the supply of and demand for money. At the present time, an interest rate is a price established in the market —actually two markets, one for investment money and another for liquid assets. In the market for investment money, investors need capital (demand) and savers provide it (supply). The price of money includes a component of compensation for the possible erosion of the value of the money due to inflation, and a real component: the ability to use the money for investments that deliver a real return. In the market for liquid assets, people surrender liquid assets and financial security in return for interest. Applying a simple theory, there would be one interest rate in the market due to the exploitation of disparities (arbitrage). Due to the existence of the risk premium, however, interest rates vary from one borrower to the next. The risk originates in uncertainty about the return on the investment or about the borrower's behavior when the loan comes due. Since economic agents are averse to risks, the greater the risk, the higher the interest rate will be.

When discussing interest in antiquity (maš—*ṣibtum*), scholars disagree about how to explain the phenomenon of interest and interest rates. One school stresses the non-monetary theory, which explains interest as derived from the productivity of capital, say, in loans of livestock or grains. In these cases, both the lender and the borrower know what the increase or yield of the capital lent (livestock or grains) will be; therefore, they know how to calculate the level of payment for it.[170] The explanation for the high 33 1/3 percent interest rate charged for loans given in barleycorn in Mesopotamia is the high rate of yield of barley, which was grown in alluvial soil with the help of advanced methods of ploughing and seeding. The yield has been calculated at 1:37, bringing the interest paid to only about 1 percent of the potential output of this loan.[171] According to another estimation, the yield came to 1:30 on average, during the Ur III period.[172] Yet another explanation has it that the procedure in leasing fields was to allot one-third of the crop to the owner of the field. A fourth explanation refers to the price differential that is created between the time the credit is received and the harvest, when prices are high, and return of the loan after the harvest, when the price and the value of the barley retained are lower.

170 Heichelheim 1958, 54*ff.*

171 According to the calculation, 240 (or 300) liters of barleycorn seeds yielded a 9,000-liter harvest —a 1:37 ratio. The interest was 80 (or 100) liters of barley per 240 (or 300) liters of barleycorns, less than 1 percent of the yield. Hudson 2000, 139; Potts 1997, 80–81.

172 Englund 1998, 181.

The sources used to determine the interest rates on loans in grain and silver leave the matter vague. The different explanations offered for interest payment practices in antiquity can be explained in part by the different meanings attributed to the word *interest* in ancient languages.[173] In Sumerian, interest, *maš*, means a calf. In ancient Egyptian, the word is *MS*, denoting birth-giving. Consequently, some scholars trace the origin of interest to the practice of lending livestock in the expectation of recovering the "principal" plus some of the offspring born to the "principal" during the term of the loan (the "interest").[174] In another practice, a borrower who used the field for grazing had to give the landlord one-third of births in the herd during the service of the field as pasture. Consequently, the concept of interest was associated with the productivity of the capital (the livestock) that had been given on loan.

Interest in the ancient world was calculated in the measurement unit of the means of exchange (barley or silver, for example) per measurement unit of the same means of exchange per month. The accepted rate for a loan of silver was one shekel per mina per month (20 percent per annum). The high interest rates in silver are explained partly by the high profit margins (up to 100 percent) that were accepted in trade. Additional explanations pertain to the acute personal, political, and security risks that were common in Mesopotamia, not to mention multiple risks associated with the vagaries of nature. Mesopotamian traders were aware of borrowers' risks and priced their loan rates accordingly, as data on the Old Assyrian trade demonstrate. As stated above, borrowers who were family members or close friends received interest-free or low-interest loans. High-risk borrowers, however—say, local inhabitants outside the traders' colony—paid exorbitant interest rates.

Additional views about interest have been posited. Those who favor the primitive-subsistence model define interest as an administrative creation that served as a fine for non-payment of tax.[175] The penalty for a loan given in silver was one shekel per mina (60 shekels) per month, i.e., 1:60, a technical ratio in accordance with a "natural calendrical" calculation using the sexagesimal (base 60) system. The interest on loans given in barley accorded with the leasing fee for the field and was paid as a penalty for the loss of output and for arrears in repaying a debt. Those who fell behind in remittances to the temple or the palace were considered debtors in arrears and were liable for the penalty.

173 Hudson 2000, 132–161.
174 Steinkeller 1981, 113–145; Veenhof 1987, 67.
175 Hudson 2000, 132–161.

The consensual interest rates in Mesopotamian society remained in effect for lengthy periods, suggesting that they may have been determined on the basis of some ancient custom irrespective of economic phenomena (money supply, money demand, risks). Credit customs varied among different areas in Mesopotamia and were reflected in the style of the loan contract and in the interest rates charged.[176]

In the Old Babylonian era (2000–1600 BCE), the number of documents associated with credit increased immensely. The topic of credit appears in many archives and information associated with it is included in statutes and royal pronouncements concerning debt forgiveness. The enormous quantity of documents originating in private archives indicates that the economy had undergone a restructuring and credit had begun to play an important role in it. Furthermore, it is hypothesized that the private sector began to serve as a mediator between the public sector—the palace and the temple—and the masses. As citizens acquired more and more access to capital that accumulated in the temples and palaces, they began to use it for loans and investments in trade and other activities.

In the Old Assyrian era, there was an official interest rate of 1 1/2 silver shekels per mina of silver per month (30 percent per annum). This rate was considered the Karum interest; it appeared on a stela as well.[177] It exceeded the rate on silver-denominated loans during the Ur III and Old Babylonian era, which was one shekel per month per mina (20 percent per annum). The Assyrian interest rate may have been influenced by the level of profit in trading with Anatolia and by the risks inherent to long-term commerce with the local inhabitants. Interest in the Old Assyrian era had four aspects: an alternative use of capital for for-profit trading; penalties to deter default; customer risk; and a favor for family members and colleagues.[178] The traders realized that once they relinquished silver to another, they could not use it for trading, profiting, and lending out at interest. Further proof of this is their use of compound interest,[179] evidently due to certain loan contracts that included a condition that if the loan was not paid back on time, the lender could take a loan from someone else and the borrower would be liable to repay it, too, plus the interest applying to it. This made the original debtor liable to the debtor who had helped him for interest on the principal and on the interest that he was paying for the silver. This procedure appears on a stela of Assyrian

176 Skiast 1994.

177 A stela (*naruā'um*) setting forth the rules and regulations of the city and the traders' colony was erected outdoors.

178 Veenhof 1989, 75.

179 See discussion of the matter and the limitations of the analysis in Veenhof 1985, 1722–1724.

traders in Kanesh. The penalties for default were usually calculated the interest rate set by the Karum (30 percent).

> As for the silver, he will take interest and compound interest according to the words of the stela.[180]

> We shall charge you interest and compound interest.[181]

The traders also understood and priced the risks that involved in credit. Credit and loans to family members, colleagues, and low-risk people were given at zero or low interest. These rates fell short of the permissible commercial rate (30 percent per annum) according to the rules inscribed in the stela, i.e., half a shekel per month per mina or 10 percent per annum.

As stated above, the traders were sensitive to their commercial reputation, for reasons including its effect on the possibility of obtaining credit and on credit terms. They attributed much importance to forming personal relations, maintaining reliability, and coping with the risk originating in people's conduct and with political risks. Reliable and well-known borrowers received loans under easier terms (in interest and terms of repayment) than did less-credible borrowers. Thus, Assyrian borrowers could borrow at 30 percent per annum, whereas local Anatolians paid twice as much. Interest rates of 40–120 percent per year appear on the tablets; they were evidently charged to local inhabitants.

> You wrote me: "PN has paid us silver and it lies here (*nadi*—idle)." The silver must not lie idle (*lā nadi*)! If PN_2 needs it, let him take it, but if not, lend it out (*tadānum*) at interest![182]

> PN brought 20 minas of silver under your seals and the son of PN_2 brought you 10 minas. Was it my instruction to have the silver sent in order to let it lie idle? Please, my brothers, if one needs silver in the Karum-office, unpack the silver and loan it at interest. If you cannot give it to the Karum-office, loan it at interest to a trader reliable as you yourself, who need not be feared![183]

> I took the silver at interest from the merchant's house, I shall be angry should too much interest accrue.[184]

> *Aššur* be (my) witness! (I swear) I shall not make you any concessions on the interest.[185]

180 MVAG 35/3 75 note c., CAD N/$_1$ 365a.
181 KTH 8:12*ff*, CAD Ṣ 159a.
182 BIN 6 25:15*ff*, Veenhof 1999, 64.
183 VS 26 69, Veenhof 1999, 64–65.
184 TCL 19 73:28*ff*, CAD Ṣ 159a.
185 TCL 20 87:18*ff*, CAD G 22a.

According to the order of the Karum, he will pay 1 1/2 shekel (per month, interest, 30 % yearly).[186]

If he does not get it to me, he will pay interest at the rate 1/3 mina per mina (per year, 33 %), reckoned the month GN eponymy PN.[187]

They will add interest at the rate 2 1/2 shekels per month per mina (50 % per year). He holds a bundle of gold under their seals as collateral security.[188]

From the eponymy of PN on for each ten shekels (of silver) one shekel per month will accrue (as interest, 120 % yearly) for him.[189]

* * *

The interest is the price the borrower pays for the use of the money for a certain period, and the consideration the lender receives for deferring the use of the money. There are several explanations for interest rates in ancient times. One refers to the interest rate as derived from capital productivity. In loans of seeds and animals, the interest rate was calculated based on the yield of the fields and the birthrate of animals. The interest was calculated as a unit of the means of exchange in which the loan was given for the month. Basic interest rates have been fixed for centuries, suggesting an ancient tradition and government involvement in determining them. The interest rates of 33 1/3 % for loans in barley and 20 % for loans in silver metal appear in the legal records from the period. According to Assyrian trading data, the basic interest rate was 30 %, and it varied from borrower to borrower, according to the particular risks.

Contracts and Bills

The institution of credit[190] cannot exist without a support system of oral and written agreements that preserve credit relations between the parties[191] and an enforcement system that, by applying social pressure or penalties, induces people to honor their contractual undertakings.[192]

A modern promissory note is a transferable document in which a buyer undertakes to pay a supplier for a shipment by an agreed-upon deadline. Similar

186 CCT 1 5a:*11ff*, CAD K 236b.
187 TC 3 91, Larsen 2002, 50.
188 CTMMA 1, 89, Larsen 2002, 199:9*ff*.
189 CCT 1 10a:19*ff*, CAD L 194b.
190 Wilcke 2007, 76–113.
191 Veenhof 2003a, 465–470.
192 Veenhof 1999, 74–75.

notes existed in the Sumerian period, the Ur III era, and the Old Babylonian age. The Assyrian traders' tablets of deposit on credit (*qīptum*) were promissory notes (*tarkistum*) as we understand them today. They could be seized by recalcitrant debtors; consequently, they could be transferred to others and anyone could present them for payment. As a result, they were highly valuable and had to be kept in safe rooms. To simplify transfer, the Assyrian traders created a bearer promissory note by identifying the lender generically as "the trader" (tamkārum). Any trader who presented the note was entitled (without challenge) to claim the proceeds of the loan repayment even though he or she had not been the lender.[193]

A bill of sale is a document that shows proof of the transfer of ownership of merchandise but not of its possession. Such a bill is accepted as an instrument/collateral for credit; the borrower holds it until the loan is paid back. Similar documents existed in the third millennium century BCE and proved the sale of assets (*kudurru*).[194] The ancients also used bills of sale to prove ownership of an asset. Contract, notes, and bills were certified under oath, by witnesses, and by the authorities either at the temple gate or in front of the emblem of Assur.

Contracts in third millennium BCE Mesopotamia, written according to a specified structure taught in the writing schools of the era, were inscribed on clay tablets.[195] In Assyrian traders' letters and legal documents that have been discovered, there appear debt repayment claims, summonses for debt repayment hearings in private and legal forums, and summaries of discussions including solutions to default-related problems. Traders invoked the procedure of "seizing" debtors in order to get them to repay. They made sure to fully document (*lapātum*) their commercial operations in agreements and contracts (*šiknātum*). After sales were consummated, documents that tallied the items sold and the terms of the sale were finalized with the help of signatories (*kunukkum*), witnesses (*šībum*), and clay envelopes. Credit documents were usually structured as follows: "Quantity X of silver [or barley] from a certain person was received by a certain person as a loan at interest," witnesses, date, and the recipient's seal. However, many contracts lacked additional clauses including the exact interest rate and repayment schedule, possibly because interest in some contracts was charged not on the credit (e.g., when merchandise was given on consignment) but for arrears in repayment. Another reason that scholars have proposed is that the interest rate was widely known and therefore did not need to be noted explicitly. Where many contracts specify interest, it expresses the rate in quantities: "The interest is one silver shekel per five silver shek-

193 Veenhof 1997, 351–363.

194 See Chapter 1, Property Rights, page 27.

195 Wilke 2007, 77–115.

els," or "one shekel per mina every [month]." Some credit notes include endorsement to another party by determining that the credit shall be paid back to someone other than its issuer. Guarantors appear in certain notes, as does collateral in the form of assets or people.

> If PN has a share in the silver, let his son stand at your side and pay strict attention to the tablet listing the purchases and sell (them) and seal half the silver and send it to me. Establish witnesses of the shipping (of) the silver so that he may not prosecute (lit. seize for oath) you some day. If his son (should say): "Give me the goods. I agree with the word of my father's house." Why has he opened up the matter with you? Then you (shall say), "Whatever he should take in (the name of) your father's house from my account. I shall take from your account. Validate your tablet and your witnesses! (and) release the merchandise!"[196]

> An addition to the one mina of silver that you loaned me at interest and (concerning which) a note is drawn up, with the month and eponym filled in.[197]

> If someone among my debtors intends to pay you silver, open my (case enclosed) tablets and make him pay silver and interest according to the tablet.[198]

> I paid x silver into your account, draw up a note for us in the present of two witnesses.[199]

> We cannot do anything until I obtain a tablet with two witnesses who are in agreement.[200]

The Assyrian promissory tablet-note is structured much like that of today. In the Assyrian era, the obligation appearing in a credit and loan agreement was absolute; anyone holding the promissory note could demand timely repayment from the debtor and the guarantors. There was no need to endorse the note to the person presenting it. Notes could be confiscated from debtors in the presence of witnesses, either directly or by court order. This is why, as stated above, promissory notes, sealed envelopes and all, were kept in a safe room. At the time of repayment, debtors took possession of the note and broke and discarded its envelope. If the note was unavailable, debtors demanded that creditors furnish them with a tablet affirming that the loan had been paid back. There is no evidence of discounting of notes on a regular basis, but there are indications that traders purchased stolen notes, evidently for less than their face value. Below is a letter from the king of Assur to the Council of the Karum in Kanesh:

> We hear that native Anatolians (*nuā'ū*) and traders (*mākīrū*) are carrying (*zabālum*) valid records belonging to merchants out of GN and that "small men" (*ṣuḫurūtum*) are buying them

196 Gwaltney 1983, 41, Pa 14, L 29–568:17–40.
197 TCL 14 49:7*ff*, CAD T 53a.
198 TCL 4 49:14*ff*, CAD Š/$_2$ 10a.
199 CCT 5 45a:3*ff*, CAD T 53a.
200 BIN 4 70:17*ff*, CAD Š/$_2$ 394b.

> all the time in the countryside. Please, as soon as you hear this letter, produce .... (missing) let them buy any tablet belonging to a merchant, which the natives have brought out of GN, collect (these) tablets and let the owner of these tablets pay you the same amount of silver you have paid (for them) and let them take their tablets (back).[201]

Loan collection was also undertaken by people whom lenders deputized for this purpose in writing (usually partners and family members). Such collectors received a copy of the original note from the lender and served it to the borrower. If the borrower paid his debt to them, the borrower wrote out an exemption (*ṭuppum ša šabā'ē*) by which he was able to ask the lender to break ("kill") the original sealed note. If the debt was repudiated on the grounds of the absence of an original sealed note or insistence that the debt had been repaid, a contract concerning the repayment could be signed in the presence of witnesses (*tarkistam laqā'um*). Under the terms of such a contract, if the lender proved his claim, the borrower would have to pay two or three times the original sum or double the interest on the outstanding amount.

> And he presented case-closed tablets concerning the silver he paid on the debts of PN and PN_2.[202]
>
> I will send to you with PN the two minas and ten shekels (of silver), the amount still outstanding on the price of the donkeys, please (lit., you are my father, you are my lord) do not withhold the tablet (stating my debt).[203]
>
> I will take the tablet and I will make the man pay the silver.[204]

Since it was accepted practice to break the loan-contract tablet at the time of repayment, the question is why so many such contracts have been found. It has been conjectured that the loans appertaining to the contracts were not paid back, for a variety of reasons, such as a deterioration of security that caused the borrower to leave home and his archive, the borrower's unwillingness or inability to sue the lender, and so on. According to another hypothesis, at the time the loan was paid back, only the envelope was broken and the contract tablet remained intact, accounting for the survival of such tablets. A borrower who claimed that he had paid back the loan had to swear that this was so. Alternatively, sometimes he had to sign a contract that obliged him, upon presentation of proof of the debt, to

201 Kt 87/k 40, Hecker 2003, 187*ff*, Veenhof 2008, 138–139.
202 TuM 1 22a:12*ff*, CAD Š/2 9a.
203 TCL 19 39:23*ff*. CAD K 100a.
204 CCT 2 22:46I, CAD Š/2 10b.

make double or even triple repayment or double interest.[205] If the tablet was not available at point of repayment, a special tablet was recorded—a "satisfaction tablet" (*ṭuppum ša šabā'ē*) affirming that repayment had been made.

> He will have paid to my father's creditors and obtain the case-enclosed tablets and they will be safekeeping with him.[206]
>
> We validated the tablets before the dagger of Assur; any earlier tablet that appears is fraudulent.[207]
>
> I paid PN and obtained the tablet (concerning the paid obligation) of our father.[208]
>
> Pay the silver otherwise my tablets remain my tablets.[209]
>
> The tablet concerning three minas of silver on which the name of the creditor is indicated is invalid, the tablet concerning two minas of silver drawn up in the name of the creditor and which the creditor has to claim from PN is (also) invalid.[210]
>
> They have requested (the return of) the tablet (recording the silver loan) but PN has declared "it is missing." I am obligated to pay the silver. If, however, the tablet recording the debt of five minas of silver due to PN_2 should surface, it is fraudulent.[211]
>
> (As for) the tablet (recording a debt) whose term is due, if he returns the silver to you, examine his tablet, and if his term has expired, then have him pay the silver and the interest on it.[212]
>
> If PN_2 cannot produce either a sealed tablet or witnesses (to prove) that PN (owes him silver, PN_2 will pay PN threefold for that silver; if he can produce either a tablet or witnesses, PN_2 is considered paid his silver.[213]

* * *

The institution of credit was supported by a set of agreements that safeguarded the parties' credit relations. The accords followed a specific structure and were usually signed by witnesses. Such documents were retained as proof of property rights and were stored in safe rooms in crates or clay containers. Loan-agreement tablets were broken when the loans were repaid, at which point they lost their value. As long as the tablet remained intact and within an envelope, its holder (any hold-

205 This also appears in Sections 106–108 of the Code of Ḫammu-rapi.
206 CCT 1 45:9*ff*, CAD A/$_2$ 377b.
207 Kültepe n/k 470:15*ff*, CAD T 138b.
208 KTB 11:15*ff*, CAD A/$_2$ 377a.
209 C 11:29*ff*, CAD Ṭ 130a.
210 ICK 1 38b:7*ff*, CAD T 128b.
211 JCS 14 1 S. 558:5*ff*, CAD Ṭ 138b.
212 VAS 26 31:27*ff*, CAD Ṭ 130b.
213 BIN 4 147:16*ff*, CAD Š/$_3$ 378a.

er) was entitled to demand repayment. Debts were collected without tablets as well; in these cases, the debtor received a "letter of exemption." Proof of debt repayment was given by means of exemption tablets or reliance on witnesses.

Collateral and Guarantors

The Assyrian traders used guarantee-collateral (*šapartum; erubbātum*) and guarantors (*qātātum*).[214] Collateral was used mainly in loans to local Anatolian borrowers and/or large loans, for example, for the purchase of houses. The collateral demanded for loans to local people usually comprised household implements, slaves, and houses; for especially large loans to Assyrian traders, collateral involved gold, silver, or houses. Collateral for supplier credit has been found in a few cases. By demanding collateral, the traders showed that they were aware of the risks and attempted to mitigate them in this manner. Assets were put up as security (*ana šapartim iddiamma*) or held as security (*ana šapartim kullm*) or as a guarantee (*erubbātum*), making the credit secure (*rakis*). In cases of high-risk borrowers and credit, lenders obtained cumulative collateral as well as guarantors. Evidence of collateral in the context of commercial credit among Assyrians is scant. The reasons for this may be that there were other ways of applying social pressure, threats of terminating regular commercial activity, and the high profitability of trading activity that made default relatively uncommon.[215]

Traders also recognized each other's promissory notes as collateral. An (unsealed) note from another trader, usually issued for the purpose of suppliers' credit, was given by the borrowing trader to the lending trader.[216] In the event of default, the lending trader could present the note to its author for repayment on its due date. The use of commercial notes for collateral purposes gives further evidence of the tradability of the traders' promissory notes.

Loan guarantors are more common than collateral in the traders' promissory notes.[217] Three kinds of guarantors appear in the traders' documents. One is a guarantor (*qātātum*), another is a partner or representative of the debtor (*šazzuztum*), and the third is an obligatory responder (*apālum*) to the lender's inquiries in regard to the loan. The promissory note lists the guarantor by name and under the guarantor's signature. There are also cases in which the partner or representative

214 See discussion in Veenhof 1999, 76–82, and Veenhof 2003a, 468–473.

215 Veenhof 2001, 93–104.

216 There are also indications of promissory notes from the palace in Anatolia and the Karum serving as collateral.

217 Veenhof 2001, 104–125.

who has to stand in for the debtor (*šazzuztum anākuma*) signs in lieu of the trader. The guarantor not only guaranteed the sum of the loan but also gave assurance that the lender would step forward when it was time to make repayment. If the guarantor had to repay the debt, he could sue the debtor for a loan that he had to take in order to pay back the debt, including the interest on that loan (plus compound interest). The Assyrian guarantees are highly complex; it is difficult to distinguish from the traders' documents the difference between a guarantor and a partner or a co-borrower in respect of repaying debts that they guaranteed or took in partnership.

> I have been entered (on the ledger) for eleven minas of silver for PN as warrantor for PN_2.[218]
>
> Inform me by sending me a message as to whether you redeemed my pledges by paying the silver to the native to whom I was indebted and who was holding my pledges.[219]
>
> For as long as they held your silver, I will give you an equivalent amount of silver, and you should hold it for as long as they held (yours).[220]
>
> In the City (i.e., Assur), your representatives begged me (for silver), (as for) PN, you took the slave girl and slaves of your agency as security, whereupon I gave them (i.e., the *sazzuztum*) the silver and they paid it to PN.[221]
>
> The (debt of) silver is secured by his house, his oxen, the fields, and whatever (else) he owns.[222]
>
> The slave PN is pledge."[223]
>
> PN is "held fast" (as pledge) by the silver (owed), if he (the debtor) returns the silver, he may take away his son wherever he pleases.[224]

* * *

Mindful of the risks, traders used collateral and guarantors with particular stringency when they lent to local inhabitants and in large sums for the purchase of properties. Guarantors issued promissory notes to secure loans; sometimes their names appear on the notes. They had to assure the debtor's presence on the repayment date. If a guarantor had to repay a debt, he could sue the debtor for the sum plus interest (including compound interest). In cases of default, a debtor might be

218 KTH 15:8*ff*, CAD L 94a.
219 BIN 6 68:26*ff*, CAD $Š/_1$ 430a.
220 IN 6 37:15*ff*, CAD K 510a.
221 TCL 4 25:15, cf. CAD $Š/_2$ 245a.
222 TCL 21 238B:16*ff*. CAD B 283b.
223 TCL 233 A 20, CAD E 327a.
224 KTH 22:8*ff*, CAD T 249a.

enserfed to the creditor for up to three years. Guarantees included family members, slaves, and various assets.

Accounting and Settling Accounts

Accounting is a method of measurement and reportage of economic events and the financial situation of a person or entity for a specified period of time. Its purpose is to provide quantitative and financial information about the activity of economic units in order to help those who make economic decisions that relate to the entity examined. The form, content, and scope of the accounting information produced at a business are derived from the demands of those who use it. The point of departure of any discussion of accounting is identifying the users of the bookkeeping information and the reasons for their necessity. Today, accounting information is consumed by controlling principals and investors, boards of directors, employees, banks and suppliers of credit, customers and suppliers, and government authorities and institutions. It is in demand in order to apply supervision, evaluate the ongoing effect of economic decisions, analyze the extent of a company's stability, assure the continued payment of its debts, and control its activity from the public standpoint.

Accounting in Mesopotamia evolved in the late fourth millennium BCE in the large temple and palace economic organizations. Excavations at Uruk yielded tablets with records of movement and inventory of goods, labor inputs, and workers' remuneration. Accounting technique and terminology were developed by the Sumerians at the temples and palaces of the mid-third millennium BCE. The special terminology that they produced was replicated and employed by the Akkadians. Many unearthed documents demonstrate the intensive use of ancient accounting techniques in the Ur III era. Accounting was performed by scribes who had learned and accustomed themselves to the techniques in scribal schools. The technique involved the recording of operations on special large tablets (*ṭuppum rabûm*), on which certain words denoted specific types of actions or assets. Quantities were recorded under these definitions. Details such as incoming goods, assets, and outgoing inventory were recorded on the horizontal line and the total appeared at the bottom of the column. The scribes used values in silver units in some cases. Two columns were inscribed on the tablets, one for recording debits and the other for credits. At the end of the term of the records (month, year), a debit or credit balance was recorded.[225] The Sumerian accounting system was designed

225 Hallo 2004, 89–106.

to satisfy the needs of the large organizations that managed the production and distribution of the goods in which they dealt; it was also meant to assure control of the economic activity of the various units of the organization in terms of inputs and outputs. Relations with customers and suppliers were given much attention but management's interest centered on the periodic state of outstanding credits and debits. The state of these balances was the basis for calculating with suppliers and customers, who were usually traders. The organization's debit balances usually became credit issued to traders. The organization kept track of repayment of credit.

The Assyrian traders' accounting system[226] was more complex. The traders kept their business accounts in a manner similar to the practice in the Ur III period and, perhaps, even earlier.[227] They parsed the records/accounts of their commercial activity by lines of income and expenditure and of sources of finance and use of silver. In addition to their commercial bookkeeping, there was management of accounts of joint transactions and investments. Organizations such as the Karum kept separate books of their own. At the time of accounting vis-à-vis another trader or organization, they prepared two copies of the books, one for each side. At the end of the process, the accounts (*bulluṭum*) had to be debited or credited—a process in which balances were transferred from one side to the other.[228]

Assyrian traders managed their business on the basis of two systems. One comprised a set of small tablets that recorded contracts or notes concerning transactions that they had made with other traders and sundry debtors (suppliers' credit, "accounts receivable," loans, investments, etc.). These tablets were kept in special clay containers or crates that were differentiated and marked by types of transactions. The second set was of large tablets (*ṭuppum rabûm*), on which records (*taḫsistum*) were separated by types of transactions (suppliers' credit, "accounts receivable," investment fund, long-term loans, ordinary loans, loaned capital, etc.) differentiated by the traders' names and by types of institutions (the temple, the Karum, "the City") and including a record of the movement by type of transaction and the institution of the tablet.[229] It is unclear whether the set of large tablets was managed regularly, when needed, or on demand.

> There is a tablet (which is) a memorandum, and we looked at the memorandum and (we found that your tin had been sold at the rate of 6 1/2).[230]

226 See discussion in Dercksen 2004, 191–230, and Veenhof 2003, 78–123.

227 Larsen 1976, 308–319.

228 Veenhof 1987, 52–54.

229 See, for example, *CCT* 2:8 and *ICK* 1:119 in Larsen 1982, 233–236.

230 ICK 1 81:10*ff*, CAD T 53a.

> I wrote the memorandum and gave you a copy, look up your copy and take as much as is written (therein as belonging) to you.[231]

> In your accounting the money should appear as a credit.[232]

> My memoranda as well as the depositions under oath are under seal in a tablet-container, get access to them.[233]

Another set of institutions pertained to clearing of transactions (*nikkassum*) by traders and their organizations. It was created mainly after the traders stopped traveling with their merchandise and hired agents to do this for them. Trading took place not only through means of barter, but also on credit. In addition, traders invested in other traders and issued loans to yet others. Such a highly developed system of credit required a bookkeeping system to determine and validate outstanding debts among participants in trade by means of settlement. The traders' account-settling meetings resembled the clearing systems that modern banks use to process checks and notes and the practice of firms' and organizations' accountants when periodic accounts are drawn up. The system was crucial for the efficient management of trade and the mitigation of transaction costs. Having no accountants who would apply professional and reliable management to their system of bookkeeping for joint transactions, they used scribes who produced the tallying tablets for them (the scribes had studied basic bookkeeping, as in recording debts and presenting balances) and had to meet in the presence of witnesses in order to add up the credit or debit balances in their reciprocal transactions or the income, expenses, and profits of their joint transactions.

The account-settling meetings were held periodically and were called "account-readings" (*nikkassi šasā'um*).[234] At these encounters, traders compared each other's data aloud in the presence of witnesses and presented documents that confirmed their assertions (*ina nikkassum šakānu*).[235] In the course of the meeting, traders could transfer shipment records from account to account, make deposits in another trader's name, and assume another trader's debt. The purpose of the meetings was to work out consensual balances of credit, advance payments, deposits, expenses, income, and profit, and once these were tallied, balances were determined (*nikkassum ṣabātu*). The traders then had to pay (*nipiltum*) or receive

231 TCL 20 90:10*ff* CAD $M/_2$ 55b.
232 TCL 19 59:12*ff*, CAD T 52b.
233 BIN 4 36:23*ff*, CAD T 53b.
234 Dercksen 2004, 191–217.
235 Witnesses attended only in complex cases of settlement in which the support documentation in the books was unclear or lacking. The witnesses also served as arbitrators when needed.

the balances, or have them recorded to their credit or debit in promissory notes or summarizing documents of the meeting.

Another set of accounts was kept for the investment fund (the "sack"). In this activity, which took place in Assur, each trader's investments in the "sack" were recorded in values of gold. Investment and withdrawal of sources invested took place in silver at a consensual exchange rate and were recorded in silver and gold. As the records were drawn up in "the City," each trader kept an investment fund account in which he recorded deposits to and withdrawals from a fund account in "the City" along with his profits from the use of the money. Periodic meetings were held to clear these accounts with the records in the investment fund at "the City" and the records of the traders' investment fund.

> Before PN and PN_2 our accounts have been cleared.[236]
>
> Before your father's death our father and your father settled the accounts.[237]
>
> PN and PN_2 seized us (as witnesses) and settled accounts in our presence, we concluded their business and they swore the oath by the City to the effect that: either with respect to a certified tablet or a lawsuit or anything else, one will not raise claim against the other.[238]
>
> Send me definitive information with the (next) messenger about how much is involved in long-term (outstanding) claims, direct exchange transactions, and accounts to be settled.[239]
>
> PN's representatives will deposit in the office of the Karum from the account of PN into the account of [...] at the time of my accounting.[240]
>
> PN and I cleared you of obligations at the accounting, we paid six minas of silver from the price (value) of your tin and textiles to clear you of your obligations.[241]

The organizations—the Karum and "the City"—held joint settlement meetings of their own on their premises. On these occasions, they added up the accounts of their activity and, as at the other meetings, compared the data and determined the balances, including deposits that traders had placed with them (*dātum*). They also took this opportunity to clear balances in their accounts with the trader and vice versa. The organizations' meetings were periodic, evidently once per year, and were run by a special official. Only large-scale traders who had accounts with the Karum attended.

---

236 ICK 2 139:4*ff*, CAD $N/_1$ 288a.
237 MVAG 33 No. 246:17*ff*. CAD $N/_2$ 224a.
238 CCT 5, 15a, Larsen 2002, 193:1*ff*.
239 VAT 9244:25*ff*, CAD $N/_2$ 225a.
240 TCL 20 184:17*ff*, CAD $N/_2$ 225a.
241 BIN 4 33:32*ff*. CAD $Š/_2$ 415b.

> Concerning the accounting, in the year when our father died, I was present for the accounting in place of our father.[242]
>
> No one from among the "small men" may approach the "man of accounting."[243]
>
> Make deposits for my share in the office of the Karum so that I have no balance to pay at the time of the accounting.[244]
>
> X silver PN's representatives will deposit in the office of the Karum from the account of PN into the account of [...] at the time of my accounting.[245]
>
> When PN settles accounts with his shareholders (partners) in *Aššur*.[246]

* * *

In summary, accounting in Mesopotamia evolved within the framework of large organizations and included recordkeeping of movements of inventory of goods in storage, traders' outstanding debts, and labor input and remuneration. The Assyrian traders' bookkeeping system was more complex. In addition to the accounts of movement and balances of their predecessors, they tracked joint transactions, credit, and investments. These accounts were managed with the help of small tablets for recording transactions and large ones for parsing the inventories shown on the small tablets by types of transactions. They maintained a periodic accounting system in order to validate balances in credit accounts among trading partners (including settling of accounts with the trade organization, the Karum). Another set of accounts was kept in the context of the investment "sack."

242 BIN 6 91:3 & 5. CAD $N/_2$ 224a.
243 JSOR 11 122 No. 19:16 (statutes), CAD $N/_2$ 224a.
244 CCT 2 1:37*ff*, CAD $N/_2$ 225a.
245 TCL 20 184:17*ff*, CAD $N/_2$ 225a.
246 KTH 19:14*ff*, CAD $N/_2$ 224a&b.

Chapter 4
Enforcement

The topic of enforcement institutions in antiquity has been thoroughly researched, primarily from its judicial, social, and political standpoints. However, the economic aspects of enforcement have been neglected. The most important works on the topic are those of Veenhof,[1] who addressed himself to law, justice, and jurisprudence, and of Larsen and Dercksen, who conducted fundamental studies on the institutions of the Old Assyrian Trade era.[2] The writer's work focuses on reviewing the studies in Institutional Economics on the rules of the enforcement system and their impact on the operations of the relevant institutions. He also provides a brief corresponding description of the way the institutions operated, how they appear in the traders' documents, and their contribution to the success of trade.

The set of economic institutions described in previous chapters were supported by an enforcement system that encouraged people to adhere to the rules of the game that underlay the institutions' existence. The enforcement system predicated its operations on two elements: the "private order," namely, the behavior of individuals in the absence of dictated rules of the game; and rules laid down by governing authorities.

Included in the rules of the "private order" were agreed upon behavioral codes, beliefs, and norms created by groups of individuals[3] who shared a common background. They established a social organization, laid down expected behaviors in coordination with each other, and disseminated information about individuals' conduct. They expected group members to engage in fair behavior in contacts between themselves, and subjected violators to collective punishment, meaning that the members of the group stopped cooperating with them. The members maintained an extensive communication system designed to promote their commercial affairs and communicate information about individuals' conduct, a necessity for attaining their long-term goals and punishing agents who strayed from the straight path.[4]

A distinction should be drawn between institutions and organizations.[5] "Institutions" are society's rules of the game—constraints that provide structure to in-

1 Veenhof 1991, 437–459; 1995, 1717–1744; 2001, 93–159; 2003a, 431–483.
2 Larsen 1976; Dercksen 2004.
3 Greif 2005, xv and 428–452.
4 Game theory is used to explain the behavior of the group members: Greif 1993, 525–548; 2005, 8, 407–420.
5 North 1992, 3–6.

https://doi.org/10.1515/9783111065533-007

terpersonal relations. These include formal statutes (a body of law, accepted law, regulations), unofficial limitations (conventions, behavioral norms, and behavioral rules that people impose on themselves), and the way these limits are enforced. "Organizations" in turn, are the actors, or participants—groups of individuals who unite to attain a shared goal. They include political entities (parties, legislatures, municipal councils, supervisory agencies), economic bodies (companies, labor organizations, family farms, cooperatives), social entities (temples, churches, clubs), and institutes of education (schools, colleges).

In contrast to the private order rules, rules of the game (institutions) that were dictated "from on high" were determined in a political process that dominated economic life by defining and enforcing economic institutions. These included, for example, the allocation, adjustment, and enforcement of property rights. It was these institutions, by and large, that determined the characteristics of the economic structure and the efficacy of resource use. Accordingly, creating and enforcing effective property rights lay at the core of the economic development policy. However political systems cannot always meet this challenge, and sometimes create different kinds of institutions, which neither recognize nor support property rights. Understanding these political institutions is crucial for analyzing the economic institutions and their formation and evolution in the political process. Essentially, the political institutions are the rules by which political organizations determine the process of choosing leaders and making decisions. In antiquity, these institutions rested on political organizations and interest groups, such as traders' organizations. Political institutions can be stable only when supported by organizations that have an interest in their continuation.

Researchers disagree about the extent of freedom that individuals have in choosing their institutions. According to the structural (cultural) approach, accepted in sociology and in the theories of the Old Institutional Economics, societies have a cultural immutability that determines the institutions and leaves individuals with no influence on the matter. The second approach, a functional (agency-based) one, stresses that individuals create their institutions for any number of goals. It is this latter approach I will adopt in the analysis in this chapter, as it enables me to investigate the creation of the institutions in various periods of time irrespective of any connection among them in their response to their creators' interests and needs.

Transaction cost economics completes the analysis of the institution by assuming that economic agents who respond to rules choose to implement contracts and, through them, establish organizations that mitigate transaction expenses. It should be borne in mind, however, that economic institutions and contracts amount to no more than provisions that may be disregarded. To invest them with force, individuals need incentives (a set of motivations) to act in accordance with them. When individuals have incentives, which usually originate in tradition and customs, they comply with the rules even though no third party forces them to do so (a compulsory order). Informal institutions of these kinds are considered stable social phenomena that do not change perceptibly over time. Economists apply game theory in the study of the "private order" that assures property rights and the honoring of contracts even in the absence of an effective institutionalized legal system.

* * *

The set of economic institutions described in this book rests on an enforcement system that incentivizes individuals to play by the rules of the game (the institutions). The system is predicated on the two elements of the "private order" and rules handed down "from on high." The former includes agreed-upon rules of conduct and beliefs that are shaped among groups of individuals, while the latter are determined in a political process.

Enforcement in Mesopotamia

There is a debate among scholars about the political structure of Mesopotamian societies in the fourth and third millennia BCE.[6] One school holds that the dominant political model during this period was centralized governance under the king (one-man rule), with the temple at his side. Both of these foci of governance had organizations that dominated the Mesopotamian society and economy. Alongside the central organizations were local organizations of small cities and rural localities controlled by councils composed of local leaders. In Mesopotamia, separate city-states occasionally united to establish central governance by a single city-state, as happened, for example, in the eras of King Eannatum of Uruk, Sargon of Akkad, and the Ur III empire.

Other scholars dispute this monolithic view of the Mesopotamian political system. They claim that parallel to the central governing system of the king and the temple were "primitive" political systems of people's councils and councils of elders that evidently originated in earlier (pre-historical) systems. These systems formed the basis of the legal system and, in many places, chose the king of the city-state, whose role it was, as the first among equals, to wage war and organize the temple.

The collapse of the Ur III Empire in the late third millennium BCE triggered a dramatic change in the political regime of the cities of Mesopotamia. Rule there

6 Jacobsen 1943, 159–172; Bailkey 1967, 1211–1236; Yoffee 1995a, 281–311; Postgate 1995, 275–291.

transitioned from governors appointed by the Ur III emperors to kings and to councils in which holders of political rights, such as important personages in the community—elders and/or oligarchs—were members. In Assur, for example, the king focused his attention on defense (army and fortifications) and played a central role in the temple;[7] he sat on the Council of Oligarchs, but with the status of first among equals. A dramatic change took place at this time, particularly in northern Mesopotamia, in regard to property rights and ownership of land, most of which became private.[8]

Local responsibility for upholding the order and honoring rights was tasked to the municipal council and its leader, the village, or the city mayor. According to Section 23 of the Code of Ḫammu-rapi, when a person is robbed and the thief is not caught, the village mayor and the village where the crime took place must make full restitution. The council, or its members, served as judges in appointing the council. A legal decision could be appealed to a higher judicial level, usually the council of the city-state, the king, or a panel of judges appointed by them.

The judicial code included the centralized procedure for presenting evidence and testimonies by both sides. Evidence had to be in writing; testimonies could be oral as well.[9] However, evidence could also be obtained by the "ordeal by river" or by the extraction of an oath. In the ordeal by river, the individual was tossed into a river; withstanding the rushing waters was considered proof of innocence, and drowning was considered proof of guilt. The institution of the oath played a key role in corroborating testimonies. Witnesses and litigants had to swear before the judges, or in the temple before the gods, or before the emblem of the deity, that their words were the truth. Oaths also settled conflicts relating to contracts and arbitration agreements. Finally, litigants had to substantiate their claims with documents. Written testimonies were agreements inscribed on tablets and sealed by litigants, witnesses, or officials. Certain kinds of transactions, such as those pertaining to real estate sales and credit, required that agreements be written in the presence of, and signed by witnesses. When arbitration took place, the principals could be interrogated about these documents and had to present witnesses to authenticate them. Judges' rulings were handed down in writing.

A contract is a general term referring to financial and other contracts, notes, and agreements that help in creating and using financial instruments. The agreement or contract, discussed at length in the previous chapter, makes it possible to determine the form, terms, and other particulars of the exchange.

7 Larsen 1976, 110.
8 Apart from royal and temple estates.
9 For the Old Babylonian period, see Westbrook 2003, 370–376.

The institution of credit cannot exist without a support system of written and oral agreements that document the existence of a credit relationship between the parties.[10] Nor can it be sustained without an enforcement system that uses social pressure or penalties to induce people to honor their contractual undertakings.[11]

In antiquity, contracts were inscribed on clay tablets, the written medium of documentation at the time. The contracts (tablets) were sealed in accordance with fixed procedures in the presence of witnesses and signatories. Once sealed, the tablets were placed in an envelope, on which a summary of the document was written out and signatures were affixed. At least two copies of these documents were prepared, one for the lender and one for the borrower. Once a contract was placed in a sealed envelope, it obliged the debtor to repay the sum borrowed to any person who presented it to him or her. Therefore, these documents were kept in safe rooms. In the event of default, there was a procedure whereby lenders could reclaim the debt tablets that they had signed and present them for payment. Once payment took place, the envelope was broken and the tablet lost its value.

The Mesopotamian legal system was grounded in written laws[12] that were promulgated publicly on stelae in central city locations.[13] These enactments express the essence of the customs and rulings of the judicial system, including those of the royalty. In addition to laws inscribed on stelae in Assur and Kanesh, for example, there were written rules relating to the convening and decision-making processes of "the City" and the Karum. These institutions' decisions were sent on to the colonies in Anatolia in the form of edicts. In addition to the aforementioned documents, the judicial institutions produced written documentation of their proceedings and rulings; these were used by litigants and judges, who mention them in their agreements, testimonies, and court rulings.[14]

Responsibility for carrying out the rulings was entrusted to special officials and soldiers. The array of punishments included social penalties such as "erasure of a name" (harm to reputation), ostracism, revocation of rights, and so on. There were also economic penalties, such as fines for claimants and authorities, confis-

10 Veenhof 2003a, 465–470.

11 Veenhof 1999, 74–75.

12 The most famous and complete set of laws is the Code of Ḫammu-rapi (eighteenth century BCE). This code, however, shows vestiges of earlier statutes, e.g., from the Ur III period and from Eshnunna (21st–19th century BCE).

13 No stelae have been found in archaeological excavations in Anatolia and Assur.

14 Veenhof 2003a, 431–483.

cation of property, and even revocation of freedom. Death penalties were imposed in certain cases, even for theft.

* * *

Thus, the enforcement system in Mesopotamia rested on private arrangements grounded in the expectation of fair conduct and in the dissemination of information about those who deviated from the norm. Violators faced collective punishment. Additional rules of conduct were handed down by authorities based on the social organizations of people's councils and councils of elders and rulers. Legal proceedings took place, and they included the presentation of evidence and witnesses by both sides. In the absence of evidence, oaths were used. Participants in exchange and credit documented their transactions in agreements or contracts. The legal system in Mesopotamia was based on written laws that were disseminated publicly on stela positioned in central city locations. Written rules dictated the way the legal forums were to convene and apply the litigation procedure. Special officials and soldiers held responsibility for the implementation of court rulings. There were prisons, pecuniary sanctions, and in certain cases, death sentences.

Enforcement in the Old Assyrian Trade Era

The Old Assyrian Trade was run on the basis of a "private order" as described above. A similar system, based on transactors' reputations, existed among traders in the medieval Maghreb.[15]

An Assyrian trader's reputation (*šumu*, "name") was an exceedingly important asset. A trader who lost it suffered significant financial harm; in extreme cases, it marked the termination of his commercial activity. To mitigate their commercial risks, traders sought reliable customers and agents to manage their trade and gathered information about personal and political credit risks. They also apologized when they transgressed accepted practice for any reason and did favors for others to bolster their reputation. And, when necessary, they exploited their reputation to ask for favors.

The elements of trust, solidarity, and reputation were at the foundation of the Old Assyrian trade. Trust[16] occurs when one party (**trustor**) is willing to rely on the

15 Grief 1989, 857–882.

16 Trust is "assured reliance on the character, ability, strength or truth of someone or something; one in which confidence is placed; dependance on something future or contingent; reliance on fu-

actions of another party (**trustee**), and the situation is directed to the future. The Assyrian traders were looking for trustworthy (*kēnum*) person with whom to conduct commercial and financial relations. They sought trustworthy relationships with people with whom they enjoyed solidarity, such as members of family or professional group (trader—*tāmkārum*), or people with whom they had experienced trustworthy relationships in the past. Those who were consistently trustworthy developed reputations for their status, and preference in doing business was given to them. They also probably enjoyed better terms when they contracted debt. Consequently, traders invested heavily in developing a positive reputation; it was both the most important asset that they brought to the market and the asset they most desired in the market.

In his book *The Old Assyrian City-State and Its Colonies,* M. G. Larsen quotes from an eleventh-century Arab book:

> Know, my brother—may God guide you—that the operation of the merchant who exports consist in employing in the locality to which he exports someone who takes care of the wares sent to him. The latter is then entrusted with selling the wares and buying others in exchange, and he ought to be a trustworthy, reliable and well-to-do man who has devoted himself to commerce and who is also well experienced in it.[17]

In the Old Assyrian Documents the following quotations appear:

> My dear father and lord, quickly dispatch the one mina of silver which PN brought you plus whatever goods PN_2 sent to you, so that the goods reach me to be available, and let me receive *en route* so it will be heard here and the owner of the goods entrusted to me will not demand a guarantor when I am about to leave, and I shall not be put to shame. If the goods have not left so it will not be heard here, who then will let himself be noted as my guarantor for the silver in its entirety? They will say "Go to your father! Who knows whether the father is good for its name?"[18]

> A reliable agent who gives no reason to worry.[19]

> One or two evil persons are set to cause confusion in our (family) firm (*bēt abīni*).[20]

> I shall do my duty for your firm and for you so that nobody will do damage to your (pl.) firm.[21]

---

ture payment for property (as merchandise) delivered; a property interest held by one person for the benefit of another" (*Merriam-Webster Dictionary*, 2021, Springfield, IL, U.S.).

17 Larsen 1976, 94–95.

18 CCT 3 8b:3–25, Larsen 2002, 64–65.

19 CCT 3, 49a:18–19; Larsen 2007, 96.

20 CCT 2 33:10, CAD $A/_1$ 75a.

21 KTS 1b:28 & 30, CAD $A/_1$ 75a.

> Entrust my tin and my textiles with a trustworthy agent in commission on fixed terms. The agent must be reliable! Do not attach importance to terms of one or two months.[22]

> For 30 years I have been living in the City and I always pay my accounts. Appeal to the colony authority and ask for clemency for me from the colony.[23]

> There must not be any blasphemy lest I become angry.[24]

> No outsider has denounced me, but you keep denouncing me in every Karum.[25]

> The gentleman's denunciation will take place within five days.[26]

> You owe me many favors.[27]

The institution of the oath, on which the "private order" system relied, was a civil-religious one.[28] Assyrians used it in the absence of a written agreement or if someone reneged on a debt or claimed that it had been repaid. The oath was also meant to prevent opportunism,[29] enhance trust between parties in exchange, and reduce transaction expenses. It was the practice among traders carry out exchange, issue credit, and tally bills at the gate or the courtyard of the temple in order to deter opportunistic behavior in the presences of the gods. Religious rules and literature urged individuals to refrain from opportunistic behavior and described the severe punishments that would be imposed upon violators. People swore to the gods or in their names to demonstrate their probity. It was believed that the gods would exact revenge against those who lied. People also swore in the name of rulers and risked their lives by lying. The worded structure of the oath was usually fixed and the oaths were given in the presence of witnesses or the authorities, at the temple gate or in front of the emblem of Assur (the dagger).[30] Even when agreements between cities were signed, rulers swore to the gods that they would honor them.

> PN and PN_2 presented their testimony abroad before the dagger of Assur[31]

22 Pa. 5 (L 29–558): 23–28, Larsen, 2002, 5.
23 CCT 5, 6a, 6:ff, Larsen 2002, pp. 3–4.
24 CCT 2 25:22 ff, CAD B 146b.
25 AKT 1 17:42 ff, CAD P 535b.
26 CCT 3 17a:25 ff, CAD P 535b.
27 CCT 5 17b:7 ff, CAD $M/_1$ 22a.
28 On the relationship of religion, trade, and regulation of interpersonal relations in matters of exchange and credit, see Silver 1985, 7–31.
29 Selfishness accompanied with fraud.
30 Veenhof 2003a, 445–446.
31 TCL 21 271:42 ff, CAD $Š/_2$ 400b.

> So that they will not seize you tomorrow to swear an oath, you should establish witnesses when the silver is shipped.[32]

> This tablet of agreement between PN, PN_2, and PN_3 about which they took an oath by the City.[33]

> If he denies (it), make him take an oath.[34]

> Either he should pay the silver or make him take an oath.[35]

> Keep in mind my testimony (sworn to) by an oath of the City (Assur) and the (local) ruler.[36]

The rules of the game (institutions) in the Old Assyrian Trade were also dictated by the authorities. In "the City" and the colonies, political institutions and organizations existed that, as shown in previous chapters, laid down rules for the allocation, revision, and enforcement of institutions such as property rights, markets, means of exchange, organization, and finance. In Assur city and the colonies in Anatolia, there were rules governing the election of leaders and political organizations' decision-making processes. The political institutions, themselves on traders' organizations, remained stable throughout the trade era, supported by traders' organizations that had an interest in their continuity.

The supreme political entities in Assur were the municipal council and the king. The highest officials were the king and the eponym,[37] who belonged to the municipal assembly (*puḫrum*). Two public bodies existed: the municipal assembly plenum, in which "greater men" and "lesser men" were members, and a smaller council comprised of "greater men/elders" (*rabiūtum*) along with the king and the eponym.[38] The latter engaged in municipal and commercial affairs by means of special committees called "the group of five" (*ḫamištum*), of "the three" (*šalištum*) or of "the six" (*šedištum*), used primarily for judicial purposes.

The council or its constituent entities also served as arbitrators and judges in traders' disputes. The composition of the municipal assembly is not known with certainty. Written sources speak of "greater men" (*rabiūtum*) and "lesser men" (*ṣuḫḫurūtum*), who were freemen (*awīlum*).[39] Regarding the membership of small council in Kanesh, it is conjectured that they were large-scale traders who

32 HUCA 39 25, CAD M_1 191a, Gwaltney 1983, 40–43, L 29–568:26 ff.
33 TCL 21 216B:7 ff. CAD Ṭ 130a.
34 TCL 20 129, CAD T 165b.
35 KTS 13b:24 ff, CAD T 165b.
36 BIN 4 112:34 ff, CAD Š/$_2$ 400b.
37 Larsen 1976, 288–293; Veenhof 2003a, 437–441.
38 This body was called the *ālum* in Assur and the *kārum ṣaḫer rabi* in Kaneš.
39 Larsen 1976, 288–293; Veenhof 2003a, 437–441.

paid the *dātum*, a special tax. This gives rise to the hypothesis that Assur had an oligarchic government of traders, with the king as first among equals.

The eponym (*limmum*), chosen in annual elections, was one of the "big men." As head of the institution known as "the City" (*ālum*) or the "City House" (*bēt ālim*), he managed municipal life and also trade. His control of the administration thereby balanced that of the king, who controlled the army and the religious establishment. In his role as "mayor," the eponym managed with his people: held elections for certain functions, collected certain taxes, inspected weights and containers, tested metals for purity, and dealt with and reviewed the export procedures. He was also in charge of the treasury of Assur the deity and the city-state's archives, the performance of large commercial transactions in certain goods with traders' participation, and perhaps, the management of the traders' investment funds (*naruqqum*).

The roles and status of the king-inspector (*waklum*) are less clear.[40] On the one hand, there are documents written by kings wherein they glorify themselves. In contrast, there are also documents of traders and letters from the king to traders that describe the king's role as limited to defense and religion. The king would send notices from the council to the colony in Kanesh, and in certain documents, he appears as an investor with the traders.[41]

As stated in previous chapters, traders also maintained organizations in the colonies in Anatolia. According to traders' documents, there were about forty Assyrian colonies in Anatolia.[42] The colonies were of two sizes and levels of importance: the *Kārum* and the *Wabartum*. The Karum was the higher in status; that of Kanesh is deemed the oldest and the most important, its instructions binding on the other colonies. The economic and organizational purview of the Karum institution is not totally clear. We do know that it was part of the Assyrian governing system— an extension of "the City" in Assur.

The center of the traders' self-rule in Kanesh was the "Karum house" of the colony (*bēt kārim*). It was headed by a general assembly akin to that in Assur, composed of "greater" and "lesser" members of the colony. In addition to the assembly was a council of traders composed of payers of the *dātum;* it may have been synonymous with the "greater men" (*awīlū rabi'ūtum*) and the "lesser men" (*šībū*). The council evidently had ten members. This group, together with the eponym, managed the colony's affairs. The colony had written laws, including those governing

40 In Larsen's opinion, the available material strongly implies that the king and his officials did not control economic life and administration in Assur city. See Larsen 1976, 176.

41 Larsen 2015, 101 ff.

42 Veenhof 2008, 154–155.

working procedures of the assembly and a code of jurisprudence. The laws also set forth details about the conduct of trade such as interest rates, relations among partners, and credit agreements.[43]

The Karum and its institutions—conference halls, the organization's warehouses, safe rooms, and a prison—were housed in a spacious building within the colony. No such structure has been uncovered in archaeological excavations in Kültepe, but information about it can be drawn from traders' documents.[44] The main functions of the Karum were the following:

- managing relations with local authorities and, together with "the City," to negotiate agreements that would assure the operation of the Assyrian colony in Anatolia and the traders' activities;
- serving as an umbrella authority for the network of Assyrian colonies in Anatolia, representing them before the authorities in Assur, and representing Assur in Anatolia.
- electing and operating the assembly of members and the colony council and discussing and enforcing binding rules for the organization's activity, trade, traders, and the enforcement system, as well as publishing these rules.
- electing and operating the judicial and market-management institutions—for example, inspecting weights and measures and testing metals (gold and silver) for purity, recording sales of assets such as houses and slaves, and certifying the validity of certain contracts and agreements.
- settling accounts with local rulers in regard to taxes and sales of textiles at preferential prices.
- managing and operating the enforcement system, including jails and confiscations of property, and dealing with exceptional deviations from regulations, such as smuggling, disputes with local inhabitants, robbery, and acts of violence.
- managing the bookkeeping system for joint activity, including caravans, large joint acquisitions, collection of taxes / membership dues (*dātum*) and deposits (*šipkātum*) from partners in the organization, maintaining a system of credit for members and sales to the authorities on credit, and the periodic accounting of outstanding debits and credits;
- managing public warehouses (including security rooms) for goods and notes, and building and maintaining public structures and the infrastructure of streets and gates.

43 Larsen 1976, 287–312, Larsen 2015, 146 ff.
44 Dercksen 2004, 193–194.

- electing the managers (*limmum*) and the (*ḫamuštum*) of the Karum House and managing the organization's staff (*bēruttum*), including inspectors and scribes.
- building and managing the temple/temples, in conjunction with the priests.

The organizational structures of the Karum had a statutory text that regulated how the institutions would operate. Only a few parts of them have survived in the traders' archives. The following are some examples of the written procedures:

> No one among the small men must approach a man with an account or keep lurking in the gate of the colony with a complaint. If someone does lurk in the gate of the colony with a complaint....[45]
>
> The scribe will divide...into three groups, and they will give verdict....:
>
> When they stand the scribe will divide them into three groups, and they will resolve the matter. In case they do not resolve the matter, the plenary assembly will convene, the scribe will divide them into seven groups and they will resolve the matter by a majority.[46]

Seated at the palace were various echelons of bureaucrats who ran daily life of the city, and with whom the traders maintained a complex relationship. This included commercial relations, evidence of which emerges in the following letter:

> A fire has consumed the palace here and this has completely preoccupied the court, so it is not opportune to ask the *rabi sikkitim* (probably the highest military official) for silver. The man has spent all his money for the country. I shall come over and see you personally, and then, when the country is back to normal, I shall bring five textiles of royal quality (a value of 100–150 shekels silver); I shall enter together with the envoys of the colony, and the man will become ashamed because of the five textiles I shall offering to him, and I shall be able to collect my silver.[47]

The traders established the Karum organization for political and economic motives, as stated. It allowed them to appear jointly before the authorities and leverage their financial power as the operators of trade and the suppliers of income to the rulers. It facilitated the functioning of supportive institutions such as the legal system, market inspection, the system of warehouses, and the temple. It also made it possible for them to engage in collective large-scale projects that would were beyond the capacities of individual traders. Thus, it lowered the traders' transaction costs and mitigated their business risks by establishing and managing enforcement institutions and conferring the advantages of joint large-scale activity.

45 KTP 19; cf. EL nos. 288–290; Larsen 1976, 284–285; Hertel 2013, 115–121.
46 TC 1, 112, Larsen 1976, 285–286; Hertel 2013, 121–122; Larsen 2015, 163.
47 BIN 6, 23 ff, Larsen 2015, 139.

Documents from the Old Assyrian Trade era[48] yield a picture of relations between rulers in the cities of Anatolia and the Assyrian traders. The traders' organizations, together with representatives of Assur city, negotiated with the rulers over agreements that would facilitate and support trade. The resulting accords dealt with trading procedures and relations with local authorities, but those that have been found appear to be flawed and difficult to translate According to the agreements, the local ruler in the palace was entitled to 5 percent (3 of 60) of textiles, 2/65 of the tin as a tax, and another 10 percent (6 of 60) of the textiles at a special price. There were also limitations on trading in iron meteorite and azure stone (*lapis lazuli*). The Assyrians received residency rights in a territorially defined colony (the Karum), evidently including the right to manage their own defense. They also received extraterritorial entitlements that applied the political and economic rights of the regime in Assur to the colonies, protection of the roads, and collateral against losses resulting from attack and robbery in areas controlled by the king. In addition, they were protected from theft by local inhabitants, who, if caught stealing, were extradited to the Assyrians and, by law, could face execution. Kings swore to local gods (*māmītum*) that they would honor the agreement. In one collective agreement with a local ruler, the latter undertook to prevent Babylonian traders from doing business in the city, undertaking to drive them away, and even to kill them.

Recently discovered a damaged agreement[49] with the king of Kanesh contain other clauses—such as paying a fine for murder and extraditing the murderer to the Assyrians, followed by his execution; a commitment by the king to adjudicate without bias trials concerning debts between Assyrians and local inhabitants; searching for and recovering plundered textiles and providing silver restitution if restitution in kind cannot be made; protecting Assyrian property against confiscation by royal officers; exempting Assyrians from induction into the king's army and absolving them from obeying decrees to forgive debts and release slaves; and authorizing Assyrians to continue trading even in wartime.

An example of other treaties that were concluded with municipal rulers is a draft agreement with a small unknown kingdom in southeastern Mesopotamia. The tablet, evidently from the initial period of trading of the Old Assyrian Trade, is phrased in the form of a declaration by the Assyrian representative to the negotiations:

> There shall be no loss of (property) belonging to an Assyrian in your country—rope, cone or anything at all.

---

48 Veenhof 2008, 183–218.
49 Kt 00/k 6

> If loss occurs in your country you shall search for (what was lost) and then return it to us.
>
> If bloodshed occurs in your country, you shall hand over the killers to us, so we may kill them.
>
> You may not let Akkadians come here. If they do travel to your country, you must give them to us so we may kill them.
>
> You shall not demand anything from us. Like your father you may take 12 shekels of tin per donkey-load in caravans going up (to Anatolia). You may—like your father—use 1 1/4 shekels of silver per donkey-load on the way down (to Assur). You cannot take anything more.
>
> If no caravan is coming because of warfare, they will send you 5 minas of tin from Hahhum.
>
> He raised his hand in prayer to the gods Assur and Adad, to the Netherworld and the spirit of his father; he overturned his table and his chair, filled his cup and poured it out. The king said: "May he turn to naught..." They (the dignitaries) said: "If we reject your oath, may our blood be spilled like (the wine) in this cup!"[50]

The ruler of Hahhum, for example, had to assent to the regular procedures concerning the Euphrates River crossings and the roads in his area:

> You must not give instruction to ferrymen that should falsely or with evil intent let a boat sink so that merchandise is lost. Any losses that result, whether from sinking boat or in other ways in the river, in the mountains or anywhere in your land, you must compensate all, even ropes, cones or a staff.[51]

Below a trader recounts a robbery and his expectation of receiving compensation from the palace:

> They broke into the house and removed six textiles. I poured dust on my head (in despair) for your sake, ... Then (officers of) the trading station at GN went up to the *barullu*-officers (of the palace) and said (to them): "let us search (for the textiles) and if they are lost then we shall personally give compensation."[52]

Although the traders' relations with the authorities were regulated, their documents make mention of cases of smuggling (*pazzurtum*) of goods in order to evade taxes. Not only did the local kings and the Karum authorities in Kanesh warn them against the practice,[53] but traders who were caught were jailed (*kišer-*

---

50 Kt n/k 794; Veenhof 2008, 186–187.
51 Larsen 2015, 156.
52 KTH 3, Larsen 2002, 176–177: 16 ff.
53 Veenhof 1995, 1732–1733.

tum) and fined. They could be released from prison in return for gifts or payment of ransom to the rulers.

> If you can smuggle them, then smuggle them, if you cannot smuggle them, then take them up to the palace and let the palace collect the *nisḫatum* tax on them and you bring the textiles down (again).[54]

> In the same way as you give orders concerning your own goods and they smuggle (for you) so also give orders concerning my goods so that they will smuggle for me textiles of good quality, fifty textiles.[55]

> 'You are my colleague! Just as you send an order for your own goods to be smuggled, do also send one for my goods.'"

> Heed my tablets, do not smuggle anything, the guardpost is rigorous.[56]

> PN brought his contraband to PN_2, but his contraband was seized, the palace arrested PN_2 and put him in prison, the watch is strict—the ruling queen wrote to GN, GN_2, and GN_3, and her own land concerning contraband, and there are spies around, (therefore) by all means do not try to smuggle.[57]

> The king and queen here have written to the road guards concerning smuggling, saying: "Seize anyone you observe carrying textiles and tin in the land, withhold the tin and textiles and lead the criminal to me." Furthermore, they have written to (people on) the *sukinu* road. "Urgent, do not smuggle tin and textiles and do not commit anything to the *sukinu* road. Urgent, the orders are strict. Do not send anything, for you will regret it."[58]

The Assyrians' judicial system was based on laws inscribed on stela (*naru'āum*).[59] Although the stela have not been discovered, scholars have reconstructed some passages of the statutes on them on the basis of traders' documents—such as the laws of the Karum, letters, agreements, contracts, summonses to trial, outcomes of arbitration proceedings, testimonies, court rulings, and so on. In several places, the expression "like the words on the stela" (*kīma awāt naruā'im*) appears in the documents.[60] The Assyrians' stela, like those of their contemporaries Eshnunna and Ḫammu-rapi, include many details pertaining to daily life—conflict resolution procedures and jurisprudence, wording of oaths, organizational conduct of

54 KTH 13:6 ff, CAD P 312a.
55 CCT 4 11a:19 ff, CAD P 312b.
56 CCT 4 18a:16 ff, CAD P 313a.
57 ATHE 62:28 ff, CAD P 314a.
58 AKT 6d, 771, Larsen 2015, 158.
59 Veenhof 1995, 1717–1744.
60 See Kt 394, 15–16, in Veenhof 1995, 1725.

the colony, business conduct (debts, interest), and relations with local authorities. References to prices and interest rates appear as well.

In addition to the code of laws (*awātum*), the following have been found:

- municipal rulings (*dīnum*) and permanent rules (*iṣurtam eṣārum*);[61]
- agreements with foreign rulers (*māmītum*);
- regulations of Assur city and the Karum in Anatolia, adopted by the assemblies and recorded on special tablets;
- Administrative decisions of the entities that manage municipal life in Assur and Kanesh, inscribed by those authorized to make them entities, e.g., the king and the eponym;
- decisions presented by legal authorities to litigants in the wake of legal proceedings;
- private legal documents such as loan agreements, marriages, and wills.[62]

In the Karum administration, a set of officials including the eponym held appointments that were valid for one week (*ḫamuštum*).[63] The status of the Karum eponym is not clear. Although he was part of the colony apparatus, he lacked the lofty status of the eponym of Assur. There was a secretary who managed meetings of the assemblies of the council of traders and the courts and recorded their minutes. Additional bureaucrats kept track of weights and measures and inspected the quality of metals. Others enforced court rulings and were empowered to break into traders' homes and confiscate property and documents. Additional officials appear as well. The eponym and the bureaucrats appear to have received no salary; instead, they were paid for performing a given service or enjoyed sundry benefits by virtue of their status.[64]

The traders tried to avoid resorting to judicial proceedings by applying persuasion, writing letters, and applying social pressure. Conflicts were settled at several levels.[65] On the personal level, there was a procedure that allowed a lender to seize a debtor,[66] and an attempt to collect through a joint hearing could also be made.

> Make people pay whatever is outstanding to him and convert your father's merchandise in direct exchange.[67]

61 Veenhof 2003a, 431–434.
62 Veenhof 2003a, 431–434.
63 One official or more.
64 Dercksen 2004, 232–233.
65 Veenhof 2003a, 442–443.
66 Veenhof 2003a, 471.
67 KTS 1b:15 ff, CAD B 12a.

> Seize (pl.) him and make him pay the money and much interest on it as proper, do not make any concessions to him.[68]

> Have my tablets read again and again but do not release them to PN, you yourself should keep my tables (or let them be deposited in his house under seal).[69]

At the public level, arbitration proceedings,[70] presided over by two people chosen by the parties chose also took place, and their rulings were binding.

> PN and PN_2 took hold of us (to require us to act as arbiters), and we settled their dispute.[71]

> PN and PN_2's son as representatives of PN_2 settled accounts with PN_3 and put their affair before us, and we settled all their affairs, be it that he had given him tin for an *ebuṭṭum*-loan, lent him even one shekel of silver, had given him *tadmiqtum* (-loan), or there were (payments for) votive offering.[72]

Conflicts at a higher level were settled with the help of claims (*še'āum*) presented (*redûm*) to the judicial authority of Assur or of the colony—the municipal assembly or the Karum, or groups of council members who were chosen to serve as judges. The parties approached this judicial body (*maḫārum, kašādum*) and conducted themselves in accordance with agreed-upon procedures that included presenting documents, giving written and oral testimony, and taking oaths. The judges handed down binding written verdicts.

> I shall settle the disputes and my advice will reach you with regard to everything you have to say (in court).[73]

> Our agent is dead, and we are suing for our agent's silver.[74]

> PN will take an oath and he will submit acclaim for x copper in the gate of the god.[75]

> They will entrust to you the tablets which the group of six [will seal] and they will establish witnesses for you, and you will present the tablets (provided) with the seal of the "six" to the judges where you negotiate.[76]

68 KTS 13a:20 ff, CAD G 22a.
69 CCT 3 34a:17 ff, CAD K 510a.
70 Veenhof 1991, 457–459.
71 CCT 1 48:2 ff, CAD Ṣ 11b.
72 ICK 2 113:9 ff, CAD T 36–37b&a.
73 CCT 3 15:30 ff, CAD G 26b.
74 ATHE 48:38 ff, CAD Š/$_2$ 358a.
75 MVAG 33 No. 278:5, CAD T 160b.
76 BIN 6 80:3 ff, CAD Š/$_2$ 256a.

> The creditors of PN's estate have substantiated their claims. If the creditors who, after PN died, took silver do not return it, they will substantiate their claims (under oath) before the dagger of Assur.[77]
>
> I am not the trading agent of PN—bring my affair before the plenary meeting of the Karum.[78]
>
> In accordance with the decision of the Karum, I will come and answer you in court.[79]
>
> If my case has been settled make a copy of the document (which says) that my case is settled and send (it) to me.[80]

The litigants could present or respond to a claim by dispatching a representative (an attorney) (*rābiṣum).*[81] In complex cases, the municipal judicial instance could appoint a counsel for the applicants in order to help them solve their problems. The following letter illustrates this matter:

> We have sent an attorney, and the attorney (*rābiṣum*) has in his possession a letter from the city which is authoritative, saying that no one either in the city or abroad must interfere, and that PN's money must be collected in the city. There they will divide the inheritance in accordance with their testament. Anyone who interferes abroad will be considered a thief with respect to every shekel of silver that he takes.[82]
>
> Do you know that PN opened the sealed room of our principle (lit. father) and that I will consider him responsible concerning the sealed room? heaven forbid that you(!) make demands to the palace concerning the sealed room of the palace.[83]
>
> I shall settle the disputes and my advice will reach you with regard to everything you have to say (in court).[84]
>
> The *rābiṣum*-attorney holds a valid written order to the effect that no one is to touch (it), either in the City (Assur) or abroad, and that the money of PN is to be collect in the City.[85]

Enforcement, usually a result of the courts' decisions, took place in the presence of officials and witnesses. If the debt was owed to the traders' institutions, the officers (*bērum*) effected collection by confiscating property of the debtor in accordance with the instructions of the eponym, the chief elected official. Recalcitrant

77 CCT 5 9a:7 ff, CAD T 128a&b.
78 CCT 1 49b:20 ff, CAD $Š/_1$ 292a.
79 TCL 21 268:14 ff, CAD $N/_1$ 52a.
80 TCL 19 9:16 ff, CAD $M/_2$ 55a&b.
81 Veenhof 1995, 1740; 2003a, 443.
82 TC 2, 21: Larsen 1976, 181–182; Michel 2001, 326; Larsen 2015, 229.
83 CCT 4 7c:1 ff, CAD $M/_1$ 138a.
84 CCT 3 15:30 ff, CAD G 26b.
85 TCL 14 21:8 ff, CAD E 251b.

debtors, of course, also sustained the additional punishment of the loss of their good name and their ability to make a living at trade—an exceedingly severe penalty and, therefore, a deterrent to misconduct.

> His smuggled goods were seized and the palace arrested PN and put him in prison.[86]

> You led me to the judges and deposited the document of PN and then the judge imposed a fine on me.[87]

> The City (Assur) had imposed a payment of ten minas of silver on you (the Karum of Kanesh), and they had (already) chosen a messenger to send when we pleaded with the elders, saying: Do not send any messenger.[88]

> My father's investors went to the City (Assur), obtained a tablet (with the official verdict) of the City, and made my father hear it read out in *Kāneš*, thus they received their silver.[89]

> Until I and PN received a tablet from the colony authorities concerning his extradition, he would not come.[90]

* * *

The enforcement system in the Old Assyrian Trade was based on a "private order" and rules handed down by the Assyrian political system. The trader's good name was an important asset, with risk assessment in the credit system predicated on it. Traders made intensive use of oaths to the deity at the gate of the temple. The political institutions of the city and the colonies were built upon on general councils and councils comprised of successful merchants. The king was a member of the council of "greater men" and was first among equals. Another elected official—the eponym— headed the institution known as "the City." This institution was in charge of collecting taxes, inspecting weights and containers that were used as means of exchange, testing metals (chiefly gold and silver) for purity, reviewing export and import procedures, and managing the temple's treasury of gold; it was also in charge of the archives and occasionally managed large commercial transactions of the city. Each colony had an institution parallel to "the City," known as a *Kārum* or, in small colonies, a *Wabartum*. Traders maintained formal relations with rulers in and en route to the trading cities of Anatolia. They signed documents with rulers in matters that included their special status, rules of jurisprudence, their personal safety and that of their property, and taxation arrangements. They had a legal system based on written rules and regulations set forth by

86 ATHE 62:32 ff, CAD K 450b.
87 MVAG 35/3 No. 325a:13 ff, CAD A/$_2$ 297–8b&a.
88 TCL 4 1:7&11, CAD Š/$_3$ 75/a.
89 Veenhof AV, 4:44 ff, CAD Ţ 129b.
90 TC 1, 4: 31 ff, Larsen 2002, 137.

their governing system. Conflict resolution was handled on the basis of the rules of jurisprudence. The “City” and Karum administrations had an array of bureaucrats whose task it was to enforce the decisions of the authorities and the courts.

Conclusion

This book represents the first attempt to use of the analytical tools of modern Institutional Economics and Transaction Cost Theory to profile the economic institutions that influenced the economy of Mesopotamia in the third millennium BCE. In the course of the research, it became clear that the market economy institutions of the Old Assyrian trade in the early second millennium BCE were the successors of similar institutions in Mesopotamia at the dawn of history.

As the writer delved into the era, he was increasingly drawn into the great debates over the structure of the Mesopotamian and ancient Egyptian economy and society. His training as an economist simply would not allow him to automatically accept Karl Polanyi's primitive-substantive model (Polanyi 1957, 1977), which so many researchers embrace as conventional wisdom. According to these models, factors of production in ancient Mesopotamia and Egypt belonged to a society comprised of extended families living on a subsistence basis and operating in an economy in which a certain social behavior was embedded. He saw the matter differently, viewing the ancient Sumerians as people whose mindsets and motivations resemble our own, and as people who established economic institutions that we can recognize today, with, of course, the inevitable adaptations to changes in technology and culture.

The staggering wealth of Old Assyrian trade documents persuaded him that quoting them, could provide strong support for the writer's views that the institutions of the Assyrian traders, like those of their Mesopotamian precursors, were institutions of a market economy. His assumption was that if institutions such as property rights, markets, instruments of payment, organization, and finance, which appear in documents from the time, functioned then in a manner that is recognizable until today, and were socially enforced, then their economy was indeed a market economy.

In the fourth millennium BCE, a new civilization appeared, the Uruk. Evidently of Sumerian extraction, it was typified by urban settlement in large cities, spacious temple complexes, and a society undergoing both technological and social change. The Sumerians engaged in far-reaching trade and established merchant colonies in multiple settlements across the Middle East.

The rapid technological changes in the fourth and third millennia BCE, initiated by the Sumerian people, created an infrastructure for sweeping transformations of Mesopotamian social and economic life. In agriculture, elaborate irrigation systems were introduced, productive fields were organized, and tools for cultivation and seeding were transformed. In the social domain, large organizations with advanced specialization were formed and writing to document their activities

https://doi.org/10.1515/9783111065533-008

was invented. In transport, the wheel was invented and then the cart, followed by the-domestication of the donkey. These changes gave productivity, trade, and urbanization a powerful push forward. Another immensely important change was the use of barley and copper, and subsequently of silver, as means of exchange in the markets, which enhanced exchange and interregional trade. In the second half of the third millennium BCE, rapid change also occurred in the development of writing and writing instruments.

The institution of property rights appears to have been quite an ancient one, dating from the transition to permanent settlements and the accumulation of property by individuals and families. Societies and authorities in third millennium BCE Mesopotamia recognized proprietary rights in many goods and services, both through outright ownership and in right of use enshrined in agreements and seals.[1]

This book argues that the means of exchange such as units of volume (barley) and of weight (copper and, later, silver) existed in the early Sumerian period. People traded in the markets and used measurement units of barley for bookkeeping, credit, paying wages, rents, and interest on loans. The standard unit of measurement was the sila of barley and there is evidence that there were containers of exactly this size.

Assur sat on a crossroads from east to west and north to south. Caravans passed through from the east, where tin and precious stones were sourced, to high-demand areas in the west, and from the sources of textiles in the south to those of silver and demand for tin in the north. Within Anatolia, traders participated in regional trade in copper, wool, and silver.

The traders' documents indicate that market institutions also existed and that market activity took place along modern lines, taking into account technological and cultural differences. There is evidence that various market situations emerged due to political disruptions that affected supply and demand.

Trade was subject to official supervision and regulation, and merchants enjoyed exclusivity in certain locations. Assyrian traders used weight units of high-quality silver to express the prices of goods and assets. They gathered information on activities in the markets by means of their literacy and their well-developed communication system. With the help of their status in the market, they took advantage of the supply of inexpensive tin from northern Iran, the strong demand for tin in the Anatolian bronze industry, the supply of cheap silver from the Anatolian highlands, the supply of high-quality textiles in Babylonia, and the brisk demand for silver in Mesopotamia, to make large profits from their trading activity.

1 Steinkeller 2004; Wilcke 2003, 210–18.

The traders pursued profits in silver where ever they could extract them. Their profits in the trade with Anatolia amounted to about 50 % per caravan cargo and 100 % per year assuming two caravans per year.

The Assyrian traders organized mainly at the family level, much as traders have done in all generations. In addition, there were organizations comprised of individuals, partners, and limited partners. The limited partnership, known as “the sack,” was established with the help of the authorities and was used as an instrument to facilitate management and long-term financing, and its structure seems to have been a singular one unique throughout long periods of history. It appeared in a limited form in the Roman era, but evolved primarily in modern times. The Assyrian trade organizations were designed to shift transactions to the internal level and mitigate transaction risks and the hazards associated with contracts and interactions with suppliers of labor and goods.[2]

The traders operated sophisticated institutions to finance their activity: long- and short-term investments, commercial credit, and loans from other traders (“bank” loans). They made long-term investments within the structure of the limited partnership, the “sack”; investors entered into long-term partnership agreements and, as their main return, received a share in the profits. Short-term interest-free loans were extended largely as deposits of goods on consignment for short and medium periods of time. Failures to make repayments were punished by fines in the form of interest. In addition to commercial credit, other traders provided “bank” credit at interest rates that varied according to the risk associated with the borrower. This financing system was supported by contracts, collateral, and guarantees.

The traders operated a detailed system of accounting and bookkeeping that helped them to manage their affairs, including reducing the risks and costs of their trade. These Assyrian financial institutions were continuations of similar institutions that existed in Mesopotamia from the third millennium BCE onward.

There are several explanations for interest rates in ancient times. One refers to the interest rate as derived from capital productivity. In loans of seeds and animals, the interest rate was calculated based on the yield of the fields and the birthrate of animals. The interest was calculated as a unit of the means of exchange in which the loan was given per month. Basic interest rates have been fixed for centuries, suggesting an ancient tradition and government involvement in determining them. The interest rates of 33 1/3 % per annum for loans in barley and 20 % for loans in silver metal appear in the legal records from the period. Ac-

2 See below the sub chapter on the Hansatic League page 177.

cording to Assyrian trading data, the basic interest rate was 30 % per annum, and it varied from borrower to borrower, according to the particular risks.

The traders maintained efficient enforcement mechanisms to organize their trade and manage their complex relations. The institutions operated on the basis of a "private order" in Assyrian society, which produced a set of expected behaviors and penalties for transgressors, the institution of the oath representing an important mechanism of this kind. An Assyrian trader's reputation (*šumu*, "name") was an exceedingly important asset. A trader who lost it suffered significant financial harm; in extreme cases, it marked the termination of his commercial activity. The elements of trust, solidarity, and reputation were at the foundation of the Old Assyrian trade. The Assyrian traders were looking for trustworthy (*kēnum*) person with whom to conduct commercial and financial relations.

In addition, organizations in Assur city and the Anatolian colonies dictated certain rules of commercial behavior. These organizations were controlled by the traders and run by bureaucrats. As a member of the municipal council of Assur, the king participated in trading as first among equals.

The traders anchored their enforcement arrangements in agreements with local rulers in and en route to Anatolia, which were supported by an effective judicial system that operated on the basis of laws, directives from the Assyrian institutions, and agreements with local rulers. Conflict resolution procedures were accompanied by evidence in the form of documents, testimonies, and oaths, and were resolved in arbitration proceedings and in courts of law. Traders made intensive use of oaths to the deity at the gate of the temple.

The political institutions of the city and the colonies were built upon on general councils and councils comprised of successful merchants. The king was a member of the council of "greater men" and was first among equals. Another elected official—the eponym— headed the institution known as "the City". Each of the about forty colonies of the Old Assyrian in Anatolia had an institution parallel to "the City," known as a *Kārum* or, in small colonies, a *Wabartum*. The "City" and Karum administrations had an array of bureaucrats whose task it was to enforce the decisions of the authorities and the courts.

The book ends with a short discussion on Institutional Economics and on the details of the two competing theories on the economic structure of Mesopotamia in the third century BCE. In addition, the book presents two sub chapters dealing with two economic structures that are similar to the economy of Mesopotamia in the third millennium BCE and the Old Assyrian Trade. The ancient Egyptian economy resemble the Mesopotamian one in the same period, and therefore received a description and analysis in a sub-chapter. The other subchapter is on the Hansatic League of the Middle Ages that developed independently similar institutions to the Old Assyrian ones.

Theory and Findings

Institutional Economics Theory

Institutional Economics[3] represents an effort to integrate institutional theory into neoclassical economic theory by debating the underlying assumptions of neoclassical theory—the rational individual and zero transaction costs. Institutional research is undertaken by analyzing socioeconomic situations and processes with the help of economists, sociologists, anthropologists, political scientists, and historians. The analysis of the conditions attempts to explain people's behavior by their aspiration to maximize their welfare and profits in the exchange process. The aspect of process analysis seeks to explain both the long-term development of economic institutions and its contribution to economic growth and welfare. Researchers in Institutional Economics identify institutions as socially established or politically dictated rules that regulate economic activity, or as contractual and organizational structures chosen by economic agents that interact in the markets.[4]

Individuals are influenced by cognitive and psychological models that help them interpret the world around them and interact with others. These models are derived from human nature and, in part, from cultural determinants, and are built by the intergenerational and interregional transmission of social knowledge, values, norms, and structures, among other things. One of our economic interactions is exchange. Imperfect information and limited thinking capacity, arising from in dogmas, prejudice, ideologies, and social structures, determine the outcomes of what we choose among available opportunities to carry out exchange and influence its process and outcomes. Douglass North explains the theory:

> Institutions are the humanly devised constrained that structure political, economic and social interaction. They consist of both informal constraints (sanctions, taboos, customs, traditions, and codes of conduct), and the formal rules (constitutions, laws, property rights). Throughout history, institutions have been devised by human beings to create order and reduce uncer-

---

3 There are several study areas and school of thought that uses the term Institutional Economics. In this book the study area called sometimes New Institutional Economics (Institutional Economics) is the framework used to analyze the economic history of Mesopotamia and the Old Assyrian Period. The other study areas include the school of thought that deal with the effect of social institutions like family, marriage, private property and more on economic behaviour. One of the founders of this school of thought was Thorstein B. Veblen. Others emphasizes the lack of harmony between different economic groups and the conflict between them as unavoidable. And thus, they welcome government intervention in the economy. Aveneyon E. *Dictionary of Economics* Tel Aviv 2004, 200, (Hebrew).

4 Grief 2005, xiv.

> tainty in exchange. Together with standard constraints of economics they define the choice set and therefore determine transaction and production costs and hence the profitability and feasibility of engaging in economic activity.[5]

According to Institutional Economics, interregional trade relies on economic and political institutions that are controlled by other institutions that determine the costs, profits, and viability of economic activity. Some of these institutions affect interregional trade directly, such as those that influence relations between traders and local leaders in trade destinations, and between traders and their agents in these destinations. To stabilize relations with local leaders, traders use two mechanisms. In one, they conclude agreements that regulate their security, working environment, and lives in the target markets, as well as economic relations with the rulers. In the other, they establish an organization that will coordinate their collective response and strengthen their standing vis-à-vis the rulers. To regulate relations with their agents, traders establish institutions that limit the agents' opportunistic behavior. One such institution is a social network in which the traders align their expectations and share information about the agents' behavior. The existence of this network allows multilateral punishment of deviations from expected behavior to take place. Traders can also build institutions that regulate relations in contracts and invest their enforcement mechanisms with structure.[6]

Another aspect of institutions of exchange is the use of the analytical tools of transaction costs theory to explain why people use economic institutions.[7] Transaction costs are incurred when partners to a transaction have imperfect information and limited intellectual ability to process information about the transaction, coupled with an ability to engage in opportunistic behavior. It is the existence of these costs that underlies the creation of the institutions. The act of exchange through institutions is accompanied by transaction costs (identifying partners, communication, measuring the goods, evaluating agents' performance, drawing up agreements, retaining documents, enforcing agreements). Knowing the costs is essential for the procurement and retention of the information. The command of information may be asymmetrical among the parties to the transaction. The use of institutions makes it possible to reduce transaction costs and, in turn, to improve the performance of the economy and realize the benefits of exchange and trade.

The underlying assumption in the economic analysis of the Old Assyrian Trade is the rational individual—the Homo Economicus—whose choices are motivated

5 North 1991, 97.
6 Grief 1992, 128–133.
7 North 1997, 149–160; Williamson 1979, 233–261; idem 2000, 595–613.

by the aspiration to maximize personal welfare and economic gain. It is true that Institutional Economics adds transaction costs and institutions to the process, but it continues to affirm the basic underlying assumption. Importantly, while the writer did not analyze Institutional Economics theory and its components in this book, he did use elements of the theory to characterize and analyze the phenomenon of the Old Assyrian Trade and its development. The focal question in this book concerned the extent to which the institutions identified in the Old Assyrian trade used existing institutions from the third millennium BCE to solve special problems in its own place and time. To answer this, existing definitions of these economic institutions as established in multiple studies have been referred to. The institutions have been profiled, and they have been dissected into their components, and the social and economic advantages of their use have been described. After the institutions were presented, how they appeared, operated, and were enforced in Mesopotamia in various eras was examined.

Economic Models that Explain the Era

Research has produced evidence that the economic institutions of the Old Assyrian Trade existed in Mesopotamian society from the third millennium BCE, if not earlier. The writer says this on the basis of many studies grounded in primary sources from that millennium. Proving the existence of these economic institutions required in-depth research on the institutions of Sumerian and Akkadian society of the third millennium BCE. Surveying the models that explain the economic and social structure of that millennium in this book, he reinforces the studies that point to the existence of a market economy at that time. Researchers examining the state of economic research into third-century-BCE Mesopotamia identify three main theories that shape the way scholarship views this era: the Marxist, the primitive-substantive, and the formal-modern.[8] According to the Marxist theory, there was no private ownership of land and other means of production in antiquity in Asia.[9] In Mesopotamian society, there were two main classes—the urban, dependent on the palace, and the rural, living under conditions of exploitation. The palace and the temple controlled the means of production—labor, land, and capital—creating unique systems of production, distribution, and exchange.

8 Renger 1994, 157–208; Van de Mieroop 2004, 54–64; Silver 2004, 65–87; Steinkeller 2004, 91–111; Jursa 2010, 13–26.
9 Van de Mieroop 2004, 54–56.

The second important school of thought describing the socioeconomic structure of Mesopotamia in the third millennium BCE is the primitive-substantive school, which rules out the very possibility of applying today's market economy model to the economies of the ancient world.[10] According to this theory, markets in antiquity did not enable resource allocation and the activity of the economic system is better described by other methods of allocation. These methods were based not on economic conduct but on social behavior; therefore, the analytical tools of neoclassical economics can explain only a few historical eras and are limited in their ability to describe the structure and activity of societies and economies in various times. This theory is championed by historians, sociologists, and anthropologists who doubt the relevance of classical economic theory for the analysis of ancient societies. They emphasize that the economists' assumption of wealth-maximizing behavior is unsuited to describing the economic structure and the form of activity of certain societies. Their theory, attributed to Polanyi studies, rests on anthropological foundations,[11] avails itself of Finley's theory[12] and relies on, among others, Max Weber's social theories.[13] According to this line of thought, Mesopotamian society in the third millennium BCE was primitive and tribal. It functioned as an expanded household (*oikos* in Greek) in a closed subsistence economy in which the means of production were held by the extended family. The researcher Johannes Renger describes this theory succinctly: [14]

> The *oikos* (= house; Sumerian e—Akkadian *bītum*) or household economy [....] is the basic structural element of ancient Mesopotamian economy, notably from the end of the fourth to the beginning of the second millennium B.C. Key elements in such an ideal type of household economy are the unity of labor, living together within a household, and consumption where there are no prices, no wages, no rent, no profit or capital. Household economy in a highly developed form finds its manifestation in the institutional households of the Mesopotamian palace and temple and their working.[15]

The theory is based on the models of reciprocity and redistribution and on kinship, friendship, and social status (or on a hierarchy that traces to affiliation with a political or religious organization). Another structural component is the "household," in which the principle of subsistence production applies rather than that of production for income and profit. The extended family organized itself in large organ-

10 North 1977, 703–716.
11 Polanyi 1957, 1977.
12 Finley, 1973.
13 Lessnof 2003, 258–260.
14 Gelb 1979, 1–97; Diakonoff 1971, 15–37.
15 Renger 1994, 170.

izational units of the temple and the palace that were controlled by the king, and involved economic activity in agriculture, crafts, and services. Individuals jointly cultivated fields, produced goods in workshops for the manufacture of textiles, leather goods, and processed metal, provided services such as trade, haulage, and public services, such as bureaucracy and soldiering, and pursued public works, such as building and maintaining irrigation systems, temples, fortifications, and palaces. In return for their labor services, they received rations for subsistence. According to the primitive-substantive model, people in these settings did not act out of economic motives of making a profit or gaining personal utility.[16] Some members of the organization (soldiers, temple staff, the managerial stratum, and those in special occupations) received land from the king in return for their labor services to the organization, which they cultivated for subsistence. Lessors of land or holders of rights to certain activities remitted votive gifts or other gifts (as opposed to a tax or a rent) to the central authorities. Family members exchanged surplus goods in their possession or bartered services on a social basis or on the principle of reciprocity. They used equivalencies of quantities of goods (prices) set by the authorities. There were no central marketplaces where prices were determined on the basis of supply and demand resulting from economic motives of profit and personal utility. Capital and credit were not used for production and exchange. People exchanged favors by borrowing goods (loans) and returning them along with gifts (interest) in order to express gratitude or to pay a penalty for arrears. The authorities kept records of trade and used them to determine accounts payable (debts) and set collective fines (interest) for delays in payback. Interregional trade took place mainly in luxury goods and among rulers who bartered gifts for political exigencies. Trade was managed by palace or temple officials (traders) who met with foreign traders in agreed-upon places—ports of trade—where the authorities set the prices of exchange.

According to this school of thought, neither archaeological evidence nor documents exist that relate to market places and prices set in them. Certain documents deal with the exchange of assets and price ratios among them. However, nowhere to be found are documents that describe price volatility originating in changes in supply and demand, and there are no explanations in the documents about the motives of those doing the exchange—especially explanations of their profits and personal preferences. These researchers emphasize that while market-style exchange for economic motives may have taken place, the markets where this happened were so small that there is no evidence about them in the written records. The researchers' model finds that barley and silver served as agreed means of so-

---

16 North 1977, 703–716.

cial exchange, record-keeping, and documentation. Authorities set prices to simplify exchange and realize social motives. There was no formal institution of credit; the existing documentation about credit relates to record-keeping and payment arrangements among organizations and among their members, including traders. Nonetheless, these researchers concede that amid the dominant socio-cooperative central structure of Mesopotamian society in the third millennium BCE, there were small islands of private activity that had institutions similar to the economic institutions of our time.

Douglass North agrees with Karl Polanyi that elements of reciprocity and redistribution in resource allocation exist in all societies at all times and asks how economists explain the existing alternatives to markets that set prices within the framework of families, societies, guilds, estates, labor organizations, cooperatives, governments, nonprofit organizations, and others. These allocation systems have played a central role in societies and economies past and present and should be explained by the discipline of economics. North proposes the analysis of transaction costs as a suitable framework for the investigation of the non-economic market structures (allocation systems) that researchers in the social sciences have proposed. North stresses the need for defined and enforced property rights in the markets at point of exchange. However, he adds, the costs of defining and enforcing these rights may be so steep as to rule out the use of markets for resource allocation. North also proffers Roland Coase's explanation of the internalization of market exchange within families, societies, and organizations, with the help of rules and agreements, in order to lower transaction costs.

According to the third school of thought presented and supported in this book, a market economy with local characteristics did exist in third millennium BCE Mesopotamia. The large organizations there operated as economic entities that employed wage-owners and lessors of land to produce and supply a range of goods and services. Workers served these organizations and as well as landowners who leased their land from them. They were rewarded in the form of wages and salaries that were differentiated by age, sex, and status in the organization. The use of means of production was controlled by the palace and by individuals who leased land and received loans for agricultural and other production. Individuals paid leasing fees and interest. They lived in kinship households and traded surplus wages and income in the market for goods and services. Private interests owned a wide range of assets such as fruit plantations, homes, slaves, and other goods, and bought and sold them freely, including by means of written agreements. Individuals obtained land under long-term leases, cultivated it with the help of wage-earners, and remitted leasing fees to the organizations. Private ownership of assets was marked by means of border stones, stakes, and seals. From the

Old Babylonian period—the second millennium BCE—the share of private land grew at the expense of land owned by temples and palaces all across Mesopotamia.

The main means of exchange—money—in the local market from the fourth millennium BCE onward was barley. It was used to pay wages, remit leasing fees, issue interest-bearing loans, and keep records in the organizations' accounting system. There were markets, and prices were set there in units of measure (volume) of barley. Private traders engaged in interregional trade with copper as their means of exchange and operated a credit system that featured differential interest rates according to risk. Weight units of silver became an important means of exchange in the middle of the third millennium BCE. They were the traders' principal form of money, a means of exchange for large assets such as homes, and the unit of preference in the records of the organizations' bookkeeping system. Emphasis on the use of commodities such as barley, copper, and silver as main means of exchange among the inhabitants of Mesopotamia and Egypt in antiquity helps to solve the mystery of how the economy and the markets operated at that time. People visited the markets with sacks of "money" and instruments of measurement (scales and units of volume) and conducted exchange with the help of a set of measurement units that the authorities established and inspected.

Additional Regions and Eras

Economic Institutions in Ancient Egypt

The socioeconomic structure that took shape in Mesopotamia was not unique to this region, with a highly similar structure evolving in Egypt during this same period.[17] In both societies, far-reaching technological, social, legal and economic changes took place within a short period of time. Technological advances included construction of complex irrigation systems, changes in the quality of grains and the process of working the fields, greater use of the wheel and the donkey for haulage, and, perhaps, most important, the invention of writing. Social changes, such as the central status of the King-God, Pharaoh, social stratification and the importance of the bureaucratic and priestly classes, and the formation of large palace and temple organizations, were reflected in legal and economic changes. Among the legal changes were the emergence of the importance of property rights in the ownership of assets (houses, fruit plantations, boats, and personal property) and the cultivation of the organizations' land under long-term leases, including a

17 Frankfort 1967, 96–125; Rice 1990, 1–23.

system of taxation/leasing fees that applied to farmers and others and provided the public sector of the palace and the temples a source of income in addition to votive gifts and their own economic activity. All of these changes contributed to innovations in economic activity, including the wider use of copper and bronze, the use of grains (mostly wheat) to pay wages and to make other payments as a "currency" in addition to copper, the conduct of economic activity and specialization in a wide range of domains such as agriculture, crafts, construction, transport, and services, intensive exchange activity in markets, aided by payment in grains (wheat and barley) and copper (and later, gold and silver as well), along with supervised weights and measures, employment of workers at wages that were differentiated by occupation and status in the public and private sectors, land allocation by leasing to senior workers, creating surpluses for exchange in the private sector, forced labor and slavery to carry out projects involving palaces, temples, infrastructure, mining activity, and burial monuments, and the existence and maintenance of surpluses among organizations and individuals and using them for exchange in the market, consumption, investment, and social welfare activity.

Land in Egypt, as in Mesopotamia, was considered the property of the deity, although not entirely so.[18] The large organizations in Egypt included masses of farmers who leased land on a long-term basis and remitted leasing fees and taxes to the palace and the temples, as well as on wage-earners who held various ranks in these institutions. The temples also held long-term use rights to farmland that they cultivated with the help of wage laborers. Private ownership of land existed as well, in the form of especially large estates that belonged to provincial rulers and high-ranking officials.

By recognizing and enforcing property rights, Egyptian society laid the foundations of exchange in the marketplace.[19] The efficiency of exchange and the market was enhanced by means of exchange of goods, such as grain (barley and wheat) and metals (foremost copper) that were based on agreed units of measurement (volume and weight) determined by the authorities. Traders created means of enforcement that included "private orders," such as reliance on norms that encouraged the upholding of property rights, and imposed social penalties on those who breached them. Governing authorities also established enforcement measures by dictate, such as laws and judicial systems and the implementation of court rulings.

The types and limitations of the documents found in Egypt create a perceptible bias in the description of the nature economic life by focusing on the public sec-

18 Lephorn 1995, 273–284; O'Connor 1995, 319–329.

19 Versteeg 2002, part II; Kemp 2006, 111–117.

tor.[20] No substantial body of documents has been found describing exchange activity in the private sector, the credit system, the form of the traders' organizations, market activity, and the interaction of the private and public sectors. This helps to explain why researchers of that era construct models emphasizing the centrality of the public sector in Egypt at the time. Adherents of the primitive-substantive models describe Egyptian society as a rudimentary one and the ancient Egyptian economy as one based on cooperative production, redistribution of subsistence rations to the inhabitants, and a crude system of exchange based on reciprocity and social class. In the opinion of scholars holding this view, there were no markets, no means of exchange, and no credit system.

However, the information that can be found in the extant documents lend support to a different interpretation of the conditions then. Under this alternative view, the redistributed rations were actually wages paid to workers, which were far beyond what was needed for subsistence only. Furthermore, the quantities paid out to the workers were differential, with high-status workers receiving many times more than did simple laborers. Therefore, these high-status workers had large surpluses—much more than their households needed in order to get by. The distribution of rations was measured out in the form of loaves of bread, but documents discovered include keys for the conversion of loaves into sacks of wheat or barley. Thus, it is found that the payment of wages ("rations") was measured in units of volume of grains. In addition, owners of fields and workshops received income from their activity (beyond the taxes they paid the authorities). This mode of payment, together with income from farming and other activity, allowed recipients of income from any source, including the authorities, to amass surpluses. Surpluses in private hands were used to purchase goods, procure other services, and invest in residential structures and burial monuments. The authorities used their surpluses to investment in infrastructure, buildings, tombs, management of the palace and the temples, and welfare activity, such as helping the less able and, at times of drought and famine, the population at large.

These surpluses, earned by households, the palace, and the temples, acted in combination with a demand factor for items other than food and with the system of supply of goods and services to create a developed local market throughout Egypt. Marketplaces were established in central locations, such as piers on the Nile. The market in Egypt used means of exchange to simplify exchange and mitigate transaction costs. The means of exchange ("money") that this market used, aided by the measures of volume that the authorities established, was the most common commodity that households possessed: grain (barley and wheat). The

20 Bleiberg 1995, 1373–1375.

most common unit of weight of copper for payment was the deben (91 grams in the old kingdom).[21]

In the New Kingdom era, silver and gold were increasingly used as means of exchange, particularly in transactions involving expensive assets, such as homes, cattle, and land.[22] The exchange rates among them at the time were roughly 100:1 silver to copper, 2:1 silver to gold, and half a *khar* ("sack") (8 *heqat*) of grain (38 liters) per *deben* of copper. A silver deben was worth 60 khars of grain.

Table 3: Measures of Volume in Ancient Egypt.

Name	Meaning	Volume	Number of units
Hinu	Jar	0.48 liter	
Heqat	Barrel	4.8 liters	10 hinas per heqat
Khar[23]	Sack	76.8 liters	16 heqats per khar

Source: Shaw I., *Oxford History of Ancient Egypt*, Oxford, 2000

Workers' salaries were paid in sacks of wheat. In the New Kingdom era (in Deir el-Medina), monthly salaries varied with the worker's occupation. A watchman received 1.5 khar (75 kilo) of wheat per month; a skilled worker or scribe received 7.5. For subsistence, a person needed roughly 40% of a khar as food; the rest was a surplus that could be traded in the market for other foodstuffs or sundry goods.[24] In addition to sacks of grain, workers received portions of oil, fish, fruit, and vegetables. There is evidence of the use of units of volume of grain (usually the khar—"sack") for making other payments: leasing fees for fields, paying taxes, and hiring transport services in the form of boats on the Nile.

Some examples of prices in Deir el-Medina under the New Kingdom include: 2 hinas of oil (liter)—one deben of copper; half a khar—8 heqats of wheat; 2 hinas of beer—half a deben of copper—5 heqats of wheat; 50 fish—2 debens of copper; one item of clothing—2.5 debens of copper; 1 plaited mattress—1 deben of copper; 1 young she-slave—4 debens of silver.

21 This was also the case in the New Kingdom era 16th–11th century BCE). In earlier times, the deben was 27 grams of copper.

22 Silver already appeared in ancient Egypt in the era preceding the dynasties. It was locally sourced and appeared together with gold in the form of electrum. Nicholson and Shae 2000, 170; Schorsch 2001, 55–57.

23 In the Old Kingdom and Middle Kingdom eras (3000–2250 BCE and 2250–1550 BCE, respectively), the khar was 10 heqat or 48 liters.

24 Janssen 1975.

Caches from the New Kingdom era (discovered, for example, at Tel el-Amarna) were found to contain pieces of copper, silver, and gold, as well as rings and ingots of these metals, that were evidently designed to function as units of weight (e.g., a *qedet* ring, one-tenth of a deben—9.1 grams or a deben ingot) (see photo of the cache below).[25]

Table 4: Weights in Ancient Egypt.

Name	Meaning	Volume	Number of units
Qedet-kite[26]	Qedet	9.1 grams	
Deben[27]	Deben	91 grams	10 qedets per deben (copper)

Source: Shaw I., Oxford History of Ancient Egypt, Oxford, 2000

There were permanent ratios among the units of means of exchange for goods, merging all of them into one system. Means of exchange such as copper and fish did not preclude the use of other goods as means of exchange. Measurement units of goods such as oil, salt, and textiles were used to make payments, and their exchange rates, too, were constant with the common units of means of exchange. In the New Kingdom period, the use of weight units of copper or silver is identified from the Deir el-Medina documents. Such a weight (1 seniu = 1/12 of a deben) was invoked as an abstract concept to calculate the total value of a collective of assets that was exchanged. In a document found that presents mathematical problems, students are asked to calculate the total value of weight units of gold, silver, and lead using silver seniu.[28]

The wall painting below depicts market day in ancient Egypt at a Nile River port. In the painting, from the tomb of Niankhkhnum and Khnumhotep in Saqqara, from the fifth dynasty of the Old Kingdom (2494–2345 BCE), the inscriptions and the buyers' shoulder bags (see Lines 3 and 4) and the conversation between the buyers and sellers as depicted by the hieroglyphs, are indicative of the use of commodities (pieces of copper or grains) as means of exchange.

25 Kemp 2006, 245.
26 There was a smaller unit of weight shaty/seniu. Its value was one-twelfth of a deben It was used to calculate exchange transactions in the market or in arithmetic problems. The unit was called a shat or a shaty in the Old Kingdom. In the New Kingdom, it was called a seniu. (Saifullah 2006, 6).
27 In the New Kingdom. In the Old and Middle Kingdom eras, the copper deben was 23.7 grams and the golden deben 13.6 grams. Weights found in excavations are inconsistent in the course of those periods.
28 Janssen 1975, 102–108, and Rhind Mathematical Papyrus.

Although the Sumerian and Egyptian societies were similar in terms of their form of organization and structure, they differed substantially in other respects. In Egypt, no rapid urbanization occurred as in Sumer, and its population remained essentially rural. In Sumer, the population coalesced around city-states and the structure of society settled into large units—as in the Akkadian and Ur III empires—at a later stage. Egypt became a unified entity in an early stage of the process. Pharaoh's status as a god was embedded in Egyptian religion and society and pharaonic rule remained stable for thousands of years. As the writer stated in the introduction to this book, some researchers claim that an agrarian system based on centralized delivery of water that was transparent to the authorities encouraged centralized rule, whereas a system in which information about water supply was vague (not "transparent") promoted decentralized governance. In the Egyptian system, the pharaohs had central information about the height and timing of the flooding of the Nile; this is an example of the first kind of system. The system in Mesopotamia, in contrast, fits the latter definition, because information about multiple irrigation systems there was decentralized and various organizations and numerous cities possessed it.[29]

As the large organizations in Sumer found it necessary to make production and payment more efficient, writing began to develop and undergo massive changes until it attained its final design in cuneiform. In Egypt, writing served as a cultural instrument from the outset; Pharaohs and the temples used it in its initial form, with minor changes, for thousands of years.[30] Activities associated with the construction of large monuments were of major importance in Egypt; they mostly surrounded the death rite, an essential component of culture and society. The Egyptians invested prodigious efforts in constructing memorial monuments and tombs, as they did in developing the mines from which they obtained stone for construction. The Sumerians engaged in intensive interregional trade on a private basis, while the Egyptians intermittently sent interregional trade missions, as the status of local and interregional traders was low in Egyptian society.

Epilogue: The Hanseatic League In the Middle Ages and Later

Throughout history, interregional traders have ensured their safety and benefits by establishing similar institutions wherever they operated.[31] The institutions

29 Mayshar et al., 2011, 40–42.
30 Ray 1986, 307–316; Frankfort 1967, 66.
31 Howel 2003, 486–490.

that have been researched most intensively are the medieval and modern trade organizations[32] known as "merchant guilds," which operated mainly in Western and Southern Europe. These entities, unlike the Assyrians' organizations, were based on choice and originated mainly in the absence of strong central authorities that would provide the traders with backing. As time passed, they obtained and exercised political power. The most famous organization of this kind was the Hanseatic League,[33] which was created in the twelfth century in Germany and lasted until the seventeenth century. Centering most of its activity in Northern and Western Europe, it united the maritime traders who operated out of main ports in the region, foremost in Germany, travelling to destination countries and centers of maritime trade in the eastern and western Baltic region, Norway, the Low Countries, and England. The Hanseatic traders-maintained trading posts—**Kontors**—in the destination areas. From the mid-fourteenth century onward, they had four main trading posts: in London (wool and textiles), Novgorod (furs, beeswax, and Silk Road products), Bergen (dried fish), and Bruges (textiles).

In the wake of the collapse of the Frederick II's German (Holy Roman) Empire in 1250, the German maritime traders attained more and more power in the municipal councils of the merchant-cities in Germany and organized to protect themselves against robbers, pirates, and pressure from the authorities in the ports of trade. They utilized their concerted power to negotiate with the authorities to obtain privileges in the areas of law, taxation, and living and trading conditions. The activities of the trading post, the Kontor, were conducted on the basis of agreements with local authorities. These accords cemented the traders' status, allowed them to manage their community affairs, determined the taxes they would pay on their trade, gave them exclusive trading privileges, and protected them against government intervention and crimes of the local population. The posts operated in specified and protected zones in the destination ports. Each Kontor was organized as a society with its own seal. It was run by a traders' plenary (the Steven) that elected an executive council of elders (in German: Oldermann) and assessors who managed the financial system and daily life. The traders remitted tax payments, rent, and fines to the Kontor treasury. The Kontor erected public structures, such as conference halls, offices, shops and warehouses, a church, a prison, traders' housing, and built infrastructures, such as roads, squares, and city walls and gates. It maintained judicial systems and meted out punishments for miscreants (e.g., smugglers) in ways that included imprisonment, deportation, denial of entry to the Kontor, and confiscation of merchandise.

32 Grief et al. 1994, 745–776.
33 Dolliner 1964.

The organizations of the Assyrian traders strongly resemble those of the Hanseatic League; they both developed webs of agreements with local rulers, both emphasized the political and organizational structure of colonies and services for traders, and both had similar financing and bookkeeping systems. There were, however, important differences. The Assyrian system was a continuation or an extension of the governing apparatus of Assur city, its judicial system was more developed, and the Assyrian traders used the organization as an economic instrument for the conduct of large commercial transactions.

The phenomenon of the Old Assyrian Trade was evidently unknown outside of its own period. There is no evidence of its being documented anywhere but in the collections of traders' documents, but it is not its absence in later documents that attests to its lack of influence in subsequent generations. Rather, it may be argued that it was the paucity of sources from Assur of that era and shortly thereafter that caused the phenomenon to vanish from historical memory.

Hence, the great similarity of the institutions that the traders created in the Middle Ages and those of the Assyrian traders can be explained not by the transmission of information between historical eras but by the development of institutions that met traders' needs in similar surroundings. Traders in both epochs engaged in long-term commerce (overland or marine) in a similarly structured environment of city-states. Both faced acute risks as they moved from market to market, and rulers in their markets behaved similarly. The traders had no armed forces with which they could deal with risks. They did, however, both have basic economic institutions that could be found in ancient times, including property rights, organizational structures, markets, means of exchange, agreements and contracts, and enforcement institutions. In both periods, the traders tailored these institutions to meet their needs; for example, they created trade organizations in their target regions in order to negotiate with local rulers, conduct daily life and commerce in their colonies or trading ports, and engage in enforcing the institutions of trade.

The differences between the institutions in these two eras lay mainly in the extent of the relationship between the political structure of the city and the commercial activity. In the Assyrian system, traders played central roles in the political structure and dominated the governing institutions in Assur; medieval traders had less influence on the authorities. As a result, the Assyrians could create the organizational and financial framework of the limited partnership that the authorities in Assur administered, something that the medieval traders neither knew nor operated. The Assyrian traders' efficient judicial system, comprised of courts, jurisprudence, and rules of enforcement, was also unmatched in the later era.

Thus, one may describe the systems of the Assyrian trading institutions as more advanced than those of later eras. The traders' promissory notes were self-standing and collectible by anyone who held them. The trade organizations of Assur city and the Karum of Kanesh were economic entities that engaged in large-scale commerce, much like modern trading companies. The Assyrians' financial institution of the "sack"—the limited partnership—made it possible to raise large sums of capital for the long term; it resurfaced in later times as means of financing limited maritime transactions only.

List of Tables and Maps

https://doi.org/10.1515/9783111065533-009

Abbreviations

AAA	Annals of Archaeology and Anthropology (Liverpool)
AfO	Archiv für Orientforschung (Vienna)
AKT	Ankara Kültepe Tabletleri, Ankaraner Kültepe Texte (Ankara)
AnOr	Analecta Orientalia (Rome)
ATHE	B. Kienast, Die altassyrischen Texte des Orientalischen Seminars der Universität Heidelberg und der Sammlung Erlenmeyer, Berlin, 1960.
BIN	Babylonian Inscriptions in the Collection of J. B. Nies (New Haven)
CAD	Chicago Assyrian Dictionary
CDA	A Concise Dictionary of Akkadian, Weisbaden 2000.
CCT	Cuneiform Texts from Cappadocian Tablets in the British Museum (London)
CTMMA	Cuneiform Texts in the Metropolitan Museum of Art (New York)
EL	G. Eisser et J. Lewy, Die altassyrischen Rechtsurkunden vum Kultépé MVAG 33 EL 1930 et MVAG 35/3 = EL 2, 1935
HUCA	Hebrew Union College Annual (Cincinnati)
ICK	Inscriptions Cunéiformes du Kultépé (Prague)
JCS	Journal of Cuneiform Studies (New Haven/Boston)
JSOR	Journal of the Society of Oriental Research (Chicago, Toronto)
JESHO	Journal of the Economic and Social History of the Orient (Leiden)
Kt	Unpublished Tablets from Kültepe (Ankara)
KBo	Keilinschrifttexte aus Boghazköi (Berlin)
KTB, KTH	J. Lewy, Die Kültepetexte der Sammlung, Rudolf Blanckertz, Berlin, 1929.
KTH (Hahn)	J. Lewy, Die Kültepetexte der Sammlung Frida Hahn, Berlin, 1930.
KTK	N. B. Jankowska, Klinopisnye Teksty iz Kjul'Tepe v Sobraniakh SSSR, Moscou, 1968.
KTP	F. J. Stephenes, The Cappadocian Tablets in the University of Pennsylvania Museum JSOR 11, 1927, pp. 101–136.
KTS	Keilschrifttexte in den Antiken Museen zu Stambul (Istanbul)
KUG	K. Hecker, Die Keilschrifttexte der Universitätsbibliothek Giessen. Berichte und Arbeiten aus der Universitätsbibliothek Giessen 9, Giessen, 1966.
Kültepe	Unpublished tablets from Kültepe
Landsberger	H. G. Güterbock and G. Komoróczy (eds.) Studies in Honor of Benno Landberger on his Seventy-fifth Birthday AS 16, Chicago, 1965.
MVAG	Mitteilungen der Vorderasiatisch-Aegyptischen Gesellschsaft
OIP	Oriental Institute Publications (Chicago)
Or	Orientalia (Rome)
Pa	University of Pennsylvania Museum Old Assyrian Texts
Prague I	K. Hecker, G. Kryszat and L. Matouš, Kapadokische Keilschrifttafeln aus den Sammlungen der Karlsuniversität Prag, Prague, 1998.
RA	Revue d'assyriologie et d'archéologie orientale (Paris)
RIMA I	Royal Inscriptions of Mesopotamia, Assyrian Period I: AssyrianRrulers of the Third and Second Mmillennia BCE (to 1115 BCE), Toronto 1987.
RT	Recueil de Travaux, Relatifs á la Philologie et á L'achéologie Égyptiennes et Assyriennes (Paris)
TC	Tablettes Cappadociennes du Louvre (Paris)
TCL	Textes Cunéiformes du Louvre (Paris)

https://doi.org/10.1515/9783111065533-010

TIM	Texts in the Iraq Museum
TPAK	Tablettes Paléo-Assyriennes de Kültepe (Istanbul)
TTAED	Türk Tarih, Arkeologya ve Ethnografya Dergisi (Ankara)
TTC	G. Contenau Trente Tablettes Cappadociennes, Paris, 1919.
TuM	Texte und Materialien der Frau Professor Hilprecht Collection (Leipzig)
UAR	Hirsch H., Untersuchungen zur Altassyyrischen Religion AfO 13/14, 1961.
VAS/VS	Vorderasiatische Schriftdenkmäler der (Königl.) Museen zu Berlin (Berlin)
VAT	Tablets in the Collections of the Staatliche Museen, (Berlin)
Veenhof AV	Veenhof Anniversary Volume: Studies Presented to Klaas R. Veenhof on the Occasion of his Sixty-Fifth Birthday, Leiden 2001.

Maps

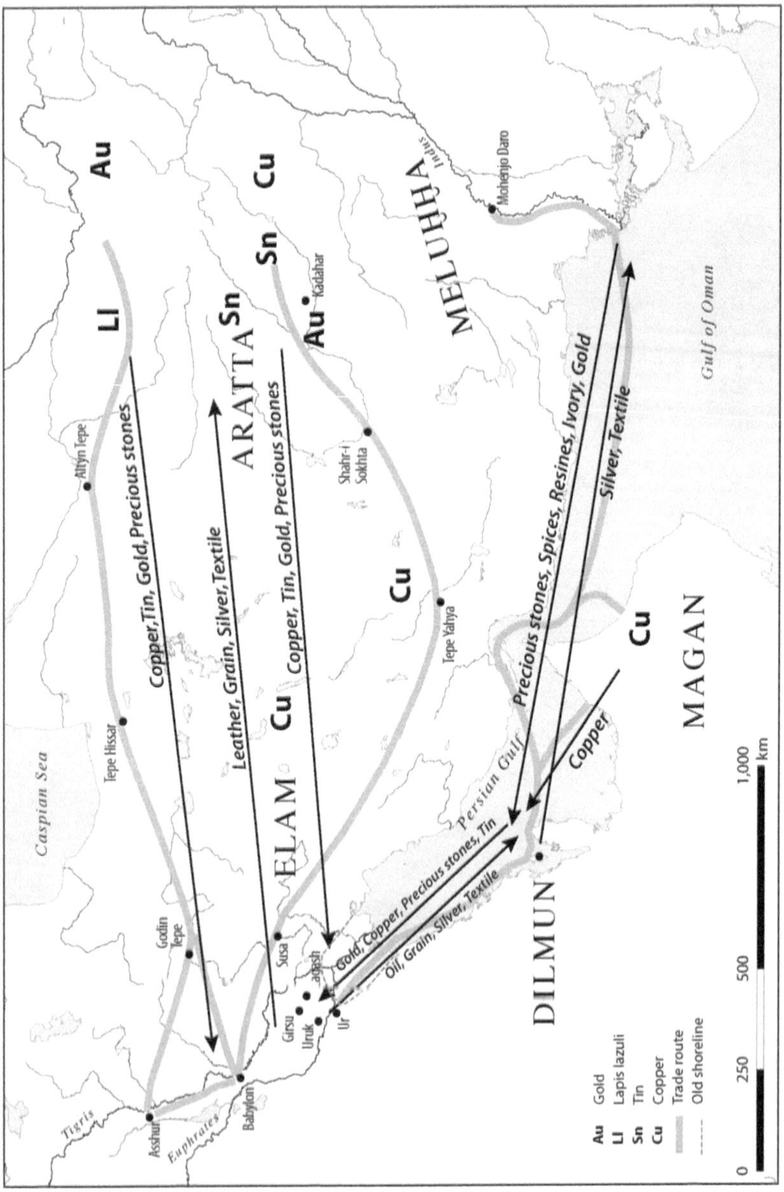

Fig. 1: Map of trade in the 3rd millenium BCE. Source: Leemans 1960; Postgate 1995, pp. 206 – 222; Potts 1994, pp. 144 – 168

https://doi.org/10.1515/9783111065533-011

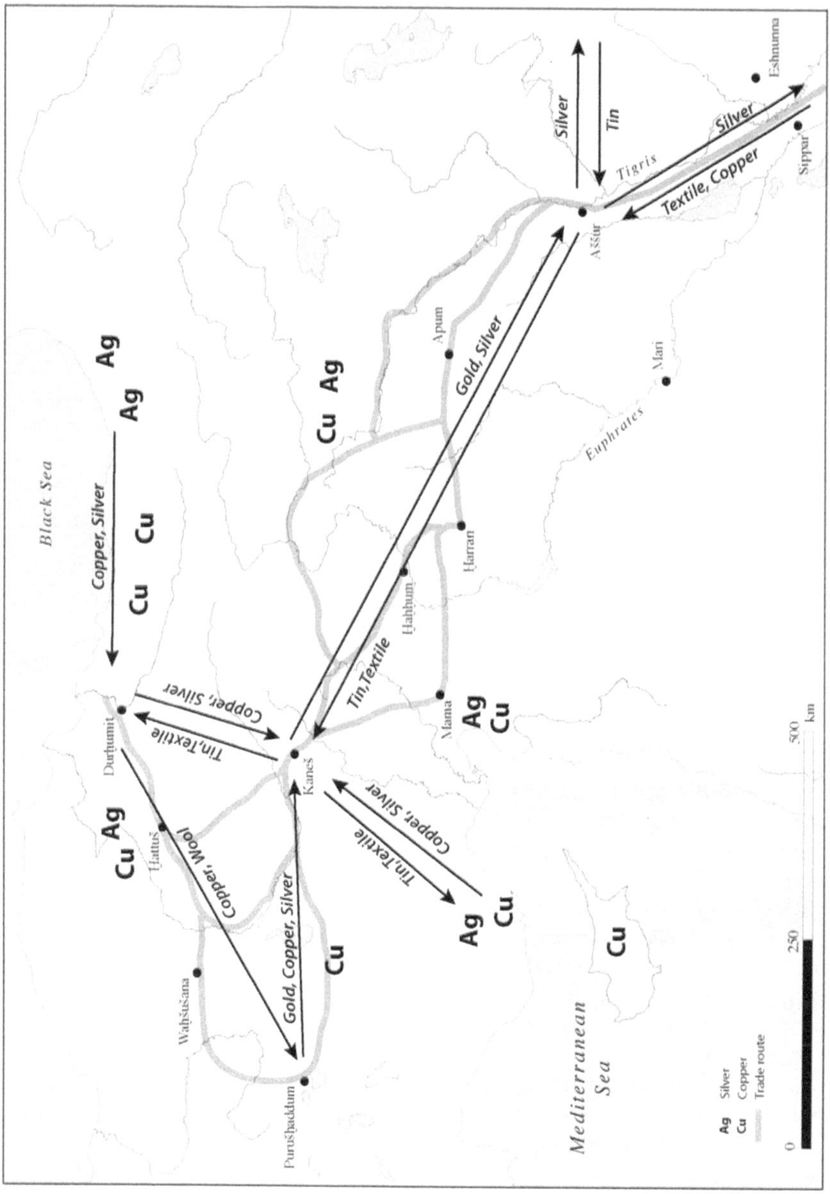

Fig. 2: Map of the Old Assyrian trade in begging of the 2nd millenium BCE. Source: Barjamovic 2011, 2008, pp. 87–100;
Michel 2004, p. 190; Veenhof 2008, pp. 79–93

Bibliography

Alchian A. A. 1977: "Why Money," *Journal of Money, Credit and Banking.* 9/ 1/2, pp. 133 – 140.

Alchian A. A. 1987: "Property Rights," *The New Palgrave: A Dictionary of Economics*, London, pp.1029 – 1034.

Alchian A. A. and Demsetz H. 1972: "Production, Information Costs, and Economic Organization," The American Economic Review, 62/5, pp. 777 – 795.

Allen W. R. 1987: "Mercantilism," in The New Palgrave: A Dictionary of Economics, Vol. 3, London, pp. 445 – 449.

Astour M. C. 1995: "Overland Trade Routes in Ancient Western Asia," in Sasson J. M. (ed.), Civilizations of the Ancient Near East, Vol. I, New York, pp. 1401 – 1420.

Bailkey N. 1967: "Early Mesopotamian Constitutional Development," The American Historical Review, 72/4, pp. 1211 – 1236.

Baltensperger E. 1987: "Credit," The New Palgrave: A Dictionary of Economics, Vol. 1, London, pp. 715 – 717.

Barjamovic G. 2008: "The Geography of Trade Assyrian Colonies in Anatolia c. 1975 – 1725 BCE and a Study of Early Interregional Networks of Exchange," in Dercksen J. G. (ed.), Anatolia and the Jazira During the Old Assyrian Period, Leiden, pp. 87 – 100.

Barjamovic G. 2011: A Historical Geography of Anatolia in the Old Assyrian Colony Period, Copenhagen.

Barjamovic G. 2018: "Interlocking Commercial Networks and the Infrastructure of Trade in Western Asia During Bronze Age," in Kristiansen K., Lindkvist T. and Myrdal J. (eds) Trade and Civilasation. Economic Networks and Cultural Ties from Prehistory to the Early Modern Era. Cambridge, pp. 113 – 142.

Barjamovic G., Hertel T. and Larsen M. T. 2012: *Ups and Down at Kanesh: Chronology, History and Society in the Old Assyrian Period,* Leiden.

Bleiberg E. 1995: "The Economy of Ancient Egypt," in Sasson J.M et al. (eds.) *Civilizations of the Ancient Near East,* Vol. III, New York, pp. 1373 – 1385.

Blum U. and Dudley L. 2003: "Standardized Latin and Medieval Economic Growth," *European Review of Economic History,* August, pp. 213 – 238.

Brezis E. S. 2003: "Mercantilism" in *The Oxford Encyclopedia of Economic History,* Vol. 3, Oxford, pp. 482 – 485.

Bulgarelli O. 2011: "Financial and Economic Activity in Mesopotamia", in Barjamovic et al (eds), *Akkade is King,* Leiden, pp 37 – 53.

Butlin R. A. 1993*: Historical Geography: Through the Gates of Space and Time*, London.

Casson L. 1974: *Travel in the Ancient World,* Toronto.

Charpin D. 1986: "Transmission des titres de propriétéet constitution des archives privées en Babylonie ancienne," in Veenhof K. (ed.), *Cuneiform Archives and Libraries*, Istanbul, pp. 121 – 140.

Charpin D. and Todd J. M. 2010: *Writing, Law, and Kingship in Old Babylonian Mesopotamia*, Chicago.

Chick V. 1987: "Finance," *The New Palgrave: A Dictionary of Economics*, Vol. 2, London, pp. 322 – 337.

Coase R.H. 1937: "The Nature of the Firm," *Economica,* new series, IV, 13 – 16, pp. 386 – 405.

Coase R.H. 1992: "The Institutional Structure of Production," *The American Economic Review,* 82/4, pp. 713 – 719.

Collon D. 1997: "Ancient Near Eastern Seals," in Collon D. (ed.), *7,000 Years of Seals*, London, pp. 11 – 22.

https://doi.org/10.1515/9783111065533-012

Contenau G. 1919: *Trente Tablettes Cappadociennes*, Paris.

Cripps E. L. 2007: *Land Tenure and Social Stratification in Ancient Mesopotamia*, BAR International Series 1676.

Dalton G. 1965: "Primitive Money," in *American Anthropologist*, New Series 67/1, pp. 44–65.

Darby H. C. 1991: "Historical Geography," in Green D. B. (ed.), *Historical Geography: A Methodological Portrayal*, Maryland, pp. 59–82.

Deimel A. 1931: *Sumerische Tempelwirtschaft zur Zeit Urukaginas und seiner Vorgänger*, Rome.

Demsetz H. 1964: "The Exchange and Enforcement of Property Rights," *Journal of Law and Economics*, 7, pp. 11–16.

Demsetz H. 1966: "Some Aspects of Property Rights," *Journal of Law and Economics*, 9, pp. 61–70.

Demsetz H. 1967: "Towards a Theory of Property Rights," *The American Economic Review*, 57/2, pp. 347–359.

Demsetz H. 1988: "The Theory of the Firm Revisited," *Journal of Law and Economics and Organization*, 4/1, pp. 141–161.

Demsetz H. 1998: "Property Rights," *The New Palgrave: Dictionary of Economics and the Law*, Vol. 3, London, pp. 144–155.

Demsetz H. 2002: "Toward a Theory of Property Rights II: The Competition between Private and Collective Ownership," *The Journal of Legal Studies*, 31/2, Part 2: The Evolution of Property Rights, pp. S653–S672.

Dercksen J. G. 1996: *The Old Assyrian Copper Trade in Anatolia*, Istanbul.

Dercksen J. G. 1997: "The Silver of Gods: On Old Assyrian *ikribū*," *Archivum Anatolicum* (ArAn) 3, Ankara, pp. 75–100.

Dercksen J. G. 1999: "On the Financing of Old Assyrian Merchants," in Dercksen J. G. (ed.), *Trade and Finance in Ancient Mesopotamia*, Leiden, pp. 85–99

Dercksen J. G. 2000: 'Institutional and Private in the Old Assyrian Period," in Bongenaar A. C. V. M. (ed.), *Interdependency of Institutions and Private Enterpreneurs*, Leiden, pp. 135–152.

Dercksen J. G. 2004: *Old Assyrian Institutions*, Leiden.

Dercksen J. G. 2008: "Observations on Land Use and Agriculture in Kaneš," in Michel C. (ed.), *Old Assyrian Studies: in memory of Paul Garelli*, Leiden, pp. 139–157.

Dercksen J. G. 2008a: The Assyrian Colony at Kanesh, in *Hattuša – Boğazköy: Das Hethiterreich im Spannungsfeld des Alten Orient*, Wiesbaden, 109–124.

Dercksen J. G. 2011: "Weeks, Months and Years in Old Assyrian Chronology," in Old Assyrian Chronology, *Bibliotheca Orientalis* N^0 3–4, 2011, pp. 233–243.

Dercksen J. G. 2011a: "The Exchange of Sacrificial Gifts Among Old Assyrian merchants," in During B. S, Wossink A. and Akkermans P. M. M. G. *Correlates of Complexity*, Leiden.

Dercksen J. G. 2014: "The Old Assyrian Trade and its Participants," in Baker H. D. & Jursa M. (ed.), *Documentary Sources in Ancient Near Eastern and Greco-Roman Economic History. Methodology and practice*, Oxford, pp. 59–112.

Diakonoff I. M. 1971: "On the Structure of Old Babylonian Society," in Klengel H. (ed.), *Beiträge zur Sozialen Struktur des Alten Vorderasien*, Berlin, pp. 15–37.

Dollinger P. 1964: *The German Hansa*, Bristol.

Driver G. R. and Miles J. C. 1952: *The Babylonian Law: Laws of Hammurabi*, Oxford.

Einzig P. 1949: *Primitive Money: in its Ethnological, Historical and Economic Aspects*, London.

Englund R. K. 1998: "Texts from the Late Uruk Period," in Bauer J., et al. (eds.), *Mesopotamien, Späturuk-Zeit und Frühdynastische Zeit*, Freiburg, pp, 15–236.

Englund R. K. 2004: "Proto-Cuneiform Account-Books and Journals," in Hudson M. and Wunsch C. (eds.), *Creating Economic Order: record-keeping, Standardization, and the Development of Accounting in the Ancient Near East*, Bethesda. pp. 21–46.

Edzard D. O. 1999: "Private Land Ownership and its Relation to 'God' and 'State' in Sumer and Akkad," in Hudson M. and Levine B. A. (eds.), *Privatization in the Ancient Near East and Classical World*, Cambridge MA, pp. 109–128.

Erol H. 2019: "Old Assyrian Metal Trade, its Volume and Interactions," in *Belleten, Turk Tarih Kurumu*, Vol LXXXIII 2019. pp. 779–806.

Finley M. I. 1973: *The Ancient Economy*, London.

Foley D. 1987: "Money in Economic Activity," *The New Palgrave: A Dictionary of Economics*, Vol. 3, London, pp. 519–525.

Foster B. R. 1977: "Commercial Activity in Sargonic Mesopotamia," *Iraq*, 39/1, pp. 31–43.

Foster B. R. 1982: *Administration and Use of Institutional Land in Sargonic Sumer*, Copenhagen.

Foster B. R. 1983: "Selected Business Documents from Sargonic Mesopotamia," *Journal of Cuneiform Studies*, 35/ 3/4, pp. 147–175.

Franfort H. and Pendlebury J. D. S. 1933: *The City of Akhenaten*, London.

Garfinkle S. J. 2004: "Shepherds, Merchants, and Credit: Some Observations on Lending Practices in Ur III Mesopotamia," *Journal of the Economic and Social History of the Orient*, 47/1, pp. 1–30.

Garelli P. 1963: *Les Assyriens en Cappadoce*, Paris.

Gelb I. J. 1965: "The Ancient Mesopotamian Ration System," *Journal of Near Eastern Studies*, 24/3, pp. 230–243.

Gelb I. J. 1979: "Household and Family in Early Mesopotamia," in Lipinski E. (ed.), *State and Temple Economy in the Ancient Near East*, Leuven, pp. 1–97.

Gelb I. J. 1982: "Measures of Dry Liquid Capacity," *Journal of the American Oriental Society*, 102/4, pp. 585–590.

Gelb I. J., Steinkeller P. and Whiting Jr. R.M. 1991: *Earliest Land Tenure Systems in the Ancient Near East: Ancient Kudurrus*, University of Chicago, Oriental Institute Publications 104.

Getzler J. 1996: "Theories of Property and Economic Development," *Journal of Interdisciplinary History*, 26/4, pp. 639–669.

Gledhill J. and Larsen M. T. 1982: "The Polanyi Paradigm and a Dynamic Analysis of Archaic States," in Renfrew C., Rowlands M. J. and Segraves B. A. (eds.), *Theory and Explanation in Archaeology*, London, pp. 197–229.

Greif A. 1989: "Reputation and Coalitions in Medieval Trade: Evidence on the Maghribi Traders," *Journal of Economic History*, 49/4, pp. 857–882.

Greif A. 1992: "Institutions and International Trade: Lessons from the Commercial Revolution," *The American Economic Review*, 82/2, pp. 128–133.

Greif A. 1993: "Contract Enforceability and Economic Institutions in Early Trade: The Maghribi Traders' Coalition," *The American Economic Review*, 83/3, pp. 525–548.

Greif A. 2000: "The Fundamental Problem of Exchange: A Research Agenda in Historical Institutional Analysis," *European Review of Economic History*, 4, pp. 251–284.

Greif A. 2005: *Institutions and the Path to the Modern Economy: Lessons from Medieval Trade*, New York.

Greif A. 2005a: "Commitment, Coercion, and Markets: The Nature and Dynamics of Institutions Supporting Exchange," in Menard C. and Shirley M. (eds.), *Handbook of New Institutional Economics*, pp. 727–786.

Greif A., et al. 1994: "Coordination, Commitment, and Enforcement: The Case of the Merchant Guild," *Journal of Political Economy*, 102/4, pp. 745–776.

Groenewegen P. 1987: "Supply and Demand" in *The New Palgrave: A Dictionary of Economics*, Vol. 2, London, p. 553.

Gwaltney Jr. W. C. 1983: *The Pennsylvania Old Assyrian Texts*, Cincinnati.

Hallo W. W. 2004: "Bookkeeping in the 21st Century BCE," in Hudson M. and Wunsch C. (eds.), *Creating Economic Order: Record-keeping, Standardization, and Development of Accounting in the Ancient World*, Bethesda, pp. 89–106.

Hecker K. 1978: "*tib'imma atalkim* – Assyerinnen im kārumzeitlichen Anatolien," *Or*, 47, pp. 404–418.

Hecker K. 2003: "kunuk kārim saher rabi," *Studied Kienast*, pp. 183–196.

Heichelheim F. M. 1958: *An Ancient Economic History*, Leiden.

Heimpel W. 2009: *Workers and Construction* Work *at Garšana*, Bethesda.

Hejeebu S. 2003: "The Firm before 1800," in *The Oxford Encyclopedia of Economic History*, Vol. 2, Oxford, pp. 315–318.

Hertel T. 2013: *Old Assyrian Legal Practices: Law and Dispute in the Ancient Near East*, Leiden.

Hill P. 1987: "Market Places," in *The New Palgrave: A Dictionary of Economics*, Vol. 3, London, pp. 332–334.

Hirsch H. 1961: *Untersuchungen zur Altassyyrischen Religion, AfO 13/14.*

Homer S. and Sylla R. 1963: *A History of Interest Rates*, New Brunswick.

Howel M. 2003: "Merchant Guilds," in *The Oxford Encyclopedia of Economic History*, Vol. 2, Oxford, pp. 486–490.

Huberman G. 1987: "Arbitrage Pricing Theory," *The New Palgrave: A Dictionary of Economics*, Vol. I, London, pp. 106–109.

Hudson M. 2000: "How Interest Rates Were Set, 2500 BCE–1000 AD," *Journal of the Economic and Social History of the Orient*, May, pp. 132–161.

Hudson M. 2002: "Reconstructing the Origin of Interest-Bearing Debt and the Logic of Clean Slate," in Hudson M. and Van de Mieroop M. *Debt and Economic Renewal in the Ancient Near East*, Bethesda, pp. 7–58.

Huehnergard J. 1997: *A Grammer of Akkadian,*Harvard.

Ichisar M. 1981: *Les Arcive cappadociennes du marchand Imdīlum*, Paris.

Janssen J. J. 1975: *Commodity Prices from the Ramessid Period*, Leiden.

Jursa M. 2010: *Aspects of the Economic History of Babylonia in the First Millennium BC*, Munster.

Kaiser B. 2003: "Market Structure," *The Oxford Encyclopedia of Economic History*, Vol. 3, Oxford, pp. 439–442.

Kemp B. J. 2006: *Ancient Egypt: Anatomy of a Civilization*, London.

Keynes J. M. 1935: *A Treatise on Money*, London.

Kienast B. 1989: "The Old Assyrian *be'ūlātum*," *Journal of Cuneiform Studies*, 41/1, pp. 87–95.

Kindleberger C. P. 1993: *Financial History of Western Europe*, Oxford.

Kramer S. N. 1977: "Commerce and Trade: Gleanings from Sumerian Literature," *Iraq*, 39/1, pp. 59–66.

Kryszat G. 2008: "The Use of Writing Among the Anatolians," in Dercksen J. G. (ed.), *Anatoliya and the Jazira During the Old Assyrian Period*, Leiden, pp. 231–238.

Kuhrt A. 1995: *The Ancient Near East 3000–330 BCE*, London.

Kulakoğlu, F. and Kangal (eds) 2010: *Anatolia's Prologue. Kültepe Kanesh Karum, Assyrians in Istanbul*, Kayseri Metropolitan Municipality Cultural Publications 78, 40–51. Istanbul: Kayseri Metropolitan Municipality.

Jacobsen T. 1943: "Primitive Democracy in Ancient Mesopotamia," *Journal of Near Eastern Studies*, 11/3, pp. 159–172.

Lafont B. and Westbrook R. 2003: "Neo-Sumerian Period (Ur III)," in Westbrook R. (ed.), *A History of Ancient Near Eastern Law*, Leiden, pp. 183–226.

De Lara Y. G. 2003: "Commercial Partnerships," in *The Oxford Encyclopedia of Economic History*, Vol. 1, Oxford, pp. 480–483.

Larsen M. T. 1967: *Old Assyrian Caravan Procedures*, Istanbul.

Larsen M. T. 1976: *The Old Assyrian City-State and its Colonies*, Copenhagen.

Larsen M. T. 1977: "Seal Use in the Old Assyrian Period,", in Buccellati G. (ed.), *Bibliotheca Mesopotamica, Vol. 6*, Malibu, pp. 92–105.

Larsen M. T. 1977a: "Partnerships in the Old Assyrian Trade," *Iraq*, 39/1, pp. 119–149.

Larsen M. T. 1982: "Your Money or Your Life! A Portrait of an Assyrian Businessman," in Diakonoff I. M. (ed.), *Societies and Languages of the Ancient Near East*, Warminster, pp. 214–245.

Larsen M. T. 1987: "Commercial Networks in the Ancient Near East," in *Center and Periphery in the Ancient World*, Rowlands M., Larsen M. T., and Kristiansen K. (eds.), Cambridge, pp. 47–56.

Larsen M. T. 2002: *The Aššur-nādā Archive*, Leiden.

Larsen M. T. 2007: "Individual and Family in Old Assyrian Society," in *Journal of Cuneiform Studies*, 59, pp. 93–106.

Larsen M. T. 2008: "Archives and Filing Systems at Kültepe," in Michel C. (ed.), *Old Assyrian Studies: In Memory of Paul Garelli*, Leiden, pp. 77–88.

Larsen M. T. 2010: "The Archives of the Salim-Assur Family Vol. I," *Ankara Kültepe Tabletleri VI-a*, Ankara.

Larsen M. T. 2015: *Ancient Kanesh, a Merchant Colony in Bronze Age Anatolia*, Cambridge.

Ledyard J. O. 1987: "Market failure," *in The New Palgrave: A Dictionary of Economics*, Vol. 3, London, 326–328.

Leemans W. F. 1950: *The Old-Babylonian Merchant, His Business and His Social Position*, Leiden.

Leemans W. F. 1960: *Foreign Trade in the Old Babylonian Period*, Leiden 1960.

Leemans W. F. 1977: "The Importance of Trade: Some Introductory Remarks," *Iraq*, 39/1, pp. 1–10.

Lephorn R. J. 1995: "Royal Ideology and State Administration in Pharaonic Egypt," in Sasson J.M et al. (eds.) *Civilizations of the Ancient Near East*, Vol. III, New York, pp. 273–284.

Lessnof M. 2003: "Weber Thesis," *The Oxford Encyclopedia of Economic History*, Oxford, pp. 258–260.

Limet H. 1987: "The Cuisine of Ancient Sumer," in *The Biblical Archaeologist'*,50/3, pp. 132–147.

Littauer M. A., and Crouwel J. H. 1979: *Wheeled Vehicles and Ridden Animals in the Ancient Near East*, Leiden.

Liverani M. 2006: *Uruk: the First City*, London.

Malul M. 2010: Collections of Laws: and Other Legal Collections from the Ancient East, Haifa. (Hebrew)

Martin H. 1988: *Fara: A Reconstruction of the Ancient Mesopotamian City of Shuruppak*, Birmingham.

Massa M. and Palmisano A. 2017: "Change and Continuity in the Long-Distance Exchange Networks between Western/Central Anatolia, Northern Levant and Northern Mesopotamia, c.3200–1600 BCE, in *Journal of Anthropological Archaeology* 49 (2018), 65–87.

Mayshar J. at al. 2011: "Transparency, Appropriability and the Early State,", in *ISET Working Papers Series*, WP 02–11, Tbilisi.

Meijer D. J. W. 2001: "Long Distance Trade: Some Remarks on the Ancient Syrian Economy," in Van Soldt W. H. et al. (eds.), *Veenhof Anniversary Volume*, Leiden, pp. 325–340.

Michalowski P. 1983: "History as Charter: Some Observation in the Sumerian King List," in *Journal of the American Oriental Society*, 103, pp. 237 ff.
Michel C. 1986: Rédition des trente tablettes "cappadociennes" de Contenau, *RA* 80, pp. 105 – 140.
Michel C. 1991: *Innāya dans les tablettes Paleo-Assyriennes*, Paris.
Michel C. 1996: "Proprietes Immobiliers dans les Tablettes Paleo-Assyriennes," in Veenhof K. R. (ed.), *Houses and Households in Ancient Mesopotamia*, Istanbul, pp. 285 – 300.
Michel C. 2001: *Correspondance des marchands de Kaneš au début du II millénaire avant J.C.*, Paris.
Michel C. 2003: *Old Assyrian Bibliography*, Leiden.
Michel C. 2004: "The *Perdum*-Mule, a Mount for Distinguished Persons in Mesopotamia during the First Half of the Second Millennium BCE," in *Men and Animals*, proceedings of the conference at the Swedish Institute, Rome, pp. 190 – 200.
Michel C. 2005/6: *Old Assyrian Bibliography 1*, Archive fur Orientforschung (AfO), Bd. 51 (2005 – 2006) pp. 436 – 449. Institut fur Orientalistik.
Michel C. 2011: *Old Assyrian Bibliography 2*, Archive fur Orientforschung (AfO), Bd. 52 (2011) pp. 416 – 437. Institut fur Orientalistik.
Michel C. 2015: *Old Assyrian Bibliography 3*, Archive fur Orientforschung (AfO), Bd. 53 (2015) pp. 525 – 559. Institut fur Orientalistik.
Michel C. 2015a: "Considerations on the Assyrian Settlement at Kaneš," in (Eckart Frahm dir.) Halshs-01186440, archives-ouvertes.fr
Michel C. 2017: Economic and Social Aspects of the Old Assyrian Loan Contract', in (Eckart Frahm dir.) Halshs-0146527, archives-ouvertes.fr
Michel C. 2018: "Women and Real Estate in the Old Assyrian Texts," in (Eckart Frahm dir.) Halshs-01674007, archives-ouvertes.fr.
Michel C. 2020: "Economy, Society, and Daily Life in the Old Assyrian Period," in (Eckart Frahm dir.) Halshs-02421686, archives-ouvertes.fr
Moorey P. R. S. 1994: *Ancient Mesopotamians Materials and Industries*, Oxford.
Muhly J. D. 1973: *Copper and Tin. The Distribution of Mineral Resources and the Nature of the Metals Trade in the Bronze Age*, Hamden.
Muhly J. D. 1985: Sources of Tin and the Beginnings of Bronze Metallurgy, *American Journal of Archaeology*, 89/2, pp. 275 – 291.
Nicholson P. T. and Shaw I. 2000: *Ancient Egyptian Materials and Technology*, Cambridge.
Niehans J. 1987: "Transaction Costs," *The New Palgrave: A Dictionary of Economics*, London, pp. 676 – 679.
Nissen H. J. 1988: *The Early History of the Ancient Near East 9000 – 2000 B.C.*, Chicago.
North D.C. 1977: "Markets and Other Allocation Systems in History: The Challenge of Karl Polanyi," *The Journal of European Economic History*, 6/1, pp. 703 – 716.
North D.C. 1981: *Structure and Change in Economic History*, London.
North D.C. 1991: Institutions, *Journal of Economic Perspectives*, 5/1, pp. 97 – 112.
North D.C. 1992: "Institutions and Economic Theory," *American Economist*, Spring, pp. 3 – 6.
North D.C. 1997: "Transaction Costs Through Time," in Menard C. (ed.), *Transaction Costs Economics: Recent Developments*, Cheltenham, pp. 149 – 160.
North D.C. 2003: "Markets," in *The Oxford Encyclopedia of Economic History*, Vol. 3, Oxford, pp. 432 – 439.
North D.C. 2005: *Understanding the Process of Economic Change*, Princeton.
O'Connor D. 1995: "The Social and Economic Organization of Ancient Egyptian Temples," in Sasson J.M et al. (eds.) *Civilizations of the Ancient Near East*, Vol. I, New York, pp.319 – 329.

Oppenheim A. L. 1954: "The Seafaring Merchants of Ur," *Journal of the American Oriental Society* 74, pp. 6 – 17.
Orlin L. L. 1970: *Assyrian Colonies in Cappadocia*, Paris.
Panico C. 1987: "Interest Rates," in *The New Palgrave: A Dictionary of Economics*, Vol. 2, London, pp. 877 – 879.
Pettinato G. 1986: *Ebla: A New Look at History*, Baltimore.
Polanyi K. 1957: *The Great Transformation*, Boaton.
Polanyi K. 1977: *The Livelihood of Man*, New York.
Postgate J. N. 1995: *Early Mesopotamia: Society and Economy at the Dawn of History*, London.
Potts D. T. 1994: *Mesopotamia and the East*, Oxford.
Potts D. T. 1997: *Mesopotamian Civilization: The Material Foundations*, Cornell.
Powell M. A. 1977: "Sumerian Merchant and the Problem of Profit," *Iraq*, 39, pp. 23 – 29.
Powell M. A. 1978: "A Contribution to the History of Money in Mesopotamia Prior to the Invention of Coinage," in Hruška B. and Komoróczy G. (eds.), *Frestschrift Lubor Matouš*, Budapest, pp. 211 – 243.
Powell M. A. 1990: "Identification and Interpretation of Long Term Price Fluctuations in Babylonia: More on the History of Money in Mesopotamia," Altorientalische Forschungen 17, 95 – 118.
Powell M. A. 1994: "Elusive Eden: Private Property at the Dawn of History," *Journal of Cuneiform Studies*, 46, pp. 99 – 104.
Powell M. A. 1996: "Money in Mesopotamia," *Journal of the Economic and Social History of the Orient*, 39/3, pp. 224 – 242.
Powell M. A. 1999: "Monies, Motives and Methods in Babylonian Economies," in Dercksen J. D. (ed.), *Trade and Finance in Ancient Mesopotamia*, Istanbul, pp. 5 – 23.
Pryor J. H. 1977: "The Origin of the Commenda Contract," *Speculum*, 52/1, pp. 5 – 37.
Quiggin A. H. 1949: *A Survey of Primitive Money*, London.
Rahmstorf L. and Stratford E.(ed.) 2019: *Weights and Marketplace: from the Bronze Age to the Early Modern Period*, Gotingen
Read J. 1997: "Sumerian Origins," in Finkel and Geller (eds), *Sumerians Gods and their Representations*, Groningen, pp. 221 – 229.
Ray J. D. 1986: "The Emergence of Writing in Egypt," in *World Archaeology*, 17/3, pp. 307 – 316.
Renger J. M. 1984: "Patterns of Non-Institutional Trade and Non-Commercial Exchange in Ancient Mesopotamia at the Beginning of the Second Millennium B.C.," in Archi A. (ed.), *Circulation of Goods in a Non-palatial Context in the Ancient Near East*, Incunabula Graeca 82, pp. 31 – 123.
Renger J. M. 1994: "On Economic Structures in the Ancient Mesopotamia," *Orientalia*, 63, pp. 157 – 208.
Renger J. M. 1995: "Institutional, Communal, and Individual Ownership or Possession of Arable Land in Ancient Mesopotamia from the end of the Fourth Millennium B.C.," in *Chicago-Kent Law Review*, 71/1. pp. 269 – 319.
Renger J. M. 2003: "Trade and Markets in the Ancient Near East. Theoretical and Factual Implications," in Zaccagnini C. (ed.), *Mercanti e Politica Nel Mondo Antico*, Roma, pp. 15 – 137.
Renger J. M. 2007: Economy of Ancient Mesopotamia: A General Outline, in Leick G. (ed.) *The Babylonian World*, New York & London, pp.187 – 209.
Ribstein L. E. 1998: "Partnership," *The New Palgrave: A Dictionary of Economics*, 3, London, pp. 10 – 13.
Rice M. 1990: *Egypt Making: The Origin of Ancient Egypt 5000 – 2000BCE*, London.
Robertson J. F. 1995: "The Social and Economic Organization of Ancient Mesopotamian Temples," in Sasson J. M. (ed.) *Civilizations of the Ancient Near East*, Vol. I, New York, pp. 443 – 500.

Roth M. T. 1997: *Law Collections from Mesopotamia and Asia Minor*, Atlanta.
Rutherford D. 1992: *Rutledge Dictionary of Economics*, London.
Rutherford D. 2002: *Rutledge Dictionary of Economics*, London and New York.
Ryan A. 1987: "Property," *in The New Palgrave: A Dictionary of Economics*, Vol. 3, London, pp. 1029–1031.
Scherer F. M. 1987: "Market Structure," *in The New Palgrave: A Dictionary of Economics*, Vol. 3, London, pp. 342–345.
Shavell S. 1998: "Contract," *The New Palgrave: Dictionary of Economics and the Law*, Vol. 1, London, pp. 436–445.
Silver M. 1985: *Economic Structures of the Ancient Near East*, Totava.
Silver M. 1995: "Economic Structure of Antiquity," in Schwab G. (eds), *Contributions in Economics and Economic History* 95–159, London.
Silver M. 2004: "Modern Ancients," in Rollinger R. and Christoph U. (eds.), *Commerce and Monetary Systems in the Ancient World: Means of Transmission and Cultural Interaction*, Stuttgart, pp. 65–87.
Skaist A. 1994: *The Old Babylonian Loan Contract: Its History and Geography*, Ramat Gan.
Smith A. 1976: *An Inquiry into the Nature and Causes of the Wealth of Nations*, Campbell R.H. and Skinner A.S. (eds.), Oxford.
Snell D. C. 1982: *Ledgers and Prices. Early Mesopotamian Merchant Accounts*, New Haven.
Snell D. C. 1995: "Methods of Exchange and Coinage in Ancient Western Asia," in Sasson J.M. (ed.), *Civilizations of the Ancient Near East*, Vol. I, New York, pp. 1487–1497.
Snell D. C. 1997: *Life in the Ancient Near East*, New Haven.
Schorsch D. 2001: "Precious-Metal Polychromy in Egypt in the Time of Tutankhamun," *The Journal of Egyptian Archaeology*, Vol. 87, pp. 55–71.
Steinkeller P. 1981: "The Renting of Fields in Early Mesopotamia and the Development of the Concept of 'interest' in Sumerian," *Journal of the Economic and Social History of the Orient*, 24, pp. 113–145.
Steinkeller P. 1987: "The Administrative and Economic Organization of the Ur III State: The Core and the Periphery," in Gibson M. and Biggs R. D. (eds.), *The Organization of Power: Aspects of Bureaucracy in the Ancient Near East*, Chicago, pp. 19–41.
Steinkeller P. 2001: "The Ur III Period," in Westbrook R. and Jansnow R. (eds.), *Security for Debt in Ancient Near Eastern Law*, Leiden, pp. 47–61.
Steinkeller P. 2002: "Money-Lending Practices in Ur III Babylonia: The Issue of Economic Motivation," in Hudson M. and Van de Mieroop M. (eds.), *Debt and Economic Renewal*, Vol. III, Bethesda, pp. 109–137.
Steinkeller P. 2004: "Towards a Definition of Private Economic Activity in Third Millennium Babylonia," in Rollinger R. and Christoph U. (eds.), *Commerce and Monetary Systems in the Ancient World: Means of Transmission and Cultural Interaction*, Stuttgart, pp. 91–111.
Steinkeller P. 2016: "The Role of Iran in the Inter-Regional Exchange of Metals: Tin, Copper, Silver and Gold in the Second Half of the Third Millennium BCE," in Maekawa K. (ed.) *Ancient Iran: New Prospective from Archaeology and Cuneiform Studies*, Ancient Text Studies in the National Museum of Iran, Vol 2. pp. 127–150.
Stiglitz J. E. 1987: "Principle and Agent," *The New Palgrave: A Dictionary of Economics*, Vol. 3, London, pp. 966–971.

Stol M. 2004: “Wirtschaft und Gesellschaft in altbabylonischer Zeit,” in Charpin D. et al., *Mesopotamien. Die altbabylonische Zeit.* (Orbis Biblicus et Orientalis 160/4), Fribourg, pp. 641–975.

Stratford E. D. 2010: “Agents, Archives, and Risk: A Micronarrative Acount of Old Assyrian Trade Through Salim-Ahum’s Activities in 1890 BCE,” PhD Dissertation, University of Chicago.

Stratford E. D. 2014: “’Make Them Pay’: Charting the Social Topography of an Old Assyrian caravan Cycle,” in *Journal of Cuneiform Studies*, Vol. 66 (2014), pp.11–38.

Stratford E. D. 2019: “Markets and Marketplaces in Middle Bronze Age Anatolia Particularly during the ‘Colony’ period, in Rahmstorf L. and Stratford E.(ed.), *Weights and Marketplace: From the Bronze Age to the Early Modern Period,* Gotingen, Vol. I, pp. 219–236.

Syla R. 2003: “Interest Rates,” in *The Oxford Encyclopedia of Economic History*, Vol. 3, Oxford, pp. 113–116.

Teissier B. 1984: *Ancient Near Eastern Cylinder Seals,* Berkeley.

Vaggi G. 1987: ‘Market Price,’ in *The New Palgrave: A Dictionary of Economics*, Vol. 3, London, pp. 334–335.

Van de Mieroop M. 1992: *Society and Enterprise in Old Babylonian Ur*, Berlin.

Van de Mieroop M. 1997: *The Ancient Mesopotamian City*, Oxford.

Van de Mieroop M. 1999: “Thoughts on Urban Real Estate in Ancient Mesopotamia,” in Hudson M. and Levine B. A. (eds.), *Urbanization and Land Ownership in the Ancient Near East,* Vol II, Cambridge, pp. 253–287.

Van de Mieroop M. 2002: “A History of Near Eastern Debt?,” in Hudson M. and Van de Mieroop M. (eds.), *Debt and Economic Renewal,* Vol. III, Bethesda, pp. 59–94.

Van de Mieroop M. 2004: “Economic Theories and the Ancient Near East,” in Rollinger R. and Christoph U. (eds.), *Commerce and Monetary Systems in the Ancient World: Means of Transmission and Cultural Interaction,* Stuttgart, pp. 54–64.

Van de Mieroop M. 2004a: *A History of the Ancient Near East ca. 3000–323 BCE,* Oxford.

Van Driel G. 1998: “Land in Ancient Mesopotamia: That What Remains Undocumented Does not Exist, “in Hearing B. and De Maaijer R. (eds.), *Landless and Hungry? Access to Land in Early and Traditional Societies; Proceedings of a Seminar Held in Leiden, 20 and 21 June, 1996,* Leiden, pp. 19–49.

Van Driel G. 2000: “Institutional and Non-institutional Economy in Ancient Mesopotamia,” in Bongenaar A. C. V. M. (ed.), *Interdependency of Institutions and Private Entrepreneurs,* Leiden, pp. 5–15.

Veenhof K. R. 1972: *Aspects of Old Assyrian Trade and its Terminology*, Leiden.

Veenhof K. R. 1977: ’Some Social effects of Old Assyrian Trade’, *Iraq* 39/1, pp. 109–118.

Veenhof K. R. 1987: “‘Dying Tablets’ and ‘Hungry Silver’ Elements of Figurative Language in Akkadian Commercial Terminology,” in Mindlin M., Geller M. J. and Wansbrough J. E. (eds.), *Figurative Language in the Ancient Near East*, London, pp. 41 75. 1988: “Prices and Trade. The Old Assyrian Evidence,” *Altorientalische Forschungen* 15, pp. 243–263.

Veenhof K. R. 1991: “Private Summons and Arbitration Among the Old Assyrians Traders,” *Bulletin of the Middle Eastern Center in Japan*, Wiesbaden, pp. 437–459.

Veenhof K. R. 1995: “In Accordance with the Words of the Stela: Evidence of Old Assyrian Legislation,” *Chicago-Kent Law Review*, 70/3, pp. 1717–1744.

Veenhof K. R. 1996: The Old Assyrian Hamustum Period: A Seven Day Week, 1996, *JEOL* 34, pp. 5–26.

Veenhof K. R. 1997: "'Modern" Features in Old Assyrian Trade," *Journal of the Economic and Social History of the Orient*, 40/4, pp. 336–366.

Veenhof K. R. 1998: "Old Assyrian and Ancient Anatolian Evidance for Care of the Elderly," in Stol M., Vleeming S. P. (eds.), *The Care of the Elderly in the Ancient Near East*, Leiden 1998, pp. 119–158.

Veenhof K. R. 1999: "Silver and Credit in Old Assyrian Trade," in Dreckson. J. D. (ed.) *Trade and Finance in Ancient Mesopotamia*, Leiden, pp. 55–83.

Veenhof K. R. 1999a: Law and Trade in Ancient Mesopotamia and Anatolia: Selected papers by K. R. Veenhof, in Dreckson. J. D. (ed.) *Trade and Finance in Ancient Mesopotamia*, Leiden.

Veenhof K. R. 2001: "The Old Assyrian Period," in Wesbrook R. and Jansnow R. (eds.), *Security for Debt in Ancient Near Eastern Law*, Leiden, pp. 93–159.

Veenhof K. R. 2003: "Archives of Old Assyrian Traders," in Brosius M.(ed.), *Ancient Archives and Archival Traditions: Concepts of Record-Keeping in the Ancient World*, Oxford 2003, pp. 78–123.

Veenhof K. R. 2003a: "Old Assyrian Period," in Westbrook R. (ed.), *A History of Near Eastern Law*, Leiden, pp. 431–483.

Veenhof K. R. 2003b: *The Old Assyrian List of Year Eponyms from Karum Kanish and its Chronological Implications*, Publication of the Turkish Historical Society VI/64, Ankara.

Veenhof K. R. 2003c: "Trade and Politics in Ancient Assur. Balancing of Public, Colonial and Entrepreneurial Interests," in Zaccagnini C. (ed.), *Mercanti e Politica Nel Mondo Antico*, Roma, pp. 69–118.

Veenhof K. R. 2008: *The Old Assyrian Period*, Leiden.

Veenhof K. R. 2008a: "Communication in the Old Assyrian Trading Society by Caravans, Travelers and Messengers," in Michel C. (ed.), *Old Assyrian Studies: in Memory of Paul Garelli*, Leiden, pp. 199–246.

Veenhof K. R. 2010: "The Archives of Kuliya, Son of Ali-abum," in *Ankara Kültepe Tabletleri V*, Ankara.

Veenhof K. R. 2010a: "The City, its Traders, and its Commercial Network," in *Journal of the Economic and Social History of the Orient*, Vol. 53, 1/2, Empires and Emporia: The Orient in the World Historical Space and Time (2010), pp. 39–82.

Veenhof K. R. 2013: "The Archives of Old Assyrian Traders: their Nature, Functions and Use," in Faraguna M.(ed), *Archives and Archival Documents in Ancient Societies: Legal Documents in Ancient Societies* IV, pp. 27–71.

Veenhof K. R. 2014: "Silver in Old Assyrian Trade. Shapes, Qualities and Purification," in Zoltán Csabai (ed.), *Studies in Economic and Social History of the Ancient Near East in Memory of Péter Vargas* (Ancient Near Eastern and Mediterranean Studies 2), L'harmattan, Budapest, pp. 393 ff.

Versteeg R. 2002: *Law in Ancient Egypt*, Durham.

von Soden W. 1994: *The Ancient Orient: An Introduction to the Study of the Ancient Near East*, Grand Rapids.

Waetzoldt H. 1987: "Compensation of Craft Workers and Officials in the Ur III Period," in Powell M. (ed.) *Labor in the Ancient Near East*, New Haven, pp. 117–141.

Wasserman N. and Bloch Y. 2019: *The Amorites: Mesopotamia in the Early Second Millennium BCE.* Jerusalem. (Hebrew)

Weber M. 1976: *The Agrarian Sociology of Ancient Civilizations*, London.

Wells B. 2005: "Law and Practices," in Snell, D. C., *A Companion to the Ancient Near East*, Oxford, pp. 183–195.

Westbrook R. 1988: *Old Babylonian Marriage Law*, Horn, Austria.

Westbrook R. 2003: "Old Babylonian Period," in Westbrook R. (ed.), *A History of Ancient Near Eastern Law*, Leiden, pp. 361–430.

Wheeler J. O. and Muller P. O. 1986: *Economic Geography,* New York.

Wilcke C. 1989: "Genealogical and Geographical Thought in the Sumerian King List," in Behrens et al. (eds.), *Studies Sjöberg,* Philadelphia, pp. 557 ff.

Wilcke C. 2003: "Early Dynastic and Sargonic Period," in Westbrook R. (ed.), *A History of Ancient Near Eastern Law,* Leiden, pp.141–181.

Wilcke C. 2007: "Market und Arbeit im Alten Orient am Ende des 3. Jahrtausends v. Chr.," in Reinhard W. and Stagl J. (eds.), *Menschen und Market. Studien zur historischen Wirtschaftsanthropologie,* Wien, pp. 71–132.

Williamson O.E. 1979: "Transaction-cost Economics: The Governance of Contractual Relations," *Journal of Law and Economics,* 22 (2), pp. 233–261.

Williamson O.E. 2000: "The New Institutional Economics: Taking Stock, Looking Ahead," *Journal of Economic Literature,* 38/3, pp. 595–613.

Wilson R. B. 1987: "Exchange," in *The New Palgrave: A Dictionary of Economics,* Vol. 2, London, pp. 202–206.

Wright G. A. 1969: *Obsidian analyses and Prehistoric Near Eastern Trade: 7500 to 3500 B.C.,* Museum of Anthropology, University of Michigan, Anthropological Papers 37, Ann Arbor.

Yenar K. A. 2000: *The Domestication of Metals: The Rise of Complex Metal Industries in Anatolia,* Eden.

Yoffee N. 1981: "Explaining Trade in the Ancient Western Asia," in Buccellati G. and Kelly-Buccellati M. (eds.), *Sources and Monographs on the Ancient Near East,* pp. 1–40.

Yoffee N. 1995: "The Economy of Ancient Western Asia," in Sasson J. M. (ed.), *Civilizations of the Ancient Near East,* Vol I, New York, pp. 1387–1399.

Yoffee N. 1995a: "Political Economy in Early Mesopotamian States," *Annual Review of Anthropology,* 24, pp. 281–311.

Zarins J. 1992: "The Early Settlement of Southern Mesopotamia: A Review of Recent Historical, Geological and Archeological Research," *Journal of the American Oriental Society* 112, 55 ff.

Index

https://doi.org/10.1515/9783111065533-013

www.ingramcontent.com/pod-product-compliance
Lightning Source LLC
Jackson TN
JSHW070446300626
104572JS00003B/423
9783111065106